D1441864

The World of Sport Aviation

**Popular Mechanics and
The Experimental
Aircraft Association**

The World
of Sport
Aviation

Budd Davisson

Color photographs by Budd Davisson

Foreword by Paul H. Poberezny,
President and Founder
Experimental Aircraft Association

Survey of Experimental Aircraft Plans and Kits
by Harvey R. Swack

Hearst Books
New York

This book is dedicated to those sport aviation pioneers, such as Ed Heath, whose love of aviation and faith in its future for every man and woman have created a movement and an industry that are bringing the joy of flight down to earth.

Copyright © 1982 by the Hearst Corporation

All rights reserved. No part of this book may be reproduced or used in any form or by any means—graphic, electronic, or mechanical, including photocopying, recording, taping, or information storage and retrieval systems—without written permission of the publishers. For information, address Hearst Books, 224 West 57th Street, New York, New York 10019.

Library of Congress Cataloging in Publication Data

Davisson, Budd.
    The world of sport aviation.

    Includes index.
    1. Aeronautical sports—History. I. Title.
GV753.D38   797.5   82-1054
ISBN 0-87851-151-2   AACR2

10 9 8 7 6 5 4 3 2 1

Printed in the United States of America

Contents

List of Color Photographs

Two rare warbirds team up. An **FM-2 Wildcat** and a **TBM "Turkey"** torpedo bomber.

When General Doolittle's B-25 Mitchell bombers roared across Japan in 1942, it was America's first good news and Japan's first bad news.

Mustang at sunset.

Between pages 114 and 115

August afternoon in Iowa. An **Arrow Sport** shows what it used to be like.

The unmistakable lines of a **WACO** cabin biplane at sunset.

The **WACO UPF-7** saw service as a military trainer but today it's far better known as a "good old airplane."

Fifty years old, the **J-3 Cub** will outlive us all.

A **Travel Air D4D** and a quiet meadow—how memories are made.

The handsome lines of the **Stearman N2S** (PT-17 in the army) made it world famous and widely popular.

The **Tiger Moth** was England's primary trainer for decades.

That rarest of birds, a completely stock 85-hp **Swift.**

Takeoff! The **Airmaster** shows how it's done.

The taperwing **WACO** Johnny Livingston used to win the 1929 trans-continental race.

Between pages 146 and 147

A pair of WACOs—a **YOC** in the background and a **VKS** up front.

The pilot's hat and cigar, and the **Cessna Airmaster's** classic form set the calendar back to 1937.

Wings over mid-America. A **Ryan SCW.**

Fun in the air and on the water is what ultralights are all about.

Pterodactyls can be led around by the nose.

The **Mohawk** shows how ultralights are developing into the true airplanes of a new category—Aircraft Recreational Vehicles.

The **Swallow** hides its Cuyuna two-cylinder engine under a fiberglass cowl.

The **Invader**—a new ultralight design shown at Sun 'n Fun 1982.

The **Swallow** rolls over and dives away, showing the maneuverability true ailerons provide.

Acknowledgments

Special credit is given to those who were instrumental in completing this book. Jack Cox and Michael O'Leary put up with a thousand telephone calls while facts were checked. Phil Edwards at the National Air and Space Museum supplied photographs of sport aviation's beginnings; dozens of others provided photographs of specific aircraft.

Thanks go to the casts of camera plane pilots and formation pilots who are always involved in air-to-air photography missions. The best photographer in the world can't shoot what isn't there, but good pilots can always make up for a bad photographer. I wish to thank, in particular, Harry Shepard, Ron Donley, Fred Wilner, and George Enhorning. They've put their time and talent on the line many times, and the quality of the photographs I've produced is due solely to their efforts and the efforts of pilots of their caliber.

Foreword

Through his comprehensive research, Budd Davisson has brought together, in one book, a sport aviation menu that will be of use and interest to the experienced homebuilder and pilot and to the non-flying aviation enthusiast as well. He touches on every major aspect of the sport today. Those who are familiar with only one or two aspects of sport aviation will find this book a revelation.

Putting wings on dreams has long been one of the goals of the Experimental Aircraft Association. This book is a tribute to the dedicated men and women who have accomplished that dream of flight through their own hard mental and physical labor, by building or restoring aircraft in their hangars, garages, basements, and even attics. The chapter on homebuilts will provide good advice to the aviator who is planning to build his first machine; it also gives a few construction tips that even experienced designers and builders may find interesting. Budd also describes the simple, yet important, government regulations that pertain to homebuilt aircraft. In thirty years of EAA homebuilding experience, these rules have stood the test of time, allowing innovative, new designs that are safe, economical, and useful.

However, homebuilts are only one aspect of sport aviation. Warbirds, ultralights, antiques and classics are all part of sport aviation, and all of them are discussed here.

One of the particular joys of this book is that in many chapters Budd puts the reader into the cockpit of a rare or unusual airplane. Very few of us own one of the exotic warbirds or the very rare antiques that have been restored to mint condition, but we can all find out what it is like to fly one, if only for a few minutes, through this book. Budd also peppers each section with fascinating bits of history and interesting anecdotes in passages that make the subject come alive. They are also important because we must know where we come from before we can decide where we are going.

I think that one direction we must certainly take is toward the Aircraft Recreational Vehicle; the EAA and I personally have long promoted the lightweight, fuel-efficient, easy-to-fly, recreational airplane. The ARV concept has come of age.

So, welcome to the wonderful world of sport aviation. If you enjoy this book, I'm sure we will see you in Oshkosh!

Paul H. Poberezny
President and Founder
Experimental Aircraft Association

The World of Sport Aviation

1 In the Beginning

One of the Wright Brothers gliding off Kill Devil Hill in 1902. Visible in the distance under the airplane are the Wrights' camp and hangar buildings. (Courtesy of the National Air and Space Museum.)

It's late on a Thursday afternoon, and what's left of a hazy December sunset is about to head west, its demise hastened by a dreary, damp wind. Two men sit in a tent, their feet up on a wooden packing case. As a coffee pot changes hands, one of them looks at the other and says, "You know, there's a possibility somebody's going to think we're scientists for doing this."

The other grins and cocks his head to glance at the wing of their machine sticking out of the hangar. "Yes, Orville, you may be right, but do you think anybody's going to know how much fun we had?"

The Wright boys weren't the first to be enthralled with the concept of flight. Ever since Australopithecus first walked erect on Africa's sandy soil, mankind has dreamed of thermaling skyward with eagles. And the pursuit of flight for pure enjoyment has given rise to a world of sport aviation that today is as wildly exuberant, colorful, and individualistic as any kingdom of jungle birds. But just as birds flock together, even though they're extremely free as individuals, so man's flying machines group together into distinct species. It's similarity of breeding that makes it easy to put sport aircraft into easily recognized categories, each with its own fascination. But just when you feel you have learned all there is to know about a particular type of airplane—antiques, for instance—you notice homebuilts. You think how wonderful it would be to build your own aircraft. Or perhaps you have spent your life caressing an antique biplane when, suddenly, a World War II Mustang whirls overhead, its 1,450 hp shaking the ground and lighting a fire in yet another corner of your imagination.

This book devotes a separate chapter to each of the sport airbird species. But before the serious reading begins, here is a short introduction to the airplanes and organizations that make sport aviation one of the fastest growing sports in America.

Homebuilts

Here is an amazing fact: today, the fourth most heavily populated airplane category in the world—well ahead of commercial aircraft and business aircraft—is home-built or amateur-built aircraft. The number varies from season to season, but more than 9,500 of these aircraft are now flying the airways. And that doesn't include thousands of ultralights. Some homebuilts get no more than a few miles from home, but a few have flown around the world. Many people find it incredible that there are such things as home-built aircraft. But in thousands of garages, basements, and attics at this moment, ordinary people are building airplanes.

The home-built airplane may be a biplane, or it may be a super-slick high-speed racing machine. It may be a very slow, antique airplane, or something right out of Star Wars. The varieties of antiques and warbirds are limited by the types of aircraft that have already been built, but home-building is limited only by the imaginations of the people involved. Home-builders and their aircraft follow only the rules of physics and aerodynamics. In many respects, Wilbur and Orville were home-builders eighty years ago.

2

Antiques of the golden age line up for inspection at a Florida fly-in. (Credit: Budd Davisson.)

Antiques

Although the history of aviation is not even a century old, its artifacts have been disappearing at an alarming rate. This sad situation is being remedied by active individuals throughout the world whose prime aim in life is to preserve pieces of flying history. They are finding them in barns and attics, and tracking down wrecks in mountains and forests.

By definition, an antique airplane is a flying machine designed and built before December 31, 1945, so the category includes about forty years of aircraft production. Restoring these airplanes can be one of the most frustrating and, at the same time, one of the most rewarding experiences in a person's life. It isn't easy to find the parts, track down the history, or match the color of the paint, but the search often leads you into the living room of someone who was part of the history your aircraft represents. While you are rebuilding a piece of mechanical history, you are uncovering human history and helping to keep alive the unwritten past of the aviation pioneers.

Classics

Aircraft can live long, useful lives, and thirty years is not an unusual life span for an aircraft. They change hands again and again, acquiring the patina of age. Eventually, yesterday's used airplanes become today's not-quite-antiques. These twenty-five- to thirty-five-year-old used aircraft now have their own designation: they are called classic airplanes. The formal definition of *classic* is any aircraft that was built or designed prior to December 31, 1955.

For the most part, classic airplanes used technology made popular during World War II. Right after the war, a huge number of aircraft were designed for the postwar aviation boom that never came. Despite all the industry's marketing optimism and all the engineering excellence that came out of the war, America just was not ready to replace the automobile with the airplane. However, the thousands and thousands of airplanes built during those years today provide opportunities for anyone who loves older aircraft to get into aviation at a lower price.

A **P-40** bares its teeth at a fly-in. The owner camps out in a tent under the wing. (Credit: Budd Davisson.)

Warbirds

It's sad, but much of our technological progress has been made during, and because of, war. The combat and training aircraft of World War II, for example, represent the pinnacle of propeller-driven aircraft development. Fighters and bombers of those days are much more than aluminum mounts that warriors rode into battle—they are mechanical legacies left to us by a generation of men and women who, under intense pressures, were able to push a technology further than the wildest dreams of aviation's pioneers. But when a war is over, weapons are discarded. Warbirds survive in the air today only because of the sometimes heroic efforts of private individuals.

Ultralights

As unlikely as it seems, the oil embargoes of 1973 and 1978 may have done sport aviation a favor. The intolerable rises in the costs of fuel and materials led to the development of the ultralight airplane—the very lightest, most inexpensive, and most easily operated aircraft possible. Many of these airplanes are so rudimentary that they make the Wright brothers' airplane look like an airliner. They're small, made of aluminum tubing and polyester, and use engines taken out of chain saws, snowmobiles, and go-carts. They originally began as powered hang gliders, but they have since metamorphosed into true small airplanes. Most of them now take off,

4

The Canadian-designed **Lazair** is one of the few ultralights with airplane-type ailerons, which give it better control in crosswinds. (Credit: Budd Davisson.)

land, and fly as do conventional airplanes, but they do so on less than 30 hp, and they burn only a gallon or so of fuel an hour.

When an ultralight flies overhead, you see a brightly colored sail of polyester, usually in a wildly gyrating pattern of colors, with the pilot strapped into a framework of aluminum tubing beneath it. That human being is as close to flight as you can get without being a bird. The machinery and expense are minimum, but the excitement is maximum.

Ultralights hold the true future of light aviation, because the major experimentation in engines and airframes is being done in that field. The ultralight section of this book should have been done in pencil—that's how temporary the situation is. They are in a state of tremendous technological advancement, and changes occur almost daily. All this book can do is outline the trends to give you an idea of how ultralights may develop.

Aerobatics

Man had been off the ground only seven years when Lincoln Beachey, growing tired of flying around straight and level, became the first American to loop the loop. In those days, that event had the same impact as breaking the sound barrier or landing on the moon; people thought it was impossible for a man to fly upside down. Today, nobody thinks about it twice.

The adventurous acrobats of sport aviation have developed into a specialized breed. It may be a grandfather out on a Sunday

5

afternoon doing a few loops, spins, and barrel rolls. Or it may be someone like six-time national champion Leo Loudenslager, honing his precision to a fine, razor edge, as he prepares for competition with the very best pilots in the world. These three-dimensional gymnasts work at speeds of up to 200 mph and at G forces that quadruple and pentuple their weight. They have had to design and build their own aircraft to withstand such forces and provide dazzling agility and precision.

EAA's current headquarters near Milwaukee, Wisconsin, houses the EAA Association and Foundation headquarters as well as the museum and the restoration shops. (Courtesy of EAA.)

Organizations

The national government of sport aviation is the Experimental Aircraft Association, first formed in 1953 to foster the home-built aircraft movement, which at that time must have been considered very experimental, indeed. However, from that legendary beginning in Paul Poberezny's Milwaukee basement, the EAA has grown into an organization of 80,000 members which oversees and shepherds all of the different factions of sport aviation.

The Experimental Aircraft Association, a non-profit organization located in Hales Corners, Wisconsin, has formed five divisions: warbirds, antiques/classics, ultralights, aerobatics, and homebuilts. Each of these divisions has its own directors and members. The EAA oversees the membership of all the divisions, publishes a monthly magazine, and works closely with a sister organization, the EAA Aviation Foundation, which maintains one of the nation's largest civilian aviation museums. The EAA and the Aviation Foundation cosponsor the world's largest aviation event, the annual Oshkosh fly-in.

Although the EAA oversees all different types of aviation activities and represents the sport aviation community in Washington, D.C., there are many other associations which serve sport aviation enthusiasts. There is the Antique Airplane Association based in Blakesburg, Iowa, which has its own fly-in and caters to the hard-core antique and classic owner. Then there is the Confederate Air Force, based in Harlingen, Texas, whose aim is to keep in the air one example of every combat aircraft that the United States flew in World War II, as a remembrance of days past. Then there is the Valiant Air Command; originally part of the Confederate Air Force, this organization decided to go its own way.

The new EAA Aviation Center, which is under construction on the EAA's Convention grounds at Oshkosh, will house the headquarters, offices, and museum. It is next door to the Kermit Weeks Flight Research Center, which is already in operation. (Courtesy of EAA.)

Overleaf.
Top: That week in August—the EAA Fly-in at Oshkosh. Some 1,600 homebuilts and 9,000 commercially built aircraft attend.
Bottom, left: Early morning in the camping area at Oshkosh. This one-week camp-out is often the high point of a family's year.
Bottom, right: *Everyone* gets involved at a fly-in camp-out.

(Credits: Budd Davisson.)

Fly-ins

What good is an airplane if you don't go somewhere with it? More important what fun is it going somewhere by yourself? Sport aviation is, if nothing else, an extremely social activity in which the camaraderie is as important as the hardware. Therefore, the birds of sport aviation flock together year-round—weather permitting, of course.

It's seldom that you see pilots of normal, factory-built airplanes going places in large numbers, or planning to gather somewhere every year for an outing, but that's the rule with the sport aviation group. On any weekend during the year, and especially during the summer months, there are dozens of fly-ins across the nation, where owners of sport aircraft gather to swap lies, fly airplanes, and generally have a good time.

The king of the fly-ins, of course, is the EAA convention held at Oshkosh, Wisconsin. During the first week of August each year, the largest aviation event held anywhere in the world literally takes off in Oshkosh, and trying to describe it is like trying to describe the Rockies. If you haven't been there, the words don't mean a thing. You can hear somebody talk all day about rows of airplanes stretching as far as you can see, about spending an entire week walking around a field almost a mile long and still not seeing it all, but the reality has to be experienced to be believed. In the world of sport aviation, if you haven't been to Oshkosh, you really haven't been anywhere.

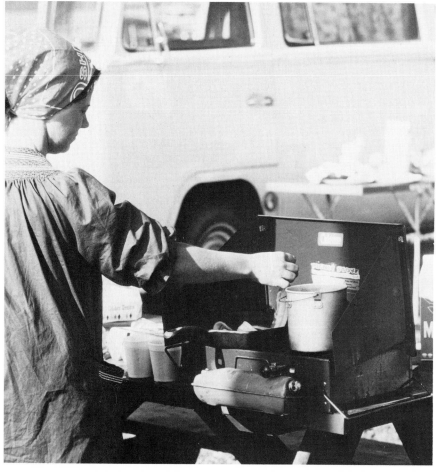

An Oshkosh tradition is the airplane raffle. Tickets cost a dollar each—undoubtedly the cheapest way to get into aviation. (Credit: Budd Davisson.)

The modern fly-in bridges three generations; in a few years these youngsters will be bringing their own kids to Oshkosh. (Credit: Budd Davisson.)

A view from the busy fly-by pattern at Oshkosh. (Credit: Budd Davisson.)

2 The Home-built Airplane

Members of the Aeronautical Experimental Association examine Glenn Curtis's **Gold Bug,** c. 1908. (Courtesy of the National Air and Space Museum.)

Whether it's home-built, custom-built, or amateur-built, the airplane that has been handcrafted by an individual in his own back yard has been with us since the beginning. If not, what were the Wright brothers building? Or Lilienthal or Chanute or Langley? Or any of the thousands of others that came after them? Home-building formed a basis for aviation pioneering, and the tradition is still alive today.

The First Home-Builders: A History

It must have been exciting to be alive during those hectic years shortly after the Wright brothers proved that powered flight was indeed possible, after they broke the barriers with concepts that

One of the Aeronautical Experimental Association's 1907 gliders. (Courtesy of the National Air and Space Museum.)

One of Chanute's gliders shown ready for launch. Compare this photo with some of the current ultralights and see how little progress has been made in the past 85 years. (Courtesy of the National Air and Space Museum.)

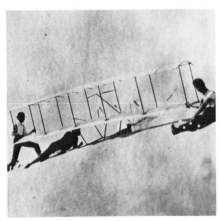

were both scientifically accurate and practical. Within months of the first flight, other pioneers were hard at work copying the Wrights' ideas. There seemed to be an almost frantic urgency among those who were interested in aviation. It was as if a source of great energy had been bottled up since time immemorial, and the Wright brothers had pulled the cork. And when the cork popped, some of the things that flew out of the bottle were too mechanically naive to be believed.

The first flying machines were nothing but bamboo, spruce pine, and canvas, wrapped in a stabilizing cocoon of wire, and the consensus of opinion was that just about anybody could build one. That this was not the case was proved by the crumpled piles of canvas and wood strewn across the pastures of the world during the first decade of flight. But for every thousand homebuilt failures, there were a few homebuilt successes.

It's hard to say when the commercial side of aviation came to the fore, but it is not difficult to tell what caused it: as soon as the military saw a use for the airplane, entrepreneurs saw a reason to produce it. And so names such as Martin, Curtiss, and Avro appeared. Even those two bicycle manufacturers had become the Wright Aeronautical Corporation of Dayton, Ohio. Turning their billed caps around backward and borrowing goggles from their friends with Stanley Steamers, this first group of home-builders became the embryo for the aviation industry.

By the time aircraft made sense commercially, they had evolved past the stage of fabric grasshoppers that leaped from crash to

11

The most successful of the old-time kit manufacturers, Ed Heath, shows off his well-known **Heath Parasol** on floats. The engine is a modified Henderson motorcycle engine. (Courtesy of the National Air and Space Museum.)

HEATH "SUPER PARASOL"

America's Most Popular
Sport Plane

The chance to get your 200 hours conveniently and economically, cross country navigation and all in a monoplane of the conventional type of passenger plane.

Send 10c for large illustrated booklet

HEATH AIRPLANE COMPANY

1721-29 Sedgwick Street   Chicago, Illinois

Lincoln 6196

In the 1920s Heath used state-of-the-art brochures and advertising messages claiming that his kit was America's most popular sport airplane. From our vantage point of 60 years later, Heath's claim certainly proved to be correct. (Courtesy of the National Air and Space Museum.)

crash. The pilot could guide the newer breed of machine where he wanted it to go with a fair degree of certainty. The science of aeronautics had been developed to the point where designers could create airplanes that were predictable. It even became entirely possible and practical for an amateur to design an airplane using the basic aerodynamic and structural techniques that were readily available, and to produce a reasonably safe flying machine. The only remaining unreliable factors in aviation were the engine and the weather, and the latter is still unreliable.

As soon as aviation went commercial, the price of a plane became too high for the amateur. Of course the high-rolling sportsman, with his checkered knickers and his expensive sportcoat, could afford to buy a Wright or a Curtiss, an Avro or a Sopwith, and go sporting about the countryside. But if the average person wanted to fly, his only choice was to build.

A Heath price sheet. (Courtesy of the National Air and Space Museum.)

Ed Heath and his **Baby Bullet** racer, with an unidentified lady friend, possibly his wife. (Courtesy of the National Air and Space Museum.)

Post-1900 America was not the pastoral society people tend to think it was. During the first several decades—encompassing the prenatal period of the airplane—a sort of inventor's fever swept the country, sparked in part by the new technologies spawned by Edison and his peers. The airplane was just one of these fields of invention in which the do-it-yourself fever burned. The same companies that fed kits and parts to the boat and auto buffs directed their efforts toward the airplane enthusiasts; by 1910, highly organized and promotionally oriented companies were feeding the first home-builders just what they wanted: airplane parts and complete kits.

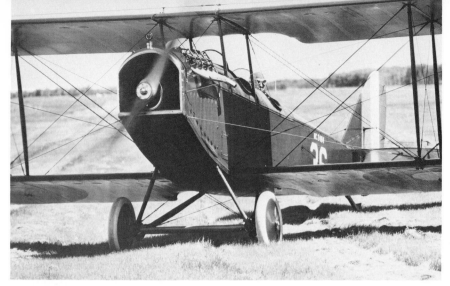

The **Curtiss JN-4 Jenny** was America's most important aeronautical contribution to the war effort in 1918; it was the primary trainer for all American flying cadets. So many were declared surplus after World War I that they became the mainstay for barnstormers, air mail pilots, and most aeronautical activities of the 1920s. Today only four or five are known to be airworthy. (Credit: Budd Davisson.)

The **Curtiss JN-4 Jenny** in its element. (Credit: Budd Davisson.)

The most prolific kit manufacturer was Ed Heath (the same Heath of Heathkit electronics fame). Heath's prewar catalogs show a bewildering variety of airplane designs and kits, as well as nearly a dozen different engines. They listed high-wing monoplanes, low-wing monoplanes, biplanes, small two-cylinder engines, converted motorcycle engines, and some "motors," as they were called, as large as twelve-cylinder radials.

After World War I, there was no reason to build your own airplane, because surplus aircraft were plentiful and cheap. Several hundred dollars bought you a Curtiss Jenny, and for a case of whiskey, you got one in nearly new condition. But by the late 1920s, the Curtiss Jennys were getting tired, and the first action of the new Civil Aeronautics Administration was to ground the entire Jenny fleet. With the prime source of cheap flying gone, the homebuilders stepped in and applied their own particular genius for coming up with the simple and the efficient.

They were fortunate in receiving a tremendous amount of help from the fledgling aviation press. When commercial manufacturers began pricing the average man out of aviation, and when the supply of Jennys started to disappear, aviation-oriented magazines jumped in to fill the gap by publishing build-this-airplane-in-your-basement designs. One was the little Lincoln Sport. When it first appeared in the 1926 *Science and Invention* magazine, the Sport was described as "an airplane that the pilot or non-pilot can build and fly with the utmost in pleasure and safety. Here is a machine with 37 horsepower that can carry you over the horizon to faraway places."

The details of the **Lincoln Sport** are typical of homebuilt construction during the 1920s. (Courtesy of the National Air and Space Museum.)

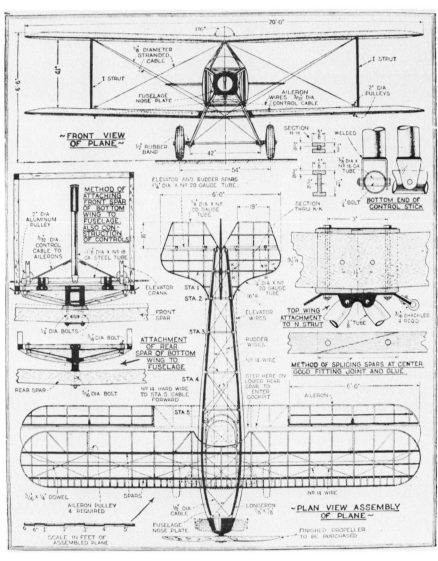

The amateur-built **Dormoy Bathtub** of the late 1920s foreshadowed many of the ultralight trends of the day. It was an efficient aircraft for its horsepower. (Courtesy of the National Air and Space Museum.)

The spirit behind this **Spirit of St. Louis** takes a break at a fly-in. The Cannavo family of Philadelphia created this exact replica of Lindbergh's famous trans-Atlantic mount. (Credit: Budd Davisson.)

Ed Heath's most successful design, called simply the Parasol, was developed in the late 1920s, and is still being built today. According to Jack Cox, editor of the EAA's *Sport Aviation*, more Heath Parasols may have been built than any other airplane in history, if units sold is the criterion.

The year 1929 was a watershed for the country in general, and for aviation in particular. By then, aviation was a full-fledged, 100 percent industrialized community. There were dozens of companies building airplanes, most of them fairly large biplanes of the Jenny type, using engines in the 90- to 200-hp category. And by 1929, it had become obvious that for the industry to survive, it was going to have to develop aircraft that would let people come into aviation at a lower financial level. Designs that answered the need for entry-level aircraft included the Aeronca C-3, the little Arrow Sport, and many other low-horsepower, low-cost, trainer-type aircraft.

The early 1930s saw the development of some highly publicized types of sport aviation craft, the most visible of which were the racers. Since some air racing events offered cash purses as rich as $22,000, self-styled designers and home-builders had strong incentives to build something that went fast. Between 1929 and 1935, the fastest land-based aircraft on the face of the earth were those homebuilts designed specifically for racing. The first land-based airplane to break 300 mph, for instance, was a Wedell-Williams Racer, built by the Wedell boys in Paterson, Louisiana. These homebuilts could blow the doors off anything the military or the commercial companies could muster. Virtually every speed record in those days was held by civilian, home-built aircraft; their success was so complete that by 1930, after suffering years of humiliating defeat, the military withdrew from racing.

But while the hoopla of the races cornered the public's attention, the ground swell of sport aviation and home-built aircraft was still growing. The most popular design of the early thirties was the famous Pietenpol. This high-wing, parasol aircraft was a long way from being jazzy, but it was cheap, and it was both buildable and affordable by the average man. The instructions even told you how to laminate and carve your own propeller! By the time the Pietenpol arrived on the scene, about 1932, it was already an

Many one-of-a-kind home-builts appeared in the 1920s and 1930s. This was George Hales' pride and joy in 1932. Where do you suppose he is today and what happened to the airplane? (Courtesy of the National Air and Space Museum.)

antique, but it offered something that captured the imagination of thousands of builders. There are still an estimated 150 of them flying today. In fact, the original designer, Bernie Pietenpol, is still building them.

But the Pietenpol wasn't alone; take the classic Knight Twister, for instance. When Vernon Payne first brought the airplane out in 1929, it looked like a bullet with two wings. Fast and unforgiving on the ground, it was light years ahead of almost every other airplane in production at the time.

And then there was the Corben Ace series. Using various automotive and aircraft engines, the different Ace models ranged from near-rocket designs to downright friendly pasture airplanes, like the Pietenpol. Here again, a good basic design can't be held down, and folks are still building them.

Throughout the 1920s and 1930s, home-building continued to flourish, but in 1938 an act of omission by the government suddenly brought the curtain down. The government, recognizing that their rules and regulations for both pilots and airplanes were sadly out of date, completely revised them, making them much more stringent. In their new form, they addressed both the technological advancements and the growth of the pilot population but failed to provide specifically for the existence of the amateur-built airplane. It was left up to the states to develop their own homebuilt regulations. Every state except Oregon decided the best way to deal with the airplane regulation game was to write one short law outlawing homebuilts, rather than a set of long ones

Traditional woodwork found in the **Pietenpol** fuselage is a series of small struts glued and gussetted together. (Credit: Budd Davisson.)

The steel tube fuselage of a **Corbin Ace** requires techniques that are as old as aircraft themselves. All the small tubes are cut, fitted, and welded together individually. (Credit: Budd Davisson.)

Paul Poberezny (left) chairs a meeting of the fledgling Experimental Aircraft Association in the early 1950s in his Milwaukee basement. (Courtesy of EAA.)

regulating them. In one sweeping action, the home-built airplane was all but eliminated.

Even if there were no regulatory problems, World War II would have brought the homebuilt movement to a standstill, as it did everything else. As soon as the war ended, however, the home-builders proved you can't hold a crowd of good people down. George Bogardus undertook a cross-country trip from Oregon to Washington in his homebuilt Little Gee Bee to publicize the problems caused by the Civil Aeronautics Administration's oversight. The CAA quickly developed a homebuilt category under their experimental licensing rules, and the amateur-built airplane took off again.

Although the popularity of the home-building movement has varied from decade to decade, there has always been a small group of experimenters and back yard builders trying to go faster, slower, farther, and shorter by building different, more individualistic airplanes. In 1953, a group of active builders and experimenters in Milwaukee, Wisconsin, decided it was time to formalize their movement. For several years they had been meeting in Paul Poberezny's basement, generally just talking about what great pilots they were and what great airplanes they were building. Poberezny and other interested individuals finally decided to form the Experimental Aircraft Association. This is a very condensed version of the birth of a legend; actually, it was largely through the support and visibility provided by the EAA that home-built aircraft attained the regulatory status they now enjoy.

What Is a Homebuilt?

According to the Federal Aviation Administration (FAA), a home-built or amateur-built aircraft is one on which an individual has done 51 percent of the work necessary to get it flying. The 51 percent ruling was established to prevent companies from manufacturing nearly completed amateur-built aircraft, which would allow them to skirt the FAA's certification processes, since a genuine homebuilt does not have to conform to FAR part 23 regulatory certification rules. In addition, the aircraft must have been built for educational or pleasure/recreational purposes only. The FAA definitions may make the subject sound dead and dry, but to a man who has spent 2,000 to 3,000 hours of his life huddled in a basement whittling on formless pieces of steel, wood, or fiberglass and making them into a thing that flies, a home-built airplane is anything but a lifeless, easily definable object.

The FAA still exercises a certain amount of control over the amateur-building process; every home-built aircraft must be licensed by the FAA. In licensing home-built aircraft, the FAA places them in a category labeled "Experimental-Amateur Built," which has its own well-defined limitations and operational parameters. The FAA's local general aviation district office (GADO) will send an inspector out to see your project while you're building it. He will inspect the welds, the fittings, and all other structural components while you are in the process of putting it together. Before you close in any portion of the structure—such as putting fabric on a wing—the FAA must inspect it. The FAA representative will sign the logbook for your airplane indicating that he has approved these construction stages.

Before the aircraft can be flown, the FAA will give it a detailed inspection. At this point, you get an entirely new view of your plane, because the man looking at it is not only a professional, but also somebody who has a great enough distance from the project to be objective. A great majority of the FAA's suggestions for modification or improvement of the aircraft before flight are worthwhile, and as often as not, they are items the builder never thought about. In one case, the aircraft, an aerobatic biplane, had two tanks, one in the wing to hold oil for the smoke system, and the other one in the fuselage for gasoline. The FAA inspector suggested that

Don Taylor of Hemet, California, taxis onto the runway for takeoff on his around-the-world flight. He was gone for sixty days and flew 171.5 hours in the first homebuilt airplane to circle the globe. (Courtesy of Ted Koston/EAA.)

the builder print "For Smoke Oil Only" on the smoke tank. While the builder was confident that he would never forget and put gasoline into the smoke system, someone else working around his airplane or someone to whom he sold his airplane might make that mistake.

Once the aircraft is flying, it must conform to all the operational rules that apply to any airplane, in terms of where it can fly and how fast or high it can fly, and it must obey all the traffic rules. However, for the annual inspection for licensing, the FAA has set up special provisions, including a test, that qualify the original builder of the airplane to make the inspection instead of an FAA-licensed aircraft inspector. This greatly simplifies the licensing process and saves considerable expense. If, however, the builder chooses not to qualify for the license to inspect his own aircraft, he must rely upon exactly the same inspection procedures that apply to normal aircraft.

Experimental amateur-built aircraft can be used just like any other airplanes, as long as it's not for commercial purposes. You can fly them at night, fly them on instruments, and fly them around the world; at least one home-built aircraft *has* flown around the world. In the fall of 1980, Don Taylor of Hemet, California, fueled up his home-built T-18 Thorp (a little 180-hp, 1,100-pound airplane) in San Francisco and took off for New Zealand and Australia. Why Australia? Because it was one of the few places in the world that he had never visited, and he had some friends there he had promised to see. But a trip like that was not unusual for Don Taylor. Before that, he made a sixty-day, 171.5-hour flight that took him all the way around the world.

Who Builds Them?

To many people the notion of building an airplane in your basement or garage is mind boggling. They assume that because somebody has built an airplane, he or she must be a super person with an elaborate workshop, someone who habitually rebuilds Formula 1 race cars and leaps tall machine shops in a single bound. That is definitely not the case. While most people who build aircraft have a high level of technical interest, there is no common thread of deep experience or of having done magnificent things with tools.

21

Not much bigger than the butterfly it's painted to represent, the **Baby Great Lakes** rivals many of the super ships for climb and maneuverability, with only 65 to 85 hp. (Credit: Budd Davisson.)

Left: Individualism and dedication—that's what sport aviation is all about. There's no clearer example than this **Pitts Special** paint job; the masking tape bill alone must have been enormous. (Credit: Budd Davisson.)

In fact, there is hardly any common ground among them at all, other than the love of flying machines and an uncommon desire to build one.

Numbered among today's aircraft builders are high school students who are part of EAA's Project School Flight, grandmothers, a group of inmates in a Canadian prison, housewives, doctors, lawyers, and Indian chiefs. The important ingredient is not skill; it is dedication—a fierce attachment to the project. If you're going to finish a 2,000-hour project, for a certain period of your life that's going to be the only thing that you do. Oh, you may still play a little golf, you may go to a dance once in a while, but the airplane is going to dominate your life. You have to be so insanely in love with the concept of fashioning shapeless matter into a flying machine that you don't miss other activities. Some families have found this to be a problem, but more often than not, the airplane has become a family project. More than one wife has rib-stitched a wing of a Pitts, or helped mask off the fuselage stripe on a Thorp, and there are certainly many upholstery jobs that owe more to the wife than they do to the husband.

There is one concrete statement that can be made about building an airplane: anybody who *wants* to build an airplane *can* build one. The problems of skill, tools, and finances can all be solved. But the intangibles, the ambition, the dedication, and the emotion that must go into a project, cannot be artificially controlled, learned, or purchased. These intangibles are within you, and they are every bit as vital.

Skill—What You Need and Where You Get It

Some people can't imagine themselves building something as complex as an airplane seems. Since an airplane is capable of flight, they are convinced it must be based upon great complexity. But that is not the case at all. The truth is that the average car is many times more complicated than an airplane. For the most part, the only real skill required in building an airplane is the ability to give continued attention to details. It's the detailing that makes the difference, and that is not a skill; it's simply an attitude.

The skills needed depend in large part on the airplane being built and the material being used. If the airplane is made of steel tubing and fabric, for instance, you'll have to learn how to weld, or you'll have to have somebody do it for you. You also have to know how to cut and fit tubing, but this is a skill which is easily acquired.

If you are building an airplane out of wood, then you'll have to learn woodworking skills, but these are not much different from those used in building bookshelves. Other types of construction are sheet metal and composite construction—working with foam and fiberglass.

The problem of skill is really not a problem, because there is always a way you can learn each skill you need. If welding is required and you don't want to have somebody else do it for you, then adult school classes can teach you most of the basics, and a friend who does aircraft welding can give you some of the specifics. The same holds true for sheet metal construction and for woodworking.

One of the best ways to begin learning a skill is to study the publications of the Experimental Aircraft Association. The EAA has a series of manuals aimed at helping the first-time builder solve his problems, no matter what construction material he is using. In addition to that, one of the major thrusts of the EAA's annual week-long convention at Oshkosh, Wisconsin, is a schedule of twenty to thirty seminars a day; they are certain to cover whatever subject you want to learn. In addition, there are always instructors conducting workshops that teach welding, sheet metal construction, and any other skill required. While a lack of skill is not a valid reason to avoid building an airplane, it is an excellent reason to begin learning.

An idyllic setting for airplanes: the October gathering of the Tullahoma Bunch in Tullahoma, Tennessee. (Credit: Budd Davisson.)

How Do You Begin?

If you think you want to build a home-built aircraft, but you don't know exactly how to get started, the first step probably should be to take a nice, cold shower. After you've cooled off, sit down and do some logical decision making. Far too often, when people get excited about the idea of building an airplane, they rush to write checks and send them out in all directions for plans, brochures, and a thousand miles of steel and wood. Then they spend a couple of weeks cutting, welding, and making a mess in their basement before they realize they have made a mistake and gone off half-cocked. As with any other complex venture, a fair amount of planning should take place before you do anything concrete.

Familiarization

One of the first steps in the build-your-own-airplane plan is to decide exactly what it is you are going to do and how you are going to do it. Familiarize yourself with the homebuilt market, all the designs, and some of the dos and don'ts. Ideally, you should decide very early to spend at least a year looking, talking, feeling, and listening before you do anything solid on your own project. Few folks, however, are that patient. Although aerial emotions seldom run on schedule, it would be smart to start your year of learning at one Oshkosh fly-in and finish at the next one.

You can spend your first week there picking up all the information you can. The following year should be spent learning in

24

your local area, and then you cap it off with another week-long visit to the Oshkosh convention. This may sound like overkill, but for every hour you spend filling in voids in your knowledge beforehand, you will save days and months on your own project.

High on the list of things to do when getting familiar with home-built aircraft is joining the Experimental Aircraft Association. For $25 a year, you not only get their superlative magazine, *Sport Aviation*, but you also become part of the homebuilt crew; you belong. You can spot a kindred soul by the round blue EAA badge on his jacket or the decal on his car. Displaying that emblem is a way of saying, "Hey, look at me, I'm crazy about airplanes and I'll talk to anybody else who is, too." Your local EAA chapter will welcome you with open arms. The chapters usually turn out to be the most important factor in an enthusiast's learning experience.

By scanning the EAA's monthly listings of aviation events in *Sport Aviation*, you can locate any fly-in or sport aviation event in your area. And if you're building an airplane, you should accept the fact that what you consider your area is going to broaden considerably. It's no longer the closest airport or merely a thirty-mile radius; you are going to spend your weekends driving 100, 200, maybe even 300 miles to get to a gathering of the faithful, where the birds are flocking.

The Fly-in

A fly-in is a gathering to which everybody that can flies in. It's an aerial version of the Easter Parade, where everybody wants to show off his or her latest finery, except that in this case, the finery may be a biplane with 450 hp up front, or a diminutive foam airplane with the propeller in back and the tail in front. Fly-ins have taken several different paths. One type is the general fly-what-you've-got-and-drive-if-you-can't-fly event, to which everybody comes. The other type caters to owners of specific models of airplanes, such as Navions, or Cessna 195s, or to broader categories, such as antiques or warbirds. Each of the different breeds has a fly-in of its own, but those breeds may all join together in other major fly-ins.

A local fly-in, even a small one, draws in airplanes from a 200-mile radius, and it's a golden opportunity to see the machine you may decide to build later on. But more important than the

The obligatory fly-in air show beginning: A skydiver descends with smoke grenades on his feet, while a biplane encircles him with smoke. A **Fokker Triplane** replica waits patiently below. (Credit: Budd Davisson.)

William Randolph Hearst was the first owner of this ultra-rare **Vultee Vl-A**. Now it gives fly-in visitors a glimpse of old-time opulence. (Credit: Budd Davisson.)

airplanes are the people. One great thing about a fly-in is that the fellow standing next to you is there for the same reason you are—because he loves airplanes. You will find that making friends is not a problem. As a matter of fact, anybody who has been in sport aviation for any length of time counts among his very best friends those he has made attending fly-ins. And don't forget to bring the family, because the EAA and their fly-ins are very definitely family affairs. A great many people throughout the United States in their late twenties and early thirties have close friends they made in their childhood when they were brought to fly-ins by their parents. They grew up seeing each other two or three times a year under the wing of an airplane. Even though such friendships may have originally been based on a shared interest in the hardware aspect of airplanes, they have deepened into true and lasting bonds. And these are the friends you need when you build an airplane.

Every person you meet at a local fly-in has some basic skill, and he's generally glad to share it. It's not unusual for one person who's good at machining parts to apply that skill on somebody else's airplane, and that somebody might repay the favor by spraying paint or stitching fabric. What develops is a barter system, in which nobody expects payment in money. Instead, you always repay the favor in kind. You can go to all the fly-ins, and you can read all the magazines and book articles you want, but it's not until you walk into a person's workshop and look at an airplane project in progress that you can accurately judge what you're getting yourself in for.

You can learn a lot by volunteering to help somebody, but an individual who is building an airplane may not be able to use your help; the airplane-building process often goes on in areas where there's barely room for one person to work, much less two. When it comes to moving fuselages, however, or hanging wings from ceilings, or doing any one of a thousand things that need three hands, your help will be welcomed.

If you strike up a friendship with somebody who is cutting metal on an airplane who will let you sit in the corner and watch, you'll learn more than you dreamed possible. Watching somebody grinding away on a piece of metal to give it the shape that's needed for a bell crank or a fitting will eliminate your own fears of doing the same thing; looking over somebody's shoulder while he's

Contact! (Credit: Budd Davisson.)

welding tubing will convince you that welding is not a magic process—it's something that can be done by mere mortals.

Some building processes, such as working with composites, in which large amounts of foam and fiberglass are used, readily lend themselves to two-man building. If you let it be known that you're willing to spend an afternoon or evening a week helping someone building a composite airplane, your help will be greatly appreciated and quickly snapped up.

One of the last steps in the familiarization process is to go down to your local FAA office and talk to the man who will be inspecting your airplane. He'll suggest how he would like to see things done. You can also get the appropriate forms from the FAA or EAA and start a logbook for your aircraft. These forms don't

The **Mead Adventure,** one of the few foam and fiberglass composite airplanes of normal configuration, can get right out and boogie on only 100 hp, doing over 200 mph. (Courtesy of Peter Lert.)

apply to any specific airplane until you fill them out, so you don't have to decide then what you are going to build.

Setting Up Work Space

Environmental psychologists charge their clients thousands of dollars to tell them that painting the walls light green will make happier employees and more productive chickens. They will tell you exactly how many lights you should have, how many lumens should be absorbed, what color paper you should be using and how many people should be in the room at one time in order to minimize stress in today's work world. But how many psychologists have ever built an airplane?

While there's no doubt that what they are saying is true, it's certain that a great many airplanes have been built in much less than optimum situations.

The fellow who built a Pitts in his back bedroom may know nothing about the psychologists' theories, but he would be the first to admit that the project would have moved along much faster and been much more enjoyable if he hadn't had to worry about the kids running in while he was doping fiberglass, or if he hadn't had to leave one door open for the fuselage to stick through. Optimizing your work space tremendously increases the chances that you will finish your project.

First of all, your shop should be at least big enough to allow you to set up the largest piece of airplane and still have plenty of room to work around it, and house the tools you need. The arrangement of the space is important, too. If you are building the airplane in the upstairs bedroom but your tools are in the basement, you will spend more time running up and down the stairs than you will building the airplane. If you have to keep ducking under pipes and climbing over bicycles, you'll soon find it more convenient to sit in front of the TV and dream about building airplanes, rather than getting down to work and doing it. There have been many airplanes built in apartment houses and barn lofts, and probably somebody's building one in a closet today. But that's the hard way.

Here are some basic guidelines that should be followed in developing a work space:

- The shop should be big enough to give you a minimum of four or five feet around all portions of the airplane or the largest portion that you'll be working on.
- The work space should be convenient to your living quarters. You would be amazed at how much having a workshop fifty feet from the house will slow down your project.
- Have more lighting than you know what to do with. A shop that is overlit (if there is such a thing) is much easier and more pleasant to work in than one that is too dark.
- Provide good ventilation. If you don't have an exhaust fan, you should at least be able to open a window to let out noxious fumes.
- Heating a work space in a northern climate can be a major problem, and an expensive one. You may have to install a wood-burning stove (you can't use it, though, when you are shooting paint or using other explosive compounds). A kerosene heater may solve the problem if your local fire code permits. In any case, plan your shop with plenty of insulation and tight-fitting doors.
- Build in plenty of storage space, especially above head level, so the floor doesn't get cluttered.

The minimum size shop is about the size of a single garage—roughly twelve by twenty-two feet, with eight-foot clear ceilings. Properly insulated and wired single garages have probably turned out more airplanes than many factories. A double garage on the first floor level of your house provides one of the best places for a shop. This gives you excellent working space and allows you to come and go when you want; you can hook the shop into the house's heating system, and you can have an exhaust fan or an open window on the outside portion of the garage to keep odors out of the house.

Tooling Up

Although some of the largest and most complex airplanes ever built were constructed with tools not much more complicated than a hand drill, it just isn't possible to have too many or too complicated tools. You may not need lots of tools, but the *right* tools make a job go faster, more easily, and, in most cases, much more precisely.

The **Smith Mini-plane** appeared on the cover of *Popular Mechanics* in the late 1950s and became one of the most popular midget biplane homebuilts. (Credit: Budd Davisson.)

The tools you need vary according to the parameters of the project, especially what type of material you are using—wood, steel, aluminum, or fiberglass. You might say that whatever the material, the basic tools are those you'd use to build a bookcase or to do a little mechanical work on your car: a set or wrenches, hammers, nails, and saws. Besides these, you need a flat, sturdy workbench; most aircraft designs require you to build a four-by-eight-foot bench in the middle of the floor to provide a surface for building wings and tails. You need a vise, attached to a smaller, sturdy work table. A four-inch vise should be considered minimum size. Since a certain amount of precision is required in building an airplane, all measuring and squaring devices should be the highest quality you can afford. A good machinist's square, a framing square, and two levels, a long one and a short one, are essential.

Two high-quality power hand tools are required: a ⅜-inch hand drill and a sabre saw. High quality is essential; there is nothing that makes a job more difficult than cheap power tools.

Nearly all aircraft designs, regardless of the type of material, require you to shape steel. That means high quality hacksaw blades by the bundle, and fistfuls of files. Incidentally, since the most commonly used steel is 4130 chromium molybdenum, you would be well advised to get some thirty-two-tooth blades for use on the thinner stock. They save a tremendous amount of elbow grease and a lot of swearing.

A bench grinder is also a must. They are available today for very little money, and, besides being useful for making parts, they

This extensively modified **Cavalier** was given retractable gear and immaculate lines by Larry Burton. The all-wood Cavalier is one of the cleanest designs in the home-building catalog. (Credit: Budd Davisson.)

The **Evans VP-1 Volksplane** is, as its name implies, the peoples' airplane. Using a Volkswagen engine for power and wood for its primary structure, the VP-1 was designed to be the simplest aircraft possible. (Credit: Budd Davisson.)

sharpen drill bits, take care of beat-up screwdrivers, and perform many other functions.

A drill press is another tool that builders all know they should have, but they often try to get by without one because of the expense. However, once they've bought it, they're always glad they did. With a decent quality drill press, you can drill precision holes time after time; this eliminates the nagging fear of making mistakes. Although a drill press can cost several hundred dollars, it is probably the most worthwhile expenditure you will make on the entire project.

A small acetylene welding torch can help you overcome many workshop problems. As with the drill press, after you acquire one, you'll wonder how you ever got along without it. Of course, on some airplane projects, especially those made of tubing and fabric, you really can't get along without it. Even if you aren't going to do the final welding yourself, you are going to have to have an oxygen acetylene welding outfit just to tack the pieces in place temporarily until a professional welder can finish weld them. A complete welding rig can cost several hundred dollars, but it's money well spent.

Every major tool mentioned so far—drill presses, welding rigs, and even power hacksaws and band saws—is usually available at 30 percent of the price of the same tool new through local classified ads. Most major metropolitan areas have a "Penny Saver" or "Want Ad Press," a small newspaper dedicated to turning over used merchandise. These can be your most important sources for tools. While it makes sense to buy the smaller hand drills and hand saws new, it makes no sense at all to spend all that money for a brand new drill press, welding rig, or band saw. Keeping your eyes glued to the classified ads keeps you informed on when there are auctions, garage sales, or individuals who have decided to get rid of their tools and move on. After a while, the search for tools becomes fun, like a treasure hunt; you never know when you're going to run across that drill attachment you've been looking for, or when you might find some lady selling off her ex-husband's lathe or roll-around tool chest at a garage sale.

Shop Safety

Owning tools and knowing how to use them safely are two entirely different things. Most people, by the time they have decided to build an airplane, are already familiar with tools. But even if you think you know what you're doing, it's wise to read through the manufacturer's manuals for each of your power tools. If it saves snipping off a piece of a finger or getting a piece of grinding dust in your eye, it's certainly time well spent. If you buy a power tool you've never used, it's especially important.

Certain safety procedures should become ingrained work habits around the shop. For instance, keep a pair of safety glasses on the grinding and drill stands; once you get into the habit of picking them up and putting them on before you turn on the machine, you'll find it's second nature and causes you no inconvenience whatsoever. A sliver of steel in your eye, while not fatal and seldom blinding, can certainly be painful. Also, it's not a wise idea to work in sloppy shirts or loose sleeves that can get caught in drill presses or be set on fire by a welding torch.

Some of the safety procedures that few people ever talk about involve the rest of the family. Your children should be carefully instructed that they must not play with the tools. Show them how these things can snip off a piece of wood or a piece of finger before the child realizes it. The entire family, and especially your spouse, must understand how dangerous it is to interrupt somebody when he or she is using tools, whether it's pounding, drilling, or making a weld.

Choosing a Design

After you spend a year immersing yourself in sport aviation and get your workshop set up, you come to the hard part—choosing a design. It may sound easy, but it's about as clear-cut as the blonde-redhead-brunette question. There are so many different factors, that picking out a design that fits you is very difficult. At the same time, the process can be fun, but there's one warning to be heeded: far too often people choose the design of an airplane based on an emotional reaction. They look at it, it tugs at their heartstrings, and they immediately reach for the telephone and their checkbook. But consider this: building that airplane is going to take over your life for the next two or three years, and wouldn't it be terrible, after spending all that time, to get in, fire it up, take off, and then decide you really don't like the airplane? The evaluation of the design is extremely important and should be approached in a cool, calculated and logical way.

First, consider your finances. Are you going to be strapped for money? Can you afford to take on one of the big designs? Can you swing the cost of tooling up for a complex airplane? Will your family put up with a financial squeeze? Next, there's the question of facilities: are you sure you've got enough space—for the tools, the supplies, *and* the airplane?

Four other questions that concern your design choice are important enough to discuss here in detail:

1. Do you really want to build an airplane?

The **Hatz biplane** is designed to counter the big engine–big bucks trend; it produces spritely performance with a small engine. (Courtesy of Ted Koston/EAA.)

2. What do you plan to do with the plane you build?
3. What kind of a builder are you?
4. What kind of a pilot are you?

The success of your project depends on honest and accurate answers to these questions, so make the critical self-evaluation they demand before committing yourself.

Do You Really Want to Build?

It is extremely important to know yourself before you get into a project as large as building an airplane. Once you do a blood-thirsty evaluation of yourself, you may find that you'd just as soon go out and *buy* an airplane, or maybe even sit on the fence and just *watch* airplanes.

Ask yourself why you want an airplane in the first place. That may sound like a silly question, but airplanes have the irresistible ability to tie your emotions in knots. Airplanes fall right in with sailing ships and railroads; they all sound that siren call. It's important for you to dig beneath your superficial reactions and discover the *real* reasons you want the airplane.

A common fantasy people spin about themselves and an airplane takes place on a late summer afternoon, with the sun just setting, and themselves in the finished airplane, winging off over the horizon, having the time of their lives. If you have that kind of dream, there's no reason to be ashamed of it, but look at the fantasy a bit more closely. Is it the act of flying in general, or is it

The **Acapella** combines 200 hp's worth of brute strength and the fuselage and wings of BD-5 kit to give fighter-like performance. Not an airplane for the timid, it is designed to get up and go. (Courtesy of Ted Koston/EAA.)

the act of flying that particular machine that sets your mind on fire? It's important that you answer that question. If all you want to do is go flying, and you view the home-built airplane as a way to do it a little less expensively, then you had better go back and reevaluate the entire project. The enormous amounts of time and effort that go into building an airplane can never be balanced by the thrill of flying. There have to be some other intangibles involved.

For a builder, the act of flying must, in many respects, be subordinated to the act of creation, to giving birth to something of your own handicraft, and in some cases, of your own design. The failure to face this fact is undoubtedly one of the primary reasons why so many home-built airplanes are never finished—

The **BJ-520,** also known as the Brokaw Bullet, is one of the most sophisticated, high-performance homebuilts available. With engines as big as 340 hp it cruises at 280 mph. (Credit: Budd Davisson.)

nine out of ten, according to the FAA. For many people, it's too easy, after they have put 500 or 1,000 tiring hours into a project and realize how far they have to go, just to sit down and say that it really isn't worth all the effort. They may realize they'd rather be out flying than huddled in the basement, grinding away on a piece of steel. The true creative urge is what's needed to finish the airplane. You have to feel as if you are building for building's sake, and every single little piece of the airplane is a separate project. You find joy in creating the little gizmo that holds the door shut, or the framus that holds the cables out of your way. You know the airplane is finished when you run out of little projects to do.

What Do You Plan to Do with the Airplane?

Of course, you want to go flying in the plane you build but it's more than that. What kind of flying do you want to do? Just being off the ground is flying, but some airplanes do a lot more than just get you up in the air. Some of them barely do that. For instance, when you're jaunting off over the horizon in your fantasies, exactly how far away is that horizon? In other words, do you want a plane for cross-country flying? Can you see yourself making 100-, 200-, 300-mile trips in it every time you fire it up? Or do you want to build the airplane just to go putting around the pasture in the late afternoon, never getting out of sight of home?

If you say, "I want a cross-country airplane," you are also saying several other things: first, that you want an airplane that is relatively fast, at least 115 to 120 mph. (These days, "fast" is defined as 150 to 170 mph.) But all that speed does you no good if you don't have enough fuel to go places; you have committed yourself to an airplane with a bigger fuel capacity as well as fair speed. But then, going places in an airplane is no fun if you can't tell where you're going. Nothing brings on a case of the sweats as fast as being lost, so you're also committed to a decent navigational/radio package on board. Then you'd better ask yourself how often you are going to go places all by yourself. Is your wife or husband going to put up with that? How about your kids? Do you need a two-place airplane, a three-place, a four-place? Do you need a six-place? How about going out and buying a bus instead? You see, if what you want to build is a traveling machine, you've got to figure out exactly how much serious traveling you are going to do. Look at your weekends. You might say, "Well, this weekend, if I had had an airplane, I could have gone somewhere, I could have taken the family, I could have done a lot of things." But you might also say, "Well, even if I had had an airplane, I couldn't have gone. Scotty had a soccer game this morning, Jennifer had to go to a ballet lesson this afternoon, I couldn't have gone anywhere. I only had an hour or two this morning that I could have flown." Look at all of these things before you decide that you want a pure cross-country airplane.

If you find in your heart that you really don't need a machine to take you bouncing over the horizon, then maybe what you want is a recreational vehicle, a just-for-fun airplane; these come in many shapes, sizes, and flavors, many of them a bit lower powered, a little slower and a whole lot less practical. But then, if you cared about "practical," you wouldn't be reading this book in the first place. The purely fun homebuilt is built to fill a purely emotional need, so it's a purely emotional airplane. It may be a funky-looking little biplane or an anachronistic-looking almost-antique. But almost without exception, the fun homebuilts are one- or two-place machines, definitely not family vehicles.

Many people decide to get into home-built aircraft because they have been to air shows where they've seen the aerobatic and stunt pilots, and they know that many home-built aircraft are aerobatic. But even in aerobatics, there is a question of degree. How far do you want to go? Do you just want to do a few rolls, spins, and loops, or a little bit of barnstorming during your off hours? If that's the case, then most of the fun aircraft will fit the bill—they will do limited aerobatics. If, however, you want to become a serious competitor, with the derring-do of Waldo Pepper, then you will have to look at some of the more specialized aerobatic machines, such as the Pitts Special or the Stephens Acro. These aircraft are designed for one purpose only: to perform any maneuver in complete safety. In most cases they are only marginally more difficult to build than the normal homebuilt, but the full-blown aerobatic specials are the hot rods of the homebuilt field; they require a hot rod builder and a hot rod pilot.

Your Ability as a Builder

Building a home-built aircraft, regardless of the type, requires only the normal do-it-yourself skills. At least one seller of plans for composite airplanes says that if you can build a straight wall and Sheetrock it, then you can build his airplane. For some aircraft that may be an oversimplification, but in general that's true. If you are not afraid to tackle normal carpentry projects or the simplest wiring projects, then you will find a home-built aircraft to be a manageable project. Don't forget it's not necessary that you know everything before you begin; it is only necessary that you be willing to learn as you go. Willingness and ability to learn are probably much more important than the skills you've already got, because there are many aspects of an airplane that you can't be expected to know the first time out. Without exception, however, the concepts and the skills are simple enough to be learned and put into practice in a relatively short time. So, ask yourself, "Am I good with my hands, and if I'm not, am I willing to develop the skills that are necessary?"

Another question that pertains to the actual construction process is whether or not you are conscious of details. Building an airplane is nothing more than a long series of small details laid end to end, and none of the pieces of the airplane, none of the separate projects, is too big or impossibly complex. However, all the parts have to fit together correctly, and there are certain finishing standards. You don't leave scratches on fittings, for instance. You don't bend pieces with a sharp radius. Proper standards of detailing that must be adhered to are easily learned and become second nature to a detail-minded person. If you tend to gloss over

39

the small things, figuring they don't really make that much difference, maybe you'd better stick to croquet. If you are a person who enjoys making sure the bolts are lined up, all the holes are clean, and there are no scratches on the pieces you are making, then you will thoroughly enjoy building an airplane.

And then there's the question of which material you prefer to work with. It's natural to feel more comfortable with one material than with another; most people, for instance, initially think they would rather work with wood, perhaps because they've built some bookcases or kitchen cabinets and it's a material with which they are familiar. It is also a material that more people are likely to be equipped to work with. However, many of these people, when they look closely at aircraft construction in wood versus aircraft construction in steel tubing or sheet metal, find that they would prefer to learn to work with steel in order to learn new skills. Steel-working is a skill easily learned, but steel tubing is a building medium that's not likely to be familiar to most people, especially since it requires some welding.

The two remaining types of material, aluminum and fiberglass composites, are generally materials with which very few people have any experience. However, if you look at the history of the amateur-built airplane movement, you can see that both of these materials require skills that are quite easily acquired, especially fiberglass composite. We'll get into each of these areas of materials in greater depth in later sections.

Another question is whether you can read blueprints. Since you will probably be working from a set of plans developed by somebody else, you'll have to visualize from those plans what you are trying to build, and what the piece is supposed to look like. You should also be able to understand the detail callouts, the type of material, the dimensions, and the tolerances that are called for. Fortunately, almost all of the plans on the market today are drawn with the amateur builder in mind. Most individuals who set out to build an airplane can study a set of plans and teach themselves the skill of reading drawings, though it may take some time.

Your Ability as a Pilot

All aircraft do not fly alike, even the ones that look very similar. This is especially true of home-built airplanes, so it's up

Ask the man who owns one: the spirit of the fly-in. (Credit: Budd Davisson.)

to you to determine your basic piloting skill level. Have you flown tail-wheel airplanes? Have you flown aircraft that are fairly demanding or aircraft that are quite forgiving? Have you flown airplanes that you can compare to the design you've chosen? The flying machine that you build will, depending on your ability to fly, give you either hours and hours of enjoyment or moments of stark, white-hot terror.

Many home-built airplanes are more spirited than the normal aircraft produced by American manufacturers. But since anybody can learn to fly any kind of airplane, the basic question is whether or not he or she wants to. The learning process can be tedious, but more often it presents challenges that some people don't want to face. For that reason, when choosing a design, you have to decide whether or not you want to grow to be a better pilot. If you choose not to increase your piloting skills, then you should select a design that is a more forgiving, docile aircraft.

But just as it's possible to build an airplane that's too complicated for the pilot, it's also possible to have a pilot too complicated for the airplane. If you are a pilot who enjoys and can handle lots of performance, you will come to a point where you are bored with a docile, low-performance airplane. As a matter of fact, you may become bored with it quite quickly. Don't build a Pietenpol if you're a speed freak. Since the amount of work that goes into a low-performance airplane is exactly the same as that which goes into a high-performance airplane, do some serious self-evaluation before you start cutting metal.

41

The final shape of a steel tube fuselage is produced by wooden stringers and formers, which are covered by doped fabric. (Credit: Budd Davisson.)

Materials and Construction Methods

The type of material you choose to build your airplane out of is really more a matter of preference than anything else. The tooling for working with wood, metal, or fiberglass is only marginally different. The same is true of skill levels. While sheet metal may require more skill in layout, steel tubing may require more skill in welding.

New builders often ask which type of construction is the fastest. Among the traditional materials, meaning wood, steel, and sheet metal, there's very little difference, although the progression rate is different at various stages of completion. For instance, in the early stages of steel tubing construction, the fuselage appears to go together quite rapidly. However, when you get to the point where you have to cover the fuselage, it takes more time to put the fabric on. In the case of a sheet metal airplane, there's more tooling involved, so it takes you longer to get to the point where you have something that looks like an airplane. But when a sheet metal fuselage is finished, all it needs is paint. The only one of the structural materials that is faster than the rest is the fiberglass composite. The composites have, in recent years, proven themselves to be quite quick to build, and the techniques are easy to learn.

Steel Tubing and Fabric

The design concept of using steel tubing for the fuselage, covering it with fabric over wooden formers, and building a fabric-covered wooden skeleton for the wings is almost as old as aviation itself. This traditional construction method, introduced before World War I, is still used today on almost all fabric-covered aircraft. In this type of construction, the fuselage is a trusswork of small steel tubes ½ to ⅞ of an inch in diameter, with wall thicknesses measured in thousandths of an inch. It's thin, light, and extremely strong. In appearance, this type of airframe construction is not much different from old stick-and-tissue rubber-band-powered model airplanes. People who have built model airplanes usually find this type of construction easy to handle.

The fuselage is built by laying out the side frames for the major structure on a plywood board. Wooden blocks glued on the

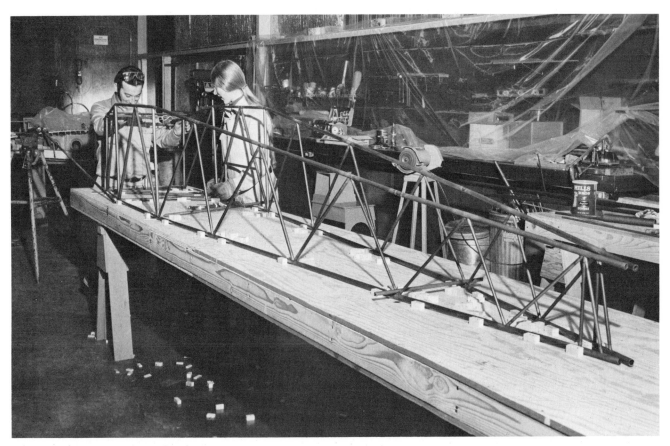

The fuselage of an **Acro Sport** begins to take shape on the jig boards where each piece is held in position by small wooden blocks. The entire assembly is tack welded together, checked for alignment, and then final welded. (Courtesy of Lee Fray/EAA.)

plywood hold the tubing in position until it is tack-welded together. This gives you two side frames that look like complex ladders. Then you stand these two ladders up, side by side, at the proper distances, and weld in the crosspieces. When you get into it, the process is not all that complicated. It's just a matter of cutting one little piece of tubing at a time and grinding the ends until they fit in place. This process is repeated dozens of times.

Welding is a procedure that scares both men and boys, but it really shouldn't. The art of welding two pieces of steel tubing together is not difficult; in fact, it's actually enjoyable. You can learn a tremendous amount about welding in a very short time, but it is very important that you have somebody looking over your shoulder to tell you what you are doing right or wrong. This is an

43

The Italian-designed **Falco** is one of the finest examples of a high-performance wooden airplane, but its structure, as shown here, is anything but simple. (Courtesy of Sequoia Aircraft.)

Left: Dorothy Ainksnoras demonstrates that building airplanes is not only a man's game; many home-built aircraft have been constructed from scratch by women. (Courtesy of EAA.)

area in which the Experimental Aircraft Association can help with their manuals and seminars.

When the entire steel framework has been welded together, wooden formers are placed around the outside and thin wood stringers run fore and aft on the airplane. The entire assembly is then covered with fabric to give it its final shape. The fabric is usually a cotton or synthetic cotton, which is doped with a type of paint that makes it shrink up taut. The wings are constructed of wood, much the same way model airplane wings are put together, and covered with the same type of doped fabric.

Wood

The use of wood in aircraft structure also goes back as far as aircraft do. Wood is one of the best materials in terms of its strength-to-weight ratio; properly used, it is quite light and very strong. It does have its drawbacks, however. Procuring high quality, aircraft-grade wood is becoming extremely difficult. Also, an aircraft is not built like a house. It does not use 2x4s stood on end, covered with ½-inch plywood. It is made up of many, many small pieces of wood, each of which is carefully shaped to carry a specific load. To a person familiar with working in wood, who is equipped for the job, normal wood airframe construction is no problem at all.

When working with aircraft wood the room temperature must normally be kept in the sixty-five- to seventy-five-degree range so that the gluing process works properly. If you have to build when the snow is heaped up against the garage, this could be difficult.

Another environmental problem is that wood supports the growth of fungus which can seriously weaken it. For that reason, the finishing of the wood is important, but certainly this task is no more difficult than varnishing a floor or a bookcase.

Aluminum

Many people are surprised to learn that all aircraft aren't made of aluminum. That's because there are very few factory-built airplanes that are made of anything but aluminum; this has given rise to the expression "Wichita Spam Can," used to refer to factory-built aircraft. In the homebuilt category, however, the all-metal airplane (meaning sheet aluminum) has to share top billing with the other three forms of construction materials. This is pri-

Stelio Frati, the famed light plane designer, designed the **Falco** in the early 1950s. Nearly 100 were produced in Italy; now the design is offered in plan and kit form to give the homebuilder a chance to own an aerial Ferrari. (Courtesy of James Gilbert/Sequoia Aircraft.)

marily because aluminum requires a few techniques not used for either wood or steel tubing. They are not particularly difficult, but working sheet metal is not something you normally learn puttering around the house.

Most sheet metal construction is known technically as "monocoque" construction. Freely translated, this means "single shell"; the outer skin of the airplane, which is very thin, is used to carry structural loads. There is no inside frame with a cosmetic shell on the outside to give it form, as there is in steel tubing and fabric construction. The sheet metal that you see on the outside is the actual load-bearing exoskeleton of the airplane.

Sheet metal requires several specific tools that are seldom needed for other types of aircraft construction. You'll need some specialty items, such as clecos, which are handy little fastening devices that you stick through a hole in two pieces of metal to hold them together. And, of course, sheet metal requires riveting equipment: rivet guns, sets, and the air compressor to drive them. Traditional riveting requires you to have not only the equipment, but also two people: one on one side to hammer the rivet, and one on the other side to hold a bucking bar against it to form the butt. The newer designs have tried to eliminate the need for two-man riveting by using pop rivets—blind rivets that are pulled with a special hand tool from one side of the sheet metal, which makes things much easier and faster. Some of the newest designs strive to eliminate rivets altogether, by attaching the aluminum skin with a special space-age adhesive.

45

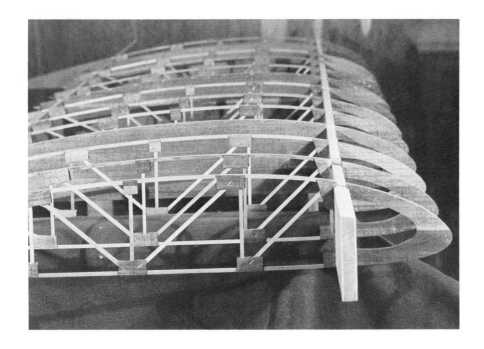

The most common structure for a fabric-covered homebuilt wing is a skeleton of wooden ribs, which give surprising strength and rigidity for a very small amount of weight. (Credit: Budd Davisson.)

Advocates of the other forms of aircraft structure inevitably say that with sheet metal you build the airplane twice: once in wood and again in sheet metal. It is true that some of the complex forms of aluminum, such as the frames on the inside of the fuselage, must be made as wooden form blocks first. Then you form the metal around the blocks. However, look at the complete project rather than just the forming process; the extra time spent on that particular part of the building is eliminated at the finishing end. In steel tube construction, after you have built the fuselage and put the formers around it, you then have to put the skin on it. On a wooden airplane, it's much the same: you have to cover it with fabric to protect the wood and then dope it. But in the case of an all-metal airplane, once you have the skin riveted in place, you're all done. You don't really need to paint an aluminum airplane except for cosmetic purposes. The thin outside layer of aluminum, much thinner than a dime, is ready to fly as soon as you have it attached. So, in the long run, the time factors are about the same.

One other distinct advantage to working with sheet metal is that temperature is not a major problem, unless, of course, you are bonding the surfaces together. The riveting process, cutting, bending, and the general handling of aluminum sheet are not much affected by low temperatures. If it's warm enough in your shop for you to work, it's warm enough to work with aluminum. A minor disadvantage in building a sheet metal airplane, however, is that the parts you make, such as the fuselage and the wings, are completely floppy and formless until the last skin is riveted in place.

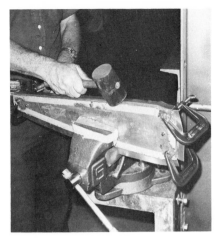

An alternative to the wooden rib is the metal rib; here one is being hammered into shape around a form block. (Courtesy of Ken Knowles.)

In a metal wing, such as this **Thorp T-18** panel, the main spar carries the load, while the ribs give the wing its shape. (Courtesy of Ken Knowles.)

This means you need jigs to hold the parts in their proper positions until the final skin is attached. Once that skin is riveted on, what you see is what you've got, because there is no way to adjust it. The only cure for a crooked or warped wing is to drill out all the rivets and reskin it.

To do clean, accurate, and safe building in sheet aluminum also requires more attention to detail, especially when it comes to protecting the aluminum surfaces. A scratch in aluminum can form the basis for a fatigue failure, so you'll have to spend more time protecting the surfaces of all the parts you make.

Composites

Originally, *composite* meant an aircraft structure that was made out of more than one type of material. For instance, an airplane with a steel tube fuselage and wood wings was once considered a composite. Today, composite is the latest buzz word in both sport and commercial aviation. It now refers to construction techniques that use a woven fabric as a thin skin, which is stabilized with a very thin layer of rigid plastic foam material, and then epoxied together with another layer of fabric. In most cases, this sandwich is a layer of fiberglass, a layer of foam, and another layer of fiberglass. It may sound outlandish that you can take something as fragile as a piece of foam and make an airplane out of it, but if you want to see how much strength you can get with foam-and-fiberglass construction, look at a foam surfboard. It weighs virtually nothing, but it's nearly as strong as a piece of wood the

47

The EAA Convention/Fly-in hosts many new designs, but none raised more eyebrows than the Rutan-designed **Quickie** when it debuted there in 1979. Made of foam and fiberglass, it cruises at over 100 mph on only 18 hp. (Credit: Budd Davisson.)

same size. The average coffee cup or a foam ice chest would make a nearly indestructible structure if you were to cover it with epoxy and fiberglass. The glass-foam-glass sandwich is currently earning acceptance as the structure of space-age airplanes.

The most efficient composite airframe structures are hollow, surrounded by a very thin skin made of the glass-foam-glass sandwich. A composite wing, for instance, is built this way. Although this is the lightest and strongest composite structure, it can also be quite complicated, because the skins must be formed into sandwiches in female molds. The average home-builder has a difficult time doing this, because making the mold is as complicated as making the airplane. To solve this problem, Burt Rutan of California has pioneered a new composite technique for home-builders in which you take blocks of foam, cut them into the shapes of the surfaces you want, and then cover them with fiberglass. In effect, you are making a foam airplane and covering it with glass, leaving the foam in place. The structures are heavier, but building progresses quickly, and it is easier to maintain accuracy. Rutan refers to this method as "moldless composite aircraft construction," but that nomenclature is not entirely accurate, because the core, which you cut out of a block of foam with a long, electrically heated wire, forms a *male* mold rather than a female one. Rutan's adaptation of this structural technique (originally employed in sailplanes) and his revolutionary aircraft designs (VariEze, Long-EZ, Defiant, Quickie) have revolutionized the home-built aircraft market. Because the material is so easily worked and gives such phenomenal structural integrity, builders have found they can turn out his designs in half the time required for a conventional home-built aircraft.

While there are clear-cut advantages to this type of structure, there are also a few disadvantages. Many people are allergic to the epoxies used in building up the fiberglass skin. Also, the dust from sanding can cause lung damage if a proper respirator system is not used; and of course, the entire process produces very strong fumes.

Kits and Parts
Somewhere in the early 1970s, a lot of entrepreneurs realized that the home-building market was not part of the lunatic fringe. It also occurred to them that although home-building movement

used to consist of individuals trying to build airplanes that were cheaper than the ones they could buy, that had changed. Today, a home-built airplane can easily cost as much as a comparable factory-built design, but it will be a truly individualistic machine. The money-saving aspect of home-building has taken a back seat to aesthetics and personal satisfaction. In short, a flourishing industry has developed to supply this high-profit market with kits, finished parts, and plans for virtually every kind of airplane imaginable.

The result of this incredible growth is that you can pick up your phone, dial a number, and have a supplier send you any part, any combination of parts, or a completed assembly. For instance, if you want wings for a Starduster TOO, you can simply place a call to the Starduster Corporation, state your requirements, and they'll send you a set of wings. There are perhaps a dozen companies putting together different parts of the fuselage, wings, and canard for VariEzes, Quickies and Long-EZs. The same is true for many other popular designs.

The purists say that anybody who buys something from a kit manufacturer is defeating the purpose of building the airplane in the first place. However, even if you bought all of the parts for the average airplane from a supplier, you would still be thousands of hours away from completing the airplane. Also, the sudden availability of parts has increased safety in many respects, because most of them are of a higher quality and consistency than many individual builders can achieve.

The extreme case of kitting an airplane is the Christen Eagle. Christen Industries designed the airplane and then developed a kit that has to be seen to be believed. You send Frank Christenson a check, and he sends back a huge number of boxes, each filled to the brim with shrink-packed parts. There's an enormous piece of cardboard, for instance, on which all of the parts for the ailerons are arranged in a specific sequence. They are then shrink-packed so that they stay in position on the cardboard when it's inserted into the box. Every nut, bolt, screw, and piece of wire that the airplane needs comes in the boxes. Along with them come thirty-two instruction manuals that use exploded isometric views and piece-by-piece drawings, to show you exactly how to assemble and finish the airplane. The practicality of this type of kit is proved by the fact that only two years after its introduction, there were dozens of Eagles flying.

All is not sunshine and roses in the kit and prefabricated parts market, however. As in any other business, there are good suppliers and bad suppliers. The best thing to do is make a list of all the suppliers for the aircraft you are interested in. Then use the network of friends you have developed over the past year to find out who has bought from these companies. Don't be fooled by the size of the outfit. In some cases, the bigger the company, the lower the quality. Conversely, some of the very smallest companies are building some of the very finest parts. Where such companies can really help a builder is in the very small fittings, such as aileron hinges, or any steel formed part that requires bending and drilling to a particular configuration. Those parts are often the most difficult for an individual to make accurately, and they are also the most critical. It makes sense to spend a few extra dollars on them; at the same time, however, it is imperative that the quality of those parts be as high as possible. What you are looking for is proper alignment of the holes, clean edges on the material with no scratches or band saw marks, surfaces without scratches, and edges of all drilled holes that are very slightly chamfered.

Plans

Plans are the very backbone of the project; a good set of plans can make things easy while a bad set can turn a project into a nightmare, especially if it's your first airplane. Unfortunately, the quality and concept of the available plans vary all over the map. Some plans, such as those for the Thorp T-18, give you a separate sheet for every part, plus assembly drawings that show how the parts go together; these plans exhibit true, professional construction quality. At the other extreme are two or three airplanes for which the plans show the complete airplane—every single part of it—on ten or twelve 8½-by-11-inch sheets; with all of the parts of the complete airplane crammed onto those sheets, it's like a jigsaw puzzle. It takes you forever to unravel things, and the drawings are so small that it's difficult to read them. One bright spot in the area of plans is the National Association of Sport Aircraft Designers (NASAD), which has established a review board to which a designer can submit his plans for a review of completeness, ac-

230 mph in a homebuilt wooden airplane? Ask the **Barracuda** pilot.

The all-composite **Dragonfly**—an example of the new wave of homebuilt technology.

The **Smith Miniplane**—one of the earliest homebuilts to gain popularity.

A Rutan design family portrait. From top to bottom:
VariViggin, VariEze, and **Defiant.**

A 150-mph Volkswagen? That's the **Sonerai II.**

Fun is where you find it, in this case in the cockpit of a **Skyotë.**

The first **VariEze** to be completed from plans shows off its unusual and effective lines.

One of the fastest and most efficient all-metal homebuilts, the **RV-3** is also one of the prettiest.

The **Quickie** established new homebuilt trends by using a motorhome auxiliary engine for power and foam and fiberglass for structure.

The unorthodox-looking **Hyper-bipe** is a classic combination of cross-country speed and acrobatic capabilities.

The **Shoestring** homebuilt racer has tremendous speed on little horsepower.

Look out below—the **Fokkers** are coming!

With the **Thorp T-18C** folding wings you can sneak in under the wing of another airplane and take absolutely no additional hangar space. (Courtesy of Ken Knowles.)

curacy, and general layout. Unfortunately, not all designers submit their plans. Here again, your best hedge against getting ripped off is to talk to friends who have bought the plans; examine them carefully and make sure they make sense before you buy them. Also make certain that the designer has an updating service that contacts builders who have bought his plans to advise them of changes or updates.

Builder Associations

To give you some idea of how all-encompassing the aviation community has become, nearly every type of home-built aircraft has formed an association that publishes a newsletter. These can be the best source of information about that particular airplane design. Take the T-18 Mutual Aid Society, for instance: for more than fifteen years, they have been cranking out a newsletter that describes the solutions builders have devised for difficulties with the T-18. The newsletter lists phone numbers and addresses of builders, so that you can contact people in your area who are bending metal on the same design. There is simply no substitute for contact with people who are building the same airplane. A phone call to somebody who has already been through the process can save you days and days of messing around on your own, and it can save you money, as well.

On Being the First

Because the home-building movement is exploding so rapidly, there is an increasing likelihood that you will pick out a design of which very few examples have been completed. This makes you a pioneer, and pioneering has its distinct disadvantages. Even the factories have troubles with airplanes after they get into the field; it often takes them several years to get an airplane completely debugged. The same thing applies to a home-built airplane. The first people who built the airplane are doing much of the debugging for the designer. That's not the designer's intent; it just works out that way. If you are already knowledgeable about homebuilts and have built one or two planes, or if you have been around them for a long time, you won't mind being a pioneer. But if you're like most people, and this is a new venture for you, it's far better to

51

pick a design that's been around for several years. As a rule of thumb, you should never build an airplane that has less than ten flying examples, and the more the better. If a design is three years old and there are no flying examples besides the prototype, that should make you stop and ask questions. On the other hand, look at a design like the VariEze: two years after the plans were released, there were more than 300 of them flying! That's the sign of a quality design.

Designing Your Own

The question is often asked, "Since I've been building model airplanes for years, why can't I design and build my own airplane?" In fact, there is no reason why you can't; it's done every day. However, it's not an easy project: Designing and engineering an airplane cannot be covered in a single book; the structural and aerodynamic analysis alone would fill several volumes. Because it is such a complex task, just doing the engineering properly takes up enough time to build half an airplane. This is not to say that designing an airplane is an impossible project for the nonprofessional, but it is certainly not an easy project. In many cases, it's neither safe nor advisable. Since there are so many fine designs already available, if you're a beginner, it makes sense to capitalize on other people's experience. Then, once you've built someone else's design and flown the airplane, if you feel you can do better, go ahead and do it.

A Homebuilt Catalog

Some of the most popular old favorites as well as some of the most promising new designs have been selected for thumbnail sketches of their construction and flight characteristics. Before getting into this subject, however, be sure to read the earlier material in this chapter about what to look for and how to evaluate your wants and needs. If you haven't answered these questions, you're likely to get very confused. These thumbnails are in no way indicative of the total breadth or depth of the homebuilt inventory. An up-to-date descriptive catalog of homebuilts would be a tome the size of the New York phone book. So, spend a little time wading through the following descriptions, and see if any of these reach in and tug at your heartstrings. A directory of available designs and their specifications is at the end of the book.

The following descriptions use commonly available training airplanes, such as the Cessna 152 and the Piper Cherokee series, for comparison. However, in many cases, the home-built airplane handles in a manner unlike that of any factory-built airplane, so there is nothing to compare it to.

The Cross-Country Machines

The primary purpose of cross-country aircraft is to take you from here to there in the shortest possible time. They are, almost without exception, two-place airplanes, because presently there are no viable three- or four-place cross-country machines—with the exception of the BD-4—in the homebuilt inventory. They are also much faster than the similarly powered store-bought airplane, and they burn much less gas.

Thorp T-18 Tiger. Originally designed in the early 1960s, the Thorp T-18 Tiger was created by aeronautical engineer John Thorp, who, among other things, did the conceptual designing for the Piper Cherokee series. The airplane was meant to be an easy-to-build, all-metal airplane for the amateur builder who desired high performance. It uses a method of assembly called "matched hole" tooling, in which the holes for the rivets are drilled into templates that are used to transfer the same set of holes from one part to the other. This ensures matching predrilled holes in the parts, eliminating the need for jigs, and greatly simplifying assembly.

The T-18 is not named Tiger by accident. This little two-place craft is one of the finest cross-country airplanes available. With a 150-hp Lycoming engine, the airplane will crank along at 165 to 170 mph with absolutely no trouble, carrying two people, adequate baggage, and plenty of radios. In the air, it is like a little fighter, quite quick in roll and pitch, but at the same time it is quite stable, and stability is a very desirable characteristic for a cross-country airplane. Its bubble canopy gives vast visibility, but you must wear a hat to avoid getting a healthy sunburn. Many builders have incorporated tinted canopies or tinted sunscreens on the top to lower the sunburn factor. This is not an airplane for the timid pilot; it takes off and lands like a mini-fighter, quickly and positively. That's

53

When John Thorp designed the **T-18 Tiger** in the early 1960s, it was meant to be the simplest aluminum sport airplane available. However, it has proved to be one of the best bases for an aerial hotrod available. With engines up to 200 hp it cruises well over 200 mph, although 170 mph with 160 hp is much more common. (Courtesy of Lu Sutherland.)

not to say that it's difficult; it's just an airplane that does exactly what you tell it to do, so if you aren't used to giving precise control inputs, you may find yourself a little over your head. However, the airplane has the reputation of being one which pilots learn to love very quickly. Once you're over the initial surge of adrenalin, it's an airplane that you have no trouble catching up with.

The Thorp has one of the most advanced mutual aid societies and newsletter systems available. In addition, its dedicated group of followers has created significant modifications for it. These include folding wings, a wider fuselage, and an advanced airfoil. The new wing lowers the stall speed and makes the landings more docile. At the same time, the new airfoil gives it a higher cruising speed. The folding wings, of course, make it possible to hangar the airplane at home in your garage, and trailer it out to the airport when you want to fly. As conventional airplanes go, the T-18 is certainly one of the best designs for cross-country traveling.

Bushby Mustang II. The Mustang II has accommodations and performance similar to the Thorp, especially when it uses the same power plants. If the Mustang has any advantage over the Thorp, it is primarily aesthetic. Many people think the boxy fuselage of the Thorp detracts from it looks. Others, of course, claim that it *adds* to the looks. The Mustang II does away with that argument by blending beautifully smooth, streamlined looks with relatively docile handling, considering the performance. Like the Thorp, the Mustang II is available in semi-kits, in which nearly all of the difficult parts come ready-made.

BD-4. The BD-4 is the only practical four-place cross county machine in the homebuilt inventory. A product of the prolific mind of Jim Bede of BD-5 fame, the BD-4 uses an unusual construction method to make things easier for the first-time builder: The fuselage is constructed of lengths of aluminum angle which are bolted together with gusset plates. The fuselage skin is then bonded in place. The foldable wings are an innovative assemblage of identical fiberglass sections that slide over a round main spar.

A reliable airplane powered by engines in the 150–200 hp class, the BD-4 can be built as a taildragger or as a tricycle geared machine. It cruises at speeds up to 190 mph.

The **Bushby Mustang II:** a popular all-metal two-place cross-country airplane. (Credit: Budd Davisson.)

The all-wood, 230-mph **Barracuda** always draws a crowd—and what proud owner can ignore an adoring audience! (Credit: Budd Davisson.)

Barracuda. Geoff Seirs designed the Barracuda as a traveling machine, and, make no mistake about it, this bird is made for going places. With engines up to 310 hp and higher, and the frontal area of a bullet, this big-engine macho machine hustles along at something over 240 mph, making it one of the fastest cross-country homebuilts available in plan form. Only the BJ-520 is any faster.

Built entirely of wood, the Barracuda demands that the pilot fly it the way it's supposed to be flown. Although not a difficult airplane to fly, it is nonetheless a true high-performance machine that tolerates few, if any, mistakes. With its retractable tricycle gear, enormous motor, fuel boost pumps, flaps, and every other operational system that a high-performance airplane is supposed to have, the airplane is not simple to build, nor is it quick. It is not inexpensive, either. For the price of the engine alone, you could build a Thorp and still have enough left over for a month's vacation. At the same time, this is an airplane that lets you run up alongside most Wichita twins, look over, smile at the pilot, and then run away and hide from him. This airplane is fast!

Wittman Tailwind. More than thirty years old, the Wittman Tailwind design just keeps soldiering ahead, especially as the cost of fuel increases. A product of the inventive mind of Steve Wittman, famed race pilot of the 1930s, the Tailwind is a study in simplicity and traditional construction. Its fuselage is a basic steel tubing box covered with fabric, and the thin-section, Hershey-bar wings are of wood and plywood construction. Its structure and basic design have been proven to be both efficient and safe.

Although the airplane is quite small, and the cockpit slightly tight, the Tailwind can be a surprisingly comfortable and easy airplane to fly. It has always been axiomatic that a tiny airplane is a difficult airplane to take off and land, but this is not the case with the Tailwind. The tapered steel tubing landing gear, a Steve Wittman patent now used by Cessna and a number of others, is designed to give soft landings and easy ground handling. This can't be said about a number of other small, tail-wheel-equipped airplanes.

As originally designed with 90 hp, the airplane cruised at 145 to 155 mph. Naturally, when the EAAers get hold of a good design, they make a hot rod out of it. Tailwinds have been flown with as much as 210 hp, although Steve Wittman himself says that 140 to 150 hp should be the absolute maximum. He flies one modified to mount a 215-cubic-inch Buick aluminum V-8 engine. This makes for an economical and easy-to-repair engine, and it also gives a rather racy-looking nose to the airplane.

The Tailwind is one of those airplanes that has been overlooked in the recent rush toward the composite machines with their exotic shapes, but it's still a good, basic, fast, and easy-to-fly cross-country airplane.

VariEze/Long-EZ. Thirty years from now, when we have a better perspective on history, Burt Rutan will be considered one of those individuals who was instrumental in setting aviation off on a new

Californian Burt Rutan has revolutionized the aircraft design field with his all-composite canard designs. (Credit: Budd Davisson.)

A bevy of Rutan's progeny, the clan **VariEze,** nuzzle up to each other on the flight line at Oshkosh. The nose gear of this design retracts to let the airplane kneel like a camel for boarding and tie-down. (Courtesy of EAA.)

path. It has been forty years since there has been major progress made in general aviation, but Rutan has started out with a clean sheet of paper and he's come up with a new design every time around. It's difficult to believe the number of airplanes he has designed, and the totally unorthodox and sometimes weird configurations of some of them.

Rutan is a zealous exponent of the old canard configuration, in which the horizontal tail surface of the airplane is mounted up front, rather than in the back. According to Rutan, the loaded canard configuration lets him design an airplane that is aerodynamically difficult to stall: therefore, it's much safer in most flight situations. This design also simplifies the fuselage and shortens it, thus reducing the wetted area and the associated drag.

Dick Rutan, test pilot for brother Burt's many designs, currently holds the world's distance record for 4,800 miles nonstop in a home-built Rutan-designed Long-EZ. (Credit: Budd Davisson.)

But Rutan's innovations are more than skin deep: his airplanes have also forged new paths in airframe construction. Every one of his newer designs uses composite construction in which the airplane's parts are first cut out of foam and then covered with fiberglass. He freely admits he did not invent the process, since the Germans have been using it in sailplanes for many years. He is, however, the first to apply it to home-built aircraft, and this innovation has whacked thousands of hours from the construction time of his airplanes. He estimates that in the next few years there will be easily a thousand of his designs flying, which would put him ahead of many of the big-time manufacturers in terms of numbers of planes in the air.

The VariEze was the first of his composite designs to take hold. Its 170-to-180-mph performance on only 100 hp coupled with its uncomplicated structure overcame any sales resistance that may have been triggered by its unusual configuration. After thousands of sets of plans were out and 300 of the airplanes were flying, Rutan chose to render his own design obsolete with an updated version called the Long-EZ.

The Long-EZ has several advantages over the VariEze. It overcame several objectionable characteristics such as low visibility, high approach speeds, and low roll rates. And it is a true long-range, cross-country machine.

Although the VariEze was capable of running across country at 170 mph, with 1,000 miles between stops, the Long-EZ, in the same configuration, with two people and only 115 hp, runs at the same speed for 1,600 miles. As if to prove that he was capable of leaping entire continents in a single bound, Rutan's test pilot, brother Dick, set a solo distance record for this class of airplane at 4,800 miles, nonstop, with extra gas tanks.

To support his new airplane and its unusual construction, Rutan developed an intense educational program during the first few years the VariEze was being built. He conducted seminars all around the country and established the Rutan Aircraft Factory newsletter, the *Canard Pusher.* This newsletter is one of the best technical publications available that deals with a single subject.

Neither the VariEze nor the Long-EZ is difficult to fly, although the VariEze does have the aforementioned problems. The VariEze is extremely light in pitch control at slow speeds, which causes overcontrolling on takeoff or landing. For this reason and others, Rutan chose to take those plans off the market when he introduced the Long-EZ.

Although you lie back in a race driver's position in the Long-EZ, the visibility and the comfort are unmatched by any other homebuilt. In takeoff and landing, you have the entire runway in view at all times, and when cruising you feel as if you are lying down in a plastic bubble. The in-flight stability matches or surpasses that of most large twin engine airplanes, yet the controls are light and delicate, and they respond to your every demand. The nose wheel is retracted by a crank mechanism, and a belly-board drag brake helps slow the airplane down for landing. Getting the airplane slowed down and keeping it slow is more of a problem than you might imagine, and this ability to glide forever is something that takes a bit of getting used to.

To demonstrate how easy the Long-EZ is to fly, Rutan had it flown by his secretary, a low-time private pilot, and by a student pilot with only twenty-five hours in her logbook. Neither one had the slightest amount of trouble. In fact, his secretary flew the airplane nonstop from California to Oshkosh, Wisconsin. Considering its performance, the Long-EZ is one of the most easily obtained tigers available. That may be why it's called an EZ.

Q2/Dragonfly. The weird-looking all-composite Q2 and Dragonfly are both outgrowths of an earlier Rutan design exercise known as the Quickie. The Quickie was a single-place airplane using an 18-hp engine that was designed to be the ultimate in light aircraft. The Q2 and the Dragonfly use the same basic configuration, but they are enlarged to accommodate two people and to use Volkswagen engines for power.

Although similar in appearance, the Q2 and Dragonfly are actually quite different airplanes. The Q2 uses a 2100-cc Volkswagen engine conversion that cranks out approximately 65 hp. It has a fairly small wing, compared to the Dragonfly. For that reason, it's quite fast—up to 180 mph with that small engine. The airplane has consistently won efficiency races. However, the same things that make it fast and efficient also make it hotter on landing, and it uses more runway because of the higher speeds. The Dragonfly, on the other hand, uses a maximum size Volkswagen

59

of 1834 cc, which eliminates the need for a stroker crankshaft and for modifying the engine to its limits—both of which reduce reliability. It may have less horsepower than the Q2, but it has much more wing area, which means that the Dragonfly can land on a much shorter runway and at slower speeds.

Both of the airplanes are intended for smooth, concrete runways, since their gear configuration will *not* allow them to be landed on grass; they can get a little hard to handle even on rough pavement.

Of the two airplanes, the Q2 has many more vendors supplying parts and semifinished fuselages. Both, however, are designed with the amateur builder in mind, and either would make an excellent choice for a cross-country airplane; of course, you have to be willing to be stared at every time you land.

Glasair. A more traditional approach to composite design is the Hamilton-Stoddard Glassair. Its configuration is like that of any other low-wing, side-by-side aircraft, but its structure is definitely space-age in concept. Rather than having foam cores with fiberglass on the outside, the Glassair uses thin glass-foam-glass sandwiches made in female molds for all skins and internal structures. The entire kit resembles a huge plastic model airplane kit: the wings are two basic pieces glued together like a model airplane, and the fuselage and tail are put together the same way.

The Glassair is designed to cruise at more than 200 mph; the 150-hp engine runs at lower rpms, giving excellent fuel economy. All of its flight and ground-handling characteristics are very normal for the type, although it might seem a little slippery to pilots not accustomed to high-performance aircraft.

The Racers

In the single-place cross-country market, many of the good designs are those airplanes originally designed as racers. Two of the front-runners are the Cassutt and the Midget Mustang. Both present entirely different approaches to single-place speed.

The Cassutt. A traditional midwing, Formula I racer, the Cassutt has a tiny fuselage made of steel tubing, covered with fabric and formers, and the wing is a one-piece plywood-covered slab that

The Hamilton-Stoddard **Glasair** is a recent kit design that comes with premolded and preshaped parts, just like a giant model airplane. But this is no model. Its 150 hp Lycoming will easily propel it at speeds of over 200 mph while burning less than 5 gallons an hour. (Courtesy of Jim Larsen.)

The single-place all-metal **Midget Mustang** that originated as a Formula I racer in 1948 has become a classic sport design. This retractable-gear version was Grand Champion Homebuilt at Oshkosh two years in a row. (Credit: Budd Davisson.)

doesn't look big enough to lift anything, much less an airplane. With a normal 100-hp engine, the Cassutt will cruise at 180 mph, depending largely on how fast you're willing to turn the engine. The airplane is uncomfortable for a large man. It is also a little short of fuel capacity, so a 400-to-500-mile cross-country would about be your limit, and you'd better not pack much more than a toothbrush. Landing the Cassutt can sometimes be a challenge, especially on pavement or with a hard crosswind; it is not an impossible airplane to land, just one that demands concentration.

Sonerais I and II. The original Sonerai was designed as a Formula V racer, meaning it had to be powered by a converted Volkswagen engine and have a minimum of 75 square feet of wing area. The Formula V racing program never really got off the ground but the Sonerai certainly did. The original racing version offered by John Monnet, the designer, in both plan and kit form was immediately picked up by homebuilders as an inexpensive mode of high speed transportation.

Monnet later brought out a two-place version—the Sonerai II—and it is enjoying even more popularity than the single place did. The Sonerai II is more comfortable flown as an occasional two-place because the provisions for the passenger are less than commodious and the airplane's performance suffers with two people on board.

All of the Sonerais have a traditional tube and fabric fuselage structure and pop-riveted aluminum wings. Monnet also offers conversion kits for the Volkswagen engine.

The Midget Mustang. One of the original Goodyear Racer designs of 1948, the Midget Mustang uses all-metal construction and a low wing configuration. Although it's not quite as fast as a Cassutt, it is much easier to land, and it's about as difficult to build. Its extreme good looks have made it a very popular airplane for more than thirty years.

The Adventure. This is one of the few traditional-looking composite homebuilts. Its structural characteristics are almost identical to those of the Long-EZ and the VariEze. Using a 100-hp Continental engine, the Adventurer cruises at 175 mph at 8,000

The **Stardusters,** designed by Lou Stolp, are among the most graceful and popular sport biplanes. (Credit: Budd Davisson.)

Left: The flight deck of a home-built such as this **Starduster TOO** is hardly as complicated as a 747, but to the pilot in command it offers more grass-roots flying than any of the more normal airplanes. (Credit: Budd Davisson.)

feet and carries enough fuel for 550 miles. Its tricycle gear takes a lot of the worry out of landing, and the cockpit was designed to be comfortable for the average-size man. Its designer, the late George Meade, consistently raced the airplane in efficiency races; he also developed a tail-wheel version of the same airplane, for those who think it's not macho to have a nose wheel on the front.

Going Places, but Not Too Far

Undoubtedly the largest category of home-built aircraft is that which includes airplanes designed for fun close to home. These airplanes may be good enough to travel 200 to 300 miles, but if you venture much farther than that, what is supposed to be a pleasurable trip becomes an arduous journey. They're designed to be a ball just putting around the airport, which is what the vast majority of pilots want. They also offer the largest number of choices, ranging from old-fashioned biplanes to modernistic little mini-rockets.

Starduster TOO.   One of the first two-place home-built biplanes, the Starduster TOO is certainly one of the prettiest. Its basic good looks and fine performance make the Starduster TOO one of the long-time favorites of almost everyone who builds airplanes. Completely traditional in its steel-tube-and-fabric fuselage and wood-frame wings with fabric covering, the Starduster TOO presents no difficult building problems. However, since it's a large airplane, it's going to be a bigger and more expensive project.

A little **Davis DA-2A** combines easy sheet metal construction with docile performance. With 85 to 100 hp it will cruise at 115 mph, carrying two people in comfort. (Credit: Budd Davisson.)

The airplane is designed to fly with anything from 150 to 260 hp, and it seems to do equally well with any engine. The cockpits are both roomy, so if you're larger than average, you will find the airplane comfortable to fly. Although the airplane wasn't designed for it, it will do basic acrobatics. You should be cautioned, however, that if you're looking for an airplane to do difficult acrobatics, the Starduster TOO is not your best choice.

The ground-handling characteristics of the Starduster require that you be something more than the complacent pilot—not a super pilot, just an attentive one.

Davis DA-2A. The little Davis DA-2A is one of the overlooked airplanes of the homebuilt movement, possibly because its designer, Leeon Davis, did not mount a major marketing program. However, it has managed to maintain solid popularity because of its ease of building and good performance. With 65 to 85 hp, the airplane will carry two people and cruise all day long at 115 mph, but you don't have to be a master metalsmith to build it. The fuselage is made up of straight, sheared sheets of aluminum with little or no curve. Although perhaps not as pleasing as one with compound curves, this rectilinear structure greatly simplifies building and does nothing to compromise the aerodynamics of the airplane.

The Davis DA-2A is an excellent choice for the first-time builder who wants to work with sheet metal. It will give him a very pleasing airplane that is as practical as it is fun to fly.

It's called the **Breezy.** Makes you wonder where it got its name, doesn't it? (Courtesy of Dick Stouffer/EAA.)

The Fun-Loving Breed

Many homebuilts are designed solely to get you off the ground and give you the most fun you have ever had. They aren't meant for running off cross-country or for doing wild aerobatics. They are meant to give you the thrill of flight as no normal aircraft can.

Breezy.   The Breezy offers a unique way to get yourself off the ground and up to where bugs can hit you in the teeth. Aptly named, the Breezy is a combination of an open fuselage structure of bridge-like tubing and airplane wings from other models, such as an Aeronca Champ or even a Cessna. Although it is usually flown as a two-place airplane, the larger engines will fly it very adequately with three people on board.

In spite of its unorthodox appearance, the Breezy has a reputation of flying more or less normally, behaving like any other small, light airplane. There is, however, one factor to be considered: from the pilot's viewpoint, there is almost no airplane, and thus it's difficult to judge your nose attitude; the first several flights are usually quite interesting.

Here's something else to think about. If you suffer from acrophobia, or fear of heights (many pilots have a touch of it), the Breezy may not be the plane for you. Some pilots have reported that their acrophobia bothers them severely in the airplane, even if it never does in a normal airplane.

Pietenpol Air Camper.   The granddaddy of the popular home-builts, the Pietenpol is, amazingly, still being built today. Every aspect of the airplane is an anachronism. It's a build-it-yourself antique, but it keeps gaining in popularity as the nation looks back with nostalgic longing. The original Air Camper used a Model A engine, but most being built today are powered by 65- to 85-hp Continentals; the Chevrolet Corvair conversion is also popular.

The Pietenpol's closest aerial cousin is a maple seed. The airplane flies easily and is unbelievably forgiving of your mistakes. Its big wing and small engine will carry two people with absolutely no problems, although, if both of you are heavyweights, it does ask that the trees at the end of the runway be fairly short. Its takeoff and landing speeds are somewhere in the neighborhood of a fast gallop, and its cruising speed is only slightly higher—in the 75-to-80-mph category. This is an airplane that's not going to take you very far, but you can have a lot of fun while you're getting there.

Recently some Pietenpols have been modified into biplanes. Rigged this way, with a slightly square nose, the plane looks for all the world like a small Jenny or any of the other trainer biplanes of 1918 or 1919. It's a pretty airplane, although the original Pietenpol was a very high-drag, high-lift, slow-speed airplane to begin with, and as a biplane it's got even more lift, more drag, and less speed.

Skyotë. The Skyotë is a recent entry into the sport biplane category. This diminutive airplane was designed specifically to use low horsepower to give blazing performance while still being a very docile machine. It's capable of aerobatics at the intermediate level and above on only 85 to 90 hp. The outrigger landing gear is calculated to give one a nostalgic feel. But though it looks like an antique, it was professionally designed by engineer Pete Bartoe. The fuselage is standard steel tubing, while the double-swept wing panels use an aluminum framework covered in fabric. Although the airplane is small and simple looking, its structure is slightly more complicated than you might expect.

The Acrobats

In the last ten years, aerobatic airplanes have developed from craft that can do a loop and a spin to machines that look as though they can fly vertically indefinitely while doing roll after roll after roll. The aerodynamics of *competition* airplanes have been refined to the point where only a handful of pilots in the world are capable of extracting all the performance they possess. At the same time, however, there exists an exciting cadre of *sport* aerobatic biplanes. These planes can perform true aerobatics, but they are not so highly honed that they belong in the unlimited arena.

Acro Sport I and II. The Acro Sport biplanes were designed by EAA president Paul Poberezny as light, easy-to-build airplanes for a serious but noncompetitive aerobatic pilot. Their straight wing panels greatly simplify construction, and the fuselage is traditional steel tubing, offering no particular challenges. Many of these airplanes have been built as projects by vocational and training schools.

65

The **Acro Sport** was designed by EAA president and founder Paul Poberezny to be an easily built and easily flown high-performance aerobatic biplane; he accomplished all his goals. (Credit: Budd Davisson.)

Although originally designed to fly on 100 to 200 hp, the Acro Sports are seldom powered with less than 150 hp, and usually with 180 hp. With any of these engines, they're docile, easy-to-fly mounts. On the runway, their manners couldn't be better, something which can't be said for all small biplanes. This basic description applies to both models, except that the Acro Sport II has a second cockpit for a passenger.

Pitts Special S-1. When one speaks of aerobatics, one is usually talking about the Pitts Special. In that field it has reigned as king for more than twenty years. Designed by Curtis Pitts shortly after World War II, the airplane has been refined from an 85-hp pasture airplane to a 200-hp screaming demon. Although several competition airplanes will outfly the Pitts Special, the Pitts is still the standard by which all the others are measured. Since more than 700 of them have been built, there is nothing about the airplane that poses a problem to the builder today.

The fuselage is of steel tubing construction, and, being quite small, it doesn't have a lot of tubing in it. The wings are traditional wood construction with the top wing a one-piece, swept-back unit with an important wood joint right in the middle of the main spar. The Pitts comes in two flavors: the symmetrical-wing referred to as the *round-wing* version, which has a symmetrical airfoil on both wings, and four ailerons; and the earlier *flat-wing* version, which has ailerons only in the bottom wing, and an airfoil with a flat bottom section. Either airplane is more airplane than the average pilot needs. However, the symmetrical-wing airplane is much better on outside maneuvers, meaning flying upside down and doing outside loops. The four ailerons of the round-wing model also give a much higher roll rate. However, it's doubtful that any sport pilot can use all of the performance a round-wing Pitts has, so a flat-wing model would satisfy just about any pilot.

Neither of the Pitts models is particularly forgiving on the runway. Because of the airplane's size and the wing loading, it comes in fast and is quite skittish on the ground. This is one of those airplanes which forces the builder/pilot to decide that he will grow to meet the challenge. However, there is one indisputable fact about the Pitts Special: you will never outgrow the thrill of a takeoff, since this is the closest you will ever come to sitting

The **Pitts Special,** a legend in tube and fabric, has reigned supreme as aerobatic king of the world for nearly 30 years; only recently developed specialty machines have been able to match its performance. Some 600 of these airplanes are flying today. (Credit: Budd Davisson.)

Which way to the front? As this ¾-scale **SE-5** and its full-scale pilot prepare to set off after the Red Baron, the fierce looks are all in fun. (Courtesy of Ted Koston/EAA.)

on the nose of a bullet. In the air, the airplane is so responsive that there are no barriers between you and flight. It is the thoroughbred of the aerobatic world and possibly the thoroughbred of the homebuilt world.

Christen Eagle. The Christen Eagle comes in two flavors, both of which are sweet and to the point: the 200 hp two-place and the fire-breathing 260 hp single-place. Both are winners in esthetics and performance. More than 500 of the two-place kits are under construction; fifty Eagles are flying, and more are taking to the air each day.

These planes are designed for competition-level aerobatics and they meet the design goals admirably. Certainly the highest-performance two-place aerobatic machines commonly available to the homebuilder, they still manage to have excellent manners, both on the ground and in the air.

A legend in embryo: a young Curtis Pitts stands in front of the diminutive biplane he called the **Pitts Special,** shortly after its first flight in 1946. (Courtesy of EAA.)

The Stephens Acro. The first airplane to challenge the Pitts Special, the Stephens Acro is also one of the first monoplanes to win national aerobatic contests consistently. All of the Stephens' accomplishments were at the hands of famed aerobatic ace Leo Loudenslager. However, the Stephens Acro which Leo Loudenslager uses for competition has been greatly modified from the original plans-built airplane. Still, the Stephens presents a pilot with one of the most tractable, easily flown, high-performance machines available.

Where the Pitts Special roars down the runway like a dragster and leaps off like a cannonball, the Stephens Acro barely takes any runway; its wing loading is so light that in a few airplane lengths it leaps off like a feather and climbs like an angel headed home after the evening rush. Everything about the airplane is civilized and smooth, and it gives even the first-time pilot very little reason for apprehension. Its landings are not only easy but in some cases almost impossible, because the airplane just does not want to slow down and land. It takes a little practice to put it exactly where you want it on the runway. In the air, however, you have absolutely no trouble putting it where you want it.

The construction of the Stephens Acro is in some places extremely simple and in other places on the difficult side. Starting

68

with the bad news: the twenty-four-foot wing is a one-piece unit, using a twenty-four-foot spar made of seven spruce laminates. This single part often presents a builder with a nearly insurmountable problem, because a clamping device must be built that can hold something twenty-four feet long. For that reason, almost all builders purchase a wing kit that includes a laminated and trimmed spar. The rest of the wing calls for straightforward wooden construction. One should pay special note to the modifications that Leo Loudenslager has made to strengthen the construction of the wing; he has twice had cracks begin to develop in the wing spar during acrobatic competition.

The Replicas: World War I

The nationwide nostalgia boom has made its way into sport aviation, especially in the homebuilt field. Those who can't afford a warbird or an antique have decided to go the model builders one better: they have built replica aircraft that fall somewhere between the size of the model and the real McCoy.

Certainly some of the most exciting replicas to build are those based on World War I fighters. Plans are currently available for Nieuport 17s, Nieuport 28s, Fokker Triplanes, and SE-5s. These are available both in full-size replicas and scaled-down airplanes. If you can get your whole neighborhood to build these, you can stage World War I all over again in your back yards.

The Fokker Triplane. It's been nearly 65 years since Manfred von Richthofen made his mark as the Red Baron of Germany. His trademarks were a bright red Fokker Triplane, and flaming piles of his enemies' airplanes. The Baron didn't live on, but his airplane did. The DR-1 Fokker is available in plans for full-size, three-quarter- and seven-eighths-scale airplanes.

The biggest problem in building any sort of replica Fokker is choosing the engine. The rotary engine originally used in the Fokker is all but impossible to find these days, and if you did, you might find it too cantankerous to fly with anyway. Most builders wind up using a flat engine in a round cowl; one of the replicas uses a Warner 145 engine, which is itself becoming rare.

In the air, the Fokker Tri is a highly maneuverable and extremely unstable airplane; but that was exactly what it was sup-

The smoke is fake and so is the **Fokker Tri-plane,** but even the Red Baron himself would have a hard time telling this replica from the real thing. (Credit: Budd Davisson.)

posed to be—agile enough for a fighter that turns on somebody else's dime. On the ground, however, it's something entirely different. The middle wing lies exactly in your field of vision, making it very difficult to see either the runway or other traffic on approach. As originally built, with a tail skid and no brakes, it's nearly impossible to handle on a paved runway, especially if there's any cross wind at all. With a tail wheel, it still is an extremely difficult machine to take off and land.

Fokker D-7. The Fokker D-7 was one of the most advanced fighters of its day, so advanced, in fact, that it was named in the Treaty of Versailles; all flying examples had to be turned over to the Allies as prizes of war. Using a steel tube fuselage and plywood-covered wings, it was one of the easiest and best flying aircraft of its day.

Plans are available for a full-size replica using the original Mercedes engine. Finding the Mercedes alone would be a major project; however, it can be replaced with a Ranger engine. Note that this aircraft is larger and far more complicated than most homebuilts. While it looks pretty, it may be more than the first-time builder wants to bite off.

The Nieuports. All three of the more common Nieuports are available in plan form: the 17, the 24, and the 28. The 17 was a little kite, the 24 was a little bit bigger but still a kite, and the 28 was nearly a regular airplane. The 28 became famous as the airplane of Captain Eddie Rickenbacker, the World War I ace. Any of the Nieuports are tractable, easily flown aircraft. The smaller ones, however, are extremely light and must be handled with great care in crosswinds. The primary problem in building a full-size Nieuport is finding the correct engine. Several have been built, especially 28s, using Warner engines, and others have been built in scaled-down versions using flat Lycoming engines buried in the cowling.

Replicas: Pearl Harbor to VJ Day

Probably no other group of airplanes ever built has the emotional impact and appeal of the World War II fighters. Models of Mustangs, P-40s, Messerschmitts, and Zeros hang from the bedroom ceilings of probably half the kids in America. But the full-

The **Nieuport 28** is one of the more tractable of the World War I designs; this example is piloted by Eric Schilling, one of World War II's legendary Flying Tigers. (Credit: Budd Davisson.)

World War I fighters will never die—as long as home-builders survive. This **Nieuport 24** replica is no more complicated than most home-builts. (Credit: Budd Davisson.)

The **Junkers JU87 Stuka** dive-bomber ⅞-scale replica is one of the most complex homebuilt replicas in existence. Constructed with a minimum of power tools, it shows what can be done with a tremendous amount of tenacity. (Credit: Budd Davisson.)

This airplane appears to be a **North American P-51**; the spectator's scale reveals the truth: it's a ¾-size replica, with a Chevrolet V-8 engine. (Credit: Budd Davisson.)

size airplanes are priced entirely out of sight and the proficiency required to fly one is all but impossible to attain. This situation has been remedied by designers of World War II replicas in all different sizes and materials.

The P-51 Mustang. Probably everybody's favorite World War II fighter is the P-51 Mustang, but it's not an easy airplane to replicate, either in full size or in miniature. Only a few of the kits for three-quarter- and seven-eighths-scale airplanes have been successfully built. The most notable one has been the Falconair modification of the Jurca design. This all-wood airplane uses a Ranger six-cylinder engine for a power plant. The design is a little on the heavy side, but it flies and, more important, it looks like a Mustang. The Stewart Mustang uses a Chevrolet or Ford engine for a power plant, and it has fiberglass shells around a steel tube frame. Only a few examples have been finished, but they're fine-looking airplanes.

The WAR Replicas. One company in California, WAR Replicas, Inc., has designed a quasi-composite structure with a wooden fuselage box and wooden spars, and plastic foam to give the final shape. The shapes can be altered to make several different World War II fighters. The first of their airplanes was the most diminutive FW-190A you've ever seen. From any distance at all it's difficult to tell whether it's the real thing or a miniature. The size

This **Hurricane** replica rendered in wood is only a fraction of the size of the original airplane, but its 150-hp Lycoming runs on a fraction of what it cost to feed the original Rolls Royce V-12 engine. (Credit: Budd Davisson.)

of the pilot's head inside sets the story straight. Using a 100-hp Continental, the airplane cruises at 150 to 160 mph, but lands a little hot. Later versions have been lightened up and appear to perform much better. The WAR repertoire includes the P-47 Thunderbolt and the F-4U Corsair. Both airplanes, because of their small size and large pilot (you can't scale the pilot down, you know), appear to be almost caricatures of the real airplane, but they are both cute as a bug. All of the successful WAR designs have had to be of airplanes using radial engines. This is because there are no suitable miniature engine replacements for the Allison and Merlin V-12s, or for in-line-engine airplanes like Mustangs. Until progress is made in that direction, it's doubtful that we'll see any little P-40s or P-51s running around the sky.

The Sidlinger Hurricane. Although the Hurricane is not as well known as the famous Spitfire, it was the true hero of the Battle of Britain; almost all of the fighting squadrons were equipped with Hurricanes. The airplane's fat wing and rather upright cockpit make it a natural for scaling down. The trick is figuring out how to put a flat engine in it and still make it look good. Fred Sidlinger has designed an all-wood seven-eighths–scale Hurricane that is a complete success. The excellent plans call for a traditional wood fuselage and wing mated to a 150-hp Lycoming engine.

Of all the replicas available, this one flies the most nearly normally, cruising at 160 mph or better.

3 The Warriors

World War II was thirty years gone, and the warhorse that I was astride was far past its fighting prime. Still, as I sat there, strapped into a plexiglass bubble filled with fire and brimstone, I had the sense of a battle about to begin, a battle that had been fought and won almost before I was born. The blurred arc of the propeller was a full twelve feet in front of me, and half of that distance was motor. The twelve cylinders of the Rolls-Royce Merlin barked with the authoritative voice of 1,450 hp. I couldn't begin to see over the nose as it pointed off in a purposeful angle toward the sky, but it was so narrow and sleek that I could easily see the edges of the runway on each side. It was a sight I had seen a thousand times in movies and a million times in my dreams. I was at the controls of a Mustang, the definitive World War II fighter, about to take off

What kind of a man flies a **Mustang**? In this particular case it's Johnny Rutherford, three-time Indianapolis 500 winner. (Credit: Budd Davisson.)

74

into a world I had visited many times in my imagination but never in reality.

My brain cells were working overtime, projecting many images at the same time on my mind's eye, making it difficult to pick out a single sensation. I was very conscious of an intense feeling of detachment, as if I were viewing myself from the outside. One facet of my mind's eye was looking at me from directly above, from which perspective I appeared to be in a fighting stance, my feet spread wide apart, my hands wrapped around the throttle and control stick. Another portion of my mind saw me from the left side, framed in the cockpit and windshield in the exact pose often seen in the late movies. The noise of the engine was so intense it became a painful pressure, making the entire experience surrealistic at best . . . exciting at the very least.

I glanced down under my left elbow and checked all the trim settings, making certain the rudder trim was set at six degrees right. The manual had said that without right rudder trim the airplane would be very willing to make a ninety-degree left turn off the runway under the influence of all that horsepower and torque. I once again surveyed the instrument panel, making sure all the needles were in the green. I retrained my eyes to become accustomed to the location of the airspeed indicator, the instrument that would be my most important guide in what I knew was going to be a tightly compressed experience. I unconsciously took a deep breath and held it, as if I were about to squeeze the trigger. I inched my left hand forward, the big cylindrical handle feeling slick with nervous perspiration. Even as I applied the slightest amount of pressure to that throttle, I knew that it was not only unleashing more horsepower than I had ever dreamed possible, but it was also opening a window in time for me to peer through and catch a glimpse of an era that I had missed, of a type of flying machine I coveted. The high, explosive bark of the twelve exhaust stacks increased in tempo until the cockpit was filled to overflowing with sound so dense it could be felt. The back of the metal bucket seat pressed against my spine, forcing me forward and dragging the edges of the runway past the wingtips with so much acceleration, I forgot to let out the breath I had taken earlier.

My right hand had been forcing the stick back against my lap in a death-like grip, and I had to force myself mentally to relax

Three of the four surviving restored **B-17s** sweep down over the south end of the Oshkosh flight line. Nearest is the EAA's own B-17; second is **Texas Raiders** of the CAF in Harlingen; **Sentimental Journey**, owned and operated by the Arizona Wing of the CAF, brings up the rear. (Credit: Budd Davisson.)

and ease the stick forward so the tail would come up and let the airplane race along the runway on its main gear. As the nose came down, I was rewarded with a view of concrete being sucked under the airplane in a swath of blurred gray, vaguely patterned by white lines and runway lights. At the same time, that enormous eleven-foot propeller and all that torque tried to turn the airplane left, and I found myself moving a rudder pedal toward the floor with my right foot to keep the Mustang perfectly lined up. It seemed I had been accelerating for an eternity when I felt the airplane get light on its feet and whisper, "Take me, let's go, let's go flying." A gentle tug on the stick made the world go away, today disappear. I was in the air—I was flying a Mustang! Yes, some dreams do come true.

Aviation can be a very emotional thing, especially when it comes to warbirds. There is something about the combat aircraft of wars we've not experienced that makes men into boys and lets boys enjoy being young. Somehow, all the emotional attractions of warbirds have nothing to do with the purpose for which they were built. Their killing days behind them, the warbirds today seem to exist as exciting monuments to men and deeds that should never be forgotten.

The artificial technological acceleration that occurs during any war was responsible for the birth and the death of the propeller-driven fighter. In five short years, technology brought the propeller-driven fighter to its absolute zenith and then killed it by developing the turbojet engine. The scream of the turbojet was so loud and so important that the sounds and smells of in-line Merlins and radial Pratt & Whitneys disappeared in an amazingly short period of time. The operational life spans of some of the airplanes we consider to be immortal, like the P-38 Lightning and the P-40 Warhawk, were in some cases no more than two or at the very most three years before they were rendered obsolete by newer designs and newer technologies. In the United States, a very few of the designs such as the Mustang soldiered on through Korea and into the mid-1950s as National Guard airplanes. But these were secondary jobs. In those days, all eyes followed the arrow-shaped outlines of the new generation of jet fighters and bombers.

Accelerated Extinction

The period right after World War II was something like the end of the era of the dinosaurs, as extinction fell upon the warbird breed like a blanket. Machines of war are not needed when there is no war, and by 1946 smelters around the world were going full blast, not beating swords into plowshares, but making once-proud fighters into beer cans and cooking pots. At disposal depots around the country, warbirds that were still stateside were gathered together. Huge auctions were held in attempts to find new owners for the airplanes, and in some cases, foreign governments did step forward to buy a few here and there. More likely than not, the winner was a private salvage contractor much more interested in the aluminum bones of the airplane than in the history it had just helped write. The contractor moved onto the airport with portable smelting rigs and cutting torches, and soon the landscape looked like an old tintype photo of the aftermath of a buffalo hunt: bones and carcasses were spread about, the creatures' precious bodily essences sinking into the ground, their valuable parts carted off to market.

Those who were truly interested in airplanes had a field day. Paul Mantz, who had a company that supplied stunt pilots and airplanes to the movies, saw an opportunity to stock up for what he was certain was to be a booming business in war pictures. When airplanes went on the auction block, he was the first one there bidding. The result was that in 1947 and 1948, Paul Mantz had

The **AD-5 Skyraider** is one of the largest single-engine aircraft ever produced. The aircraft seen here was the last Skyraider operational in the armed forces; it flew well into the 1970s. Many Skyraiders saw active duty in Vietnam. (Credit: Budd Davisson.)

The EAA's **P-51 Mustang** poses next to its **DC-3**—two classics in their categories. (Credit: Budd Davisson.)

the fifteenth largest air force on the face of the earth. Paul Mantz and his personal air force made such memorable movies as *Twelve O'Clock High* possible. When you see the original *Twelve O'Clock High* on the late show, notice the episode in which a B-17 lands on its belly and slides through a crowd of tents. That's Paul Mantz at the controls, and that's his airplane. One bidder—some say it was Mantz—is reported to have made a killing on the air force policy of filling an aircraft full of fuel before it is parked. All the airplanes he bought were full of fuel, and he drained them and sold the fuel for as much as he paid for the airplanes.

Overseas, the slaughter of metal pterodactyls went on in a less orderly fashion. It made absolutely no sense to bring back airplanes such as P-40s and Wildcats that were considered obsolete when the war began. So, they were killed exactly where they stood when the war ended. In late 1945 and 1946, thousands of troops occupied their time by cutting huge trenches in the desert and bulldozing fighters and bombers into them. In other places, such as India, they just pushed the airplanes into heaps and set fire to them. On island fortresses, Navy and Marine Corps airplanes were bulldozed off into the sea, or loaded onto barges and carted out to sea, where they were thrown overboard. Only those aircraft judged to be technologically superior, which in the case of the American airplanes meant only the P-51 and the F4U Corsair, were deemed worthy to be brought all the way back to the United States, and even the earlier versions of those aircraft were left overseas.

By 1950, for all intents and purposes, the process of extinction had run its course. The mighty air forces marshaled to defend liberty were no more, and the few remaining survivors were in the private hands of race pilots and the firms that needed high-performance airplanes to take aerial photographs. For the first twenty years after the war, few cared what had happened to those valiant airplanes. Nobody seemed to want an airplane that would burn sixty, seventy, or eighty gallons of thirty-cent gas per hour. And even as late as 1961, when the Canadians sold all of their newly rebuilt Mustangs, the prices were still in the $1,000 range.

The Ultimate Artifact

Today, although they may be airplane restorers and pilots, many sport aviators could almost be called aerial archeologists, because it's their intent to rebuild the ultimate artifact—a World War II warbird—and to do so means digging through the past to find the information and parts to assemble one of these machines.

If you look at the survival rate of World War II airplanes, it's easy to see that they fall in the rare artifact category. Take the P-47 Thunderbolt, for instance. Prior to VJ Day, more than 14,000 of them had been built. Today only eight or ten are known to exist, and only three or four still fly. And the famous P-40 Warhawk of the Flying Tigers? At least 15,000 of them came out of Curtiss Wright's factory, but today only eight or nine are still in the air.

Other countries' warbirds fared even worse. Germany built an astounding 34,000 Messerschmitt 109s between 1939 and 1945.

Today not a single original ME-109 is still airworthy, although there are several Spanish versions of the airplane flying. What's more amazing is that around the world there are no more than a half dozen original Messerschmitts, even in museums. Wing tip to wing tip, over 200 miles of ME-109s were built, but only a few hundred feet survive.

Today the warbird owner and rebuilder is somebody who has survival statistics on the top of his mind constantly. As he climbs into the cockpit or reaches up and tightens a bolt, he knows that he is a part of history, and the artifact that he is trying to save is one of the most vulnerable known to man. An airplane is much more fragile and easily destroyed than one of the fabled Clovis arrowheads, or the fossilized skull of a long-dead semierect cousin of ours.

The legendary **Messerschmitt 109** of World War II was produced in larger numbers than any other aircraft ever built, yet no original German-built Messerschmitt still flies. However, several Spanish-built 109s (HA-1112) with Merlin Rolls Royce engines are in the air. The pilot of this plane is Warbirds of America President Bill Harrison, of Tulsa, Oklahoma. (Courtesy of Jim Larson.)

Turning Over Rocks

Restoring something that is as massively complicated as a World War II combat airplane, when there are so few of them around and even fewer parts, is a truly heroic project, and one that more often than not begins with a scavenger hunt in which the prize may be something as rare as an aileron for a Corsair, or a canopy hinge bracket for an early-model Mustang. That is where the aluminum archeologist earns his title and gets his thrills.

Take Pete Regina of Van Nuys, California, for instance. In helping his brother bring a D-Model P-51 back from Israel, Pete ran across a wing for one of the very rare, very early B-Model Mustangs. At that time, only three B-Model airframes were known to exist in the world. The next leg of the scavenger hunt took him to northern California, where he found the rear eight feet of a B-Model fuselage lying in the back of a hangar. Several more years

Only a handful of the 14,000 **P-47 Thunderbolts** of World War II have survived. This restored example is owned and operated by the Kalamazoo Aviation History Museum near Kalamazoo, Michigan. (Credit: Budd Davisson.)

were spent digging through brush heaps and junk piles, coming up with a little piece here and a little piece there. He managed to scrounge up the major portions of a wing, portions of the fuselage, and a bushel or two of miscellaneous pieces. Six years later, after building a completely new fuselage and manufacturing parts that were missing, Pete sat at the controls of his completed airplane and flew it for the first time.

Then there's the story about John Paul's buried P-40. In any field of interest, whether it be antique cars, antique weapons, or antique airplanes, you always hear stories about the one that's in the barn, or the one that's buried, or the one that landed in the lake and is perfectly preserved. Ninety-nine times out of a hundred, those turn out to be old wives' tales. John Paul, who happened to own a P-40, was approached by somebody at an airport one day who told him an airplane-in-a-barn story, only in this case it was supposed to be a P-40 buried in a field. John didn't pay much attention, but after a while he began to wonder about it. He located the farmer who owned the field and started digging. At nine feet he hit a wing tip; digging underneath, he found that the landing gear was down. Excitedly excavating the canopy, which was closed, he looked down inside the fuselage to see if it had been torched off, and to his relief he found that it had not been cut off and was not even crushed! After several days of digging, he hoisted a P-40N Warhawk from a grave in which it had lain since 1948. Even more amazing, the metal on the airplane was not corroded at all; the airplane should soon be back in the air.

Other stories abound, like the tales of the Martin B-26 Marauder that was airlifted by helicopter out of the tundra in northern Alaska and the Japanese Zero that was brought back from a Pacific island where it had been shot full of holes. One of the more amazing survival stories concerns a P-40 that was sitting on Amchitka Island in the Aleutians. When the United States government announced it was going to use the island as a nuclear testing site, a gentleman in Washington State started writing everybody he could

81

This **P-40** lay on its back on Amchitka Island in the Aleutians for 30 years until a concerned Washington State enthusiast effected its rescue; the full story is told in the text. (Courtesy of George Enhorning.)

think of in an effort to save the airplane. He got no response. Then about six months later, he got a call from the dock in his home town. "What do you want us to do with your airplane?" he was asked.

His logical response was, "What airplane?" Racing down to the waterfront, he found a barge moored to the pier, and sitting in the middle of the barge was the P-40. Somehow (the details are unknown, and probably best not ferreted out), another P-40 had been saved from oblivion.

There are still some warbirds to be found. For instance, there are half a dozen P-38s sitting on the ice cap in Greenland. They were brand new, with almost no flight time on them at all, when they had to belly-land on the ice because they were running out of fuel. Their crews were picked up and parts salvaged later. Lots of folks are trying to figure out how to get those planes back. And then there are the Navy airplanes sitting on the bottom of Lake Michigan. It's fresh water, so there's some hope that they have survived. And there are stories about Spitfires in India, and FW-190s in Rumania, and Hawk 75s in Argentina . . . and the stories go on and on.

The Warbird Totem Pole

The military machines of both World War II and the period shortly thereafter seemed to be arranged into a totem pole—an aerial caste system with the glamour boys of combat at the top and the hard-working schoolteachers and scouts at the bottom. Forgetting the uses for which they were intended, the warbirds would have arranged themselves in a totem pole regardless, because their popularity seems to be as much a function of flash and performance as anything else.

The Fighters

It's no secret that every pilot who ever lived wanted at one time or another to be a fighter pilot. Somehow it fits right in with wanting to be a fireman, a Texas Ranger, and Robin Hood. The macho mystique of the fighter pilot has been the thin basis for a good many very thin movies. The one-on-one, Red Baron-versus-the-good-guy type of dogfight nags at the corners of every pilot's

In the dark early days of World War II, the Flying Tigers and their **P-40s** brought the only bright news home.

P-51D Mustang:
the name says it all.

Mustang fighter pilots like nothing better than to line up for a parade, although it's not as easy as it looks.

Wildcats were the Navy's only carrier fighters at the beginning of World War II.

Facing page: Forty years of aeronautical progress in a single frame. The structures above the tail of the **Mustang** are the assembly sheds at Cape Kennedy.

The only restored **B-17s** regularly flying form up for a portrait.

The distinctive gull-wing of the **Corsair** provided a place to mount short landing gear and still have propeller clearance.

Friends and foes. The only airworthy Japanese **Zero** in the world in formation with two old enemies, an **F6F-5 Hellcat** and a **Corsair**.

Facing page, top: The Republic **P-47 Thunderbolt** was the heaviest single-engine fighter of World War II.

Facing page, bottom: The **F4U Corsair** was a Navy/Marine mount, while the **P-51 Mustang** flew with the Air Corps.

Two rare warbirds team up. An **FM-2 Wildcat** and a **TBM "Turkey"** torpedo bomber.

When General Doolittle's **B-25** Mitchell bombers roared across Japan in 1942, it was America's first good news and Japan's first bad news.

Mustang at sunset.

The death of a legend. A British **Mosquito** fighter bomber sinks into the dirt at a California airport, its fragile plywood structure rotting away to dust. The Mosquito was intended as a high-altitude, unarmed reconnaissance airplane but was fast enough to run away from almost any fighter. (Credit: Budd Davisson.)

mind, and every pilot knows he would be the victor. Is there any difference between that and the Main Street scene of *High Noon?* Or of *Shane?* It's the classic confrontation in which an individual triumphs by virtue of his skill and daring. Thus macho nostalgia has made the fighter plane the superhero of the warbird set.

Is the reputation of the fighters justified? In the eyes of almost everybody, the answer is an unequivocal yes. You have only to look at the sleek lines of a P-51, the fastest and most versatile fighter of the war, to understand the answer. You have only to stand out on the ramp and listen once to that distinctive staccato bark of the Merlin V-12 as it flashes by at low level to understand the excitement these airplanes engender.

But no matter how much you love them, getting into the game is difficult, because the game is so small and at the same time financially so big. Worldwide, there are probably no more than 100 or 120 fighters of all nationalities still flying, out of a total that must have exceeded 500,000 or 600,000 airplanes. And of the total still in the air, fully two-thirds of them are Mustangs. The rest of the population is made up of two of this airplane, a dozen of that, and a half dozen of something else.

The reason for the Mustang's seemingly universal popularity, with both pilots and aficionados, is twofold. First, it has obvious aesthetic appeal and a remarkable performance reputation. Second, there is the simple fact that it survived in such large numbers. The Mustang owes its survival to its excellence as a fighter; shortly after the war, as we moved into jet-propelled aircraft, every under-

There is nothing more exciting than the moment of lift-off in a 2,200-hp aircraft like the **Corsair.** This particular aircraft was the lead plane in the TV series, "Baa Baa Black Sheep." (Credit: Budd Davisson.)

developed nation bought large numbers of Mustangs for its air force. In addition, our own National Guard stocked many of its squadrons with Mustangs and used them until the late 1950s.

Most recently, because of television coverage in the *Baa-Baa Black Sheep* series, the Chance-Vought F4U Corsair gained popularity almost equal to that of the Mustang. However, even with the recent influx of seven or eight Corsairs from Central America, the total flying population of F4Us is only fourteen or fifteen airplanes. As is true for so many other fighters that exist in very small numbers, a sellers' market for Corsairs has developed. However, since those planes arrived from Central America with generous quantities of military F4U spares, most of the major components for Corsairs are fairly easily acquired. This is lucky, because the big bent-wing bird uses 2,200 hp up front and is no Piper Cub when it comes to maintenance.

The Curtiss P-40 represents an excellent case study of what the warbird restorers have done to save history. In the late 1960s, when MGM filmed the movie *"Tora! Tora! Tora!"*, they needed two P-40s to represent the aircraft flown by Lieutenants Walsh and Taylor, two of the pilots who mixed it up with the Japanese Zeros during the Pearl Harbor attack. MGM was so hard-pressed to come up with the airplanes that they barely had enough spares to keep them flying. This situation has changed rapidly; in the last few years, the flying population of P-40s has been between eight and twelve at any given time. There are reportedly over twenty P-40 Warhawks under restoration, and in most cases this means extensive remanufacturing of parts, reskinning of the complete aircraft, and manufacturing of huge numbers of mechanical accessories that no longer exist.

The Corsairs are not the only Navy aircraft to have survived, but the numbers are not very high for the rest. Grumman's Cat series, the F4F Wildcat, the F6F Hellcat, and the F8F Bearcat (which never actually saw combat in World War II) are represented in the air by no more than six or seven examples. And these numbers are dwindling as more of them are relegated to museums or suffer in-flight failures and are demolished.

Of the foreign airplanes, the Spitfire is by far the most numerous, but that means three or four are flying in the U.S., and three or four overseas. However, there are a dozen or more under

The last propeller-driven fighter accepted by the U.S. military was the **F8F Grumman Bearcat.** Of the half dozen still surviving, this extremely rare **XF8F-1** is one of the original experimental pre-production aircraft. With a 2,250-hp Pratt & Whitney engine, it held a climb-to-10,000-feet record, until a second-generation jet aircraft took it away. (Credit: Budd Davisson.)

Is there another machine with the grace and lines to match a **Spitfire**? There are only two or three flying in the United States today. (Credit: Budd Davisson.)

A **B-17** (left), a **B-29**, and a
B-24 parked together make a
truly historic sight these days:
The CAF B-29 is the only one
regularly flying, and the B-24
represents half the flying Liberator population. (Credit:
Budd Davisson.)

restoration at this time. Other British fighters, such as the Hurricane, Tempest, Typhoon, and Mosquito exist in very limited
numbers, in most cases no more than four or five. Of the Axis
airplanes—German, Japanese, and Italian—the numbers are not
even worth going into, because in many cases they just don't exist.

The Bombers

Anyone thinking about private ownership of a bomber should
question his sanity, because, while a single-engine fighter is difficult to maintain, a multi-engine bomber is infinitely more so.
But today, thanks to a dedicated group of warbird fanatics, there
are combat bombers flying that otherwise would have vanished
over the horizon like the dodo bird. Even so, restored bombers are
a very rare sight today.

The B-17 Flying Fortress, "The Battle Queen," still reigns supreme in the hearts of those who remember the sacrifices made
to stamp out the various brands of tyranny. After the war, the
B-17 was quickly relegated to noncombat roles because it had been
replaced by the B-29 Super Fortress. However, it was a marvelous
flying machine and was amazingly low on maintenance; and in
spite of its complexity, many of the surplus B-17s found their way
into the work force doing all sorts of odd and sometimes dirty jobs.
It was a B-17, for instance, that was used to map most of Vietnam,
at a time when all the problems still belonged to the French. It
was the B-17 that first brought effective fire fighting right to the
door of the forest fire. "Have Borate, Will Travel" was the slogan.
The crews flying the fire-fighting B-17s put in more hazardous
combat time saving the lives of Douglas firs than they did trying
to end the war. With four 1200-hp single-row Wright radial engines, the B-17 proved itself to be tremendously adaptable to a
wide range of jobs. It soldiered on long after it was cashiered out
of the military. Unfortunately, when it was put into its other work
clothes, it was stripped of all the refinements that had made it a
bomber; top turrets, bottom turrets, gun mounts, and the bulky
bombardier radio and navigation stations all were removed. Thus,
to restore a B-17 today, an individual has to do a tremendous amount
of scrounging to come up with the parts that were at one time
nothing but junk. In the case of the top turrets, even the Air Force
museum had trouble finding one.

Proud Mary is the oldest **B-25** still flying. During World War II this plane—the fourth one built—was the personal transport of Army Air Corps Commander General "Hap" Arnold. The interior houses an executive office rather than guns and bare sheet metal. (Credit: Budd Davisson.)

Both the Navy and the Air Force used the **Beechcraft T-34 Mentor** during the 1950s as a pilot's first introduction into the air. Hundreds of these planes, sold as surplus, have been showing up as extremely usable warbirds that also double as cross-country machines. (Credit: Budd Davisson.)

Finding the working top turret was one of the hardest parts of getting this **B-25** back into wartime trim, but it's these little details that most spectators enjoy. (Credit: Budd Davisson.)

The Spitfires and Hurricanes of the world owe their survival to the movie *Battle of Britain*, for which the money was found to track down all the remaining aircraft and make them airworthy, and there's a similar story to be told about the B-25 Mitchell medium bomber. It was the B-25, in case you've forgotten, that General Doolittle launched off the deck of the carrier *Hornet* to make his famous raid on Tokyo, at the time when the Japanese empire seemed impenetrable. It was also the twin engine, twin-tailed B-25 that played the leading role in the movie version of Joseph Heller's book *Catch 22.* Had it not been for that movie, dozens of B-25s would have continued sinking into the grass at out-of-the-way airports until they were finally cut apart for junk, as so many of them had already been. It was lucky this acting job came along, because the B-25 had lost its fire-fighting job when it was found that under certain conditions it could be torn apart by the extreme turbulence of a fire.

At fly-ins around the nation, it is usually a B-25 that represents the bombers. Even though its 1,000-gallon capacity and 150-200-gallon-per-hour thirst are a little inhibiting, it is probable that B-25s will stay in the air for quite some time to come.

So many of the American bombers have approached extinction that it is an occasion of some note when even one of them becomes airworthy. The Consolidated B-24 Liberator, the B-29 Super Fortress which dropped the atom bomb, the A-20 Havoc, and the B-26 Marauders are all represented by only one or two examples. The same is true of almost every foreign bomber. Only the British and the Canadians have managed to keep a few of the Lancaster and Shackleton bombers in the air, and absolutely none of the Axis powers' bombers, with the exception of a few Spanish-built German Heinkel 111s, still fly. In most cases they don't even exist in museums.

The Schoolmarms

The training aircraft utilized during World War II and shortly thereafter are by far the most numerous in the whole warbird category. This is because the advanced trainers were used well into the 1950s, while some of the others proved to work out well for crop dusting. Still others were just neat little light aircraft that almost anybody could buy and fly.

Affectionately called "the turkey" by its pilots, the **TBM Avenger** was the last torpedo bomber adopted by the United States. It survived the war to fight fires by dropping borate, but only five remain in restored condition; a few have the rear gun turret shown here. (Credit: Budd Davisson.)

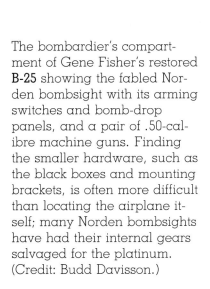

The bombardier's compartment of Gene Fisher's restored **B-25** showing the fabled Norden bombsight with its arming switches and bomb-drop panels, and a pair of .50-calibre machine guns. Finding the smaller hardware, such as the black boxes and mounting brackets, is often more difficult than locating the airplane itself; many Norden bombsights have had their internal gears salvaged for the platinum. (Credit: Budd Davisson.)

The designation system used during the war to denote the different levels of training was: PT for primary training, which is where you first got your feet wet; BT for basic training, where you got a little more flight time before you moved into more complicated machines; and AT for advanced training, which was the last step before you graduated into the real thing—fighters or bombers.

The bottom of the PT series is fairly well represented, although individual types are small in number. Take the PT-17 Kadet, known to the navy as the N2S. Popularly known as the Stearman, this big biplane formed the backbone for the training programs during World War II. It was stable, easy to fly, and, as many students proved, it was virtually indestructible. You could fly through a house with it—and this has been done several times. Today the Stearman is still being used by many crop dusters across the country, although more and more its value as a time machine is eclipsing its value as a crop duster. It has filled its role so well that even its days as a teacher are not over yet. As recently as 1980, both Mexico and Chile were purchasing newly rebuilt 1944-vintage Stearmans for use as basic trainers in their air forces. With its sturdy 220-hp Continental engine and its tank-like fabric-covered biplane chassis, the Stearman will undoubtedly outlive every other World War II vintage airplane.

The other PT series aircraft, the PT-22 Ryan (a nice little low-wing, two-place, open-cockpit bird) and the PT 19/23/26 (Fairchild made many versions of this monoplane), still exist in some numbers and are excellent flying toys for their owners.

The **Stearman trainers** were actually built by Boeing; the Navy called theirs the N2S, while the Army versions were PT-13s and PT-17s. Today they are the most numerous and most popular of the war-time trainers. (Credit: Budd Davisson.)

A few of the forty or fifty **AT-6 Texans** that always show up for the Oshkosh fly-in. (Courtesy of EAA.)

A family portrait of **T-28s**—the big 1950s trainers used by both the Air Force and the Navy: An Air Force A model in Navy colors leads the pack, with a B in the middle and a C bringing up tail-end charlie. (Credit: Budd Davisson.)

The BT category of old-time trainers has but one occupant of any note, the BT13/15 Vultee Valiant, also known as the "Vibrator." This all-metal, low-wing, fixed-gear, 450-hp trainer taught thousands of cadets how to fly on instruments and how to handle more powerful aircraft. It was decommissioned almost as soon as the war came to an end, but for no apparent reason, large numbers of these durable craft survived in derelict condition behind barns and hangars all around the country. Although many of them were stripped of their engines and propellers, which were used on Stearman crop dusters, a sizable number of the air frames have survived and are today being restored.

The AT category also has only one occupant, but its numbers are huge in comparison to those of the rest of the warbird series. During World War II, when you said you were in advanced training, that meant that you were flying the AT-6 Texan, North American's indefatigable design that first hit the runways in 1938 and was being manufactured by the Canadians as late as the 1960s. It was not phased out of the United States Air Force or United States Navy inventories until the early 1960s. By the time the T6 (or SNJ as the navy called it) was stripped of rank and privileges, it had trained many thousands of pilots to fly, and large numbers were bought at bargain basement prices of $1,000 or so by private individuals to use for aerobatics, smoke writing, or any other job where they felt they could justify flying the superlative aircraft. So many were bought by civilians that in the early 1950s, when the air force decided it really wasn't through with the Texans and

Banking away for another practice bombing run, this Air Training Command **AT-11** looks like it's ready for business. (Credit: Budd Davisson.)

would like to have another go at them, they had to buy AT-6s from private owners to be refurbished and upgraded. There are still a number of air forces around the world which use the AT-6 Texan as their basic trainer. We will probably see the turn of the century before the last AT-6 is taken out of active military service somewhere in the world.

One subvariant of the AT series, the AT-11, was a military version of the twin engine Beechcraft C45/D18 transport that was modified for use as a bombardier trainer. Complete with bomb bay doors, a glass nose, and a Norden bombsight, the AT-11 saw virtually no use as a civilian aircraft other than for mosquito control or crop dusting. It has, however, resurfaced in recent times as a classic warbird and one that's much more usable than the rest. This is one of the few warbirds that you can take to a fly-in, with your entire neighborhood on board, and be assured of lots of oohs and ahhs from enthusiasts in the audience.

The Warbugs

As a class they were known as "grasshoppers"—airplanes that could land anywhere, take off on roads, and serve as the eyes and ears of infantry units in every theater of combat operations. Officially they were designated L for liaison aircraft, and with the exception of the Stinson L-5, they were off-the-shelf civilian aircraft that had been modified to fill the grasshopper role.

L-2. The Taylorcraft L-2 was nothing more than a Taylorcraft TD wearing fatigues. It had a high wing configuration like all the others, and its 65-hp engine could lift it out of a short grass field with no effort. It was an extremely light, enjoyable aircraft to fly. Because it was so light, it didn't want to come down as quickly as it wanted to go up, so the military ordered the L-2Ms issued with spoilers across the top of the wings so the pilot could pull a handle and spoil all the lift on the wing, dropping the plane to a predetermined spot.

L-3. The L-3 Aeronca was not as well known as some of the other grasshoppers, although it is gaining in popularity. It was of the same 65-hp, high wing variety that could operate out of small areas and serve as a trainer and as a spotter as well.

The **Beechcraft AT-11,** a bombardier-training version of the civilian D18 Beech transport, is a favorite warbird restoration project. That's the Norden bombsight inside the glass nose. (Credit: Budd Davisson.)

A true warbug, the **L-2 Taylorcraft** flitted around the world's battlefields using whatever space was available as a runway. (Credit: Budd Davisson.)

The little **Aeronca L-3** never carried weapons, but it did military duty carrying officers and acting as the eyes of the artillery batteries. Today, it ranks as one of the cheapest of the warbirds: $5,000 will get you into the game. (Credit: Budd Davisson.)

The **Fieseler-Storch** was Germany's primary World War II liaison airplane. It was designed to operate in and out of almost nonexistent runways. The Storch's best known escapade involved flying into a mountaintop fortress to rescue Mussolini from insurgents late in the war. (Credit: Budd Davisson.)

This **L-5** pilot's thumbs-up shows how happy he is to possess a warbird that is authentic in every detail, yet can be flown at reasonable cost. (Courtesy of Ted Koston/EAA.)

L-4. The L-4 was a Piper J-3 Cub with more glass for better visibility. Other than that, it was, and still is, classic Cub, and it has survived in tremendous numbers to become the darling of the warbug set. It's easy to fly, fun to own, and has the nostalgia of the big birds but with the utility and fun of a tiny one.

L-5. The Stinson L-5 Sentinel was the only one of the liaison airplanes used during the war that was designed specifically for that purpose. Designed and built by Stinson Aircraft, which already was manufacturing a number of well-known private airplanes, the L-5 borrowed heavily on existing technology. The Sentinel was much larger than the rest of the liaison airplanes; some variations of it even had a large door down the side through

Britain's final propeller-driven fighter, the **Sea Fury,** lived on to see combat in Korea and to serve with foreign air forces through the 1970s. Considered by many to be the pinnacle of propeller-driven fighter development, Sea Furies have been imported in considerable numbers for restoration. (Credit: Budd Davisson.)

which a litter case could be loaded. Its 190-hp, six-cylinder engine and specially designed aerodynamics let its pilot yank it out of virtually any kind of field.

L-6 Interstate. The L-6 Interstate is probably the rarest of the World War II grasshoppers. Derived from the civilian Interstates, its extensive modifications include outward-slanting windows for greater visibility. In many ways the machine was outfitted like the L-5, but it was much smaller. The engine was a 113-hp geared Franklin—best known for its habit of self-destructing. Today, few if any of these engines are available and the L-6s still flying use modern, more reliable engines.

Getting into the Warbird Game

By now you have noticed that there are warbirds and there are warbirds, and you can jump in and get your feet wet, or you can just as easily jump in and go clear over your head. The warbirds have price tags that run from the entirely manageable to the absolutely unheard of. They bottom out at about $5,000 for a warbug that's seen better days, and run on up to $300,000 or $400,000 for the concours restorations of combat rarities, such as P-40s, top-dog Mustangs, and Spitfires. When you stand by the runway with your tongue hanging out, as echelons of fighters go roaring past, it's essential to remember that times have definitely changed; the days of the super bargains are far behind us. The value of the

average warbird has increased almost a thousand times in the past ten or twelve years, and you cannot just point at a certain warbird and say, "I want that type," "I want a Mustang," or "I want a Spitfire." Unless of course, money is no object.

The price factors that usually decide the type of airplane a pilot will buy, as opposed to what he wants, include much more than simply the cost of acquisition. Assuming you can plunk down $200,000 for an airplane, how are you going to feel about a yearly maintenance bill that may run $15,000 to $30,000, and direct operating costs (gas, oil, and insurance) that hit you anywhere from $300 to $400—*per hour*? But do you really have to spend that much to play with the warbirds? You can buy almost any one of the liaison airplanes at a price of a good used Chevy, while most of the more exotic primary trainers, such as PT-22s and Stearmans, can be had for the price of a Cadillac (and they're a lot more fun). It's not until you climb over into the advanced trainer category that you find yourself dropping Mercedes-sized bundles of cash. The trainers are also much less expensive to operate than the combat birds, and some of the liaison series, such as the L-4 Cub, could almost be considered downright cheap to run.

Restoration? Only If You're Ready

The most common fantasy to cross the mind of those wanting to get into the warbird game is that of finding a P-51 Mustang in a barn, paying the farmer $200 for it, and running home to rebuild it. Forget it! In the first place, your chances of finding a $200 Mustang, or even a $20,000 one, or even a $100,000 Mustang in a barn are at least as good as winning the Irish Sweepstakes. But finding it and buying it are nothing compared to what you're going to face getting it home and restoring it. This is another area where the difference between the big iron and the trainer/liaison categories is especially noticeable.

The total restoration of an airplane such as a P-51 Mustang, or a P-40, or, heaven help you, a B-25, is such an enormous project that it is difficult for those who haven't been through it even to imagine it. Don't make the mistake of thinking that just because the airplane is forty years old it is going to be simple and rudimentary. Nothing could be farther from the truth. Don't forget

Not normally considered a military airplane, the **WACO UPF-7** nonetheless wore an Air Force uniform when it was conscripted to do instructional duties in CPT pilot-training programs during World War II. (Credit: Budd Davisson.)

The **Junkers JU-52** was Germany's DC-3 and the backbone of its transportation command. Today, this one is the mount for well-known aviation writer Martin Caidin, who calls it *Iron Annie*. (Credit: Budd Davisson.)

that the combat aircraft of that time represent the pinnacle of propeller-driven airplane technology, and they use extremely complex control systems. Take the engines, for instance. One of the major advancements that the jet engine represents over the big reciprocating engines of World War II is that it's so simple. The Merlin engine of the Mustang was a 1,450-hp V-12 with double overhead cams and a two-stage super-charger. The 2200-hp Pratt & Whitney R2800 in the Corsairs, Thunderbolts, and Hellcats had no less than eighteen cylinders and thirty-six spark plugs. Your local fix-it shop is going to be no help when it comes to overhauling one of these! The same is true of almost every part of a big-engine warbird. The parts are expensive, they are rare, and in some cases, they are all but impossible even to move. You can pick up the propeller of an L-4 with your little finger, but three men can't carry a P-38's propeller—assuming you can find one.

All of the foregoing explains why most of the restorations of fighters and bombers in the United States are done in one of half a dozen shops that specialize in this type of work. That's not to say that a man can't tackle one of these airplanes single-handed and get it flying again, but it's not easy. In restoring his B-Model Mustang, Pete Regina farmed out only those parts that required machinery he couldn't possibly lay his hands on; the project took six years and cost well over $100,000 for parts alone.

From the rear, the **Yak-11's** clear lines and tiny cockpit reveal how the designer made certain it would go fast, regardless of how little the pilot could see. (Credit: Budd Davisson.)

The restoration story takes on a whole different, much lighter complexion when you start talking about even the most complex of the trainers, such as the AT-6 Texan. Although it still has a 1,000-pound, 650-hp engine up front and weighs over 3,000 pounds empty, the AT-6 is an airplane that can be rebuilt by any competent mechanic at any airport and is well within the grasp of the more advanced do-it-yourselfers. Also, most trainers, like the BTs and the ATs, were designed to be flown hard and maintained by nineteen-year-old kids who had been in the service exactly six months. They are robust and rudimentary, qualities that endeared them not only to our armed forces, but to armed forces throughout the world, which is why there are so many surplus parts, for the AT-6 Texan, at least. Although the parts may not be at bargain basement prices, they are available, something which can't be said for the big iron.

Then there are the PTs, the primary trainers: these restorations are, for the most part, the simplest of the simple. With the exception of the woodwork in the Fairchild PT 19s, 23s, and 26s, almost none present anything more complex than fabric and tubing with built-up wooden wings. The popular PT-17 Stearman biplane trainer is a good-size airplane but still presents no unsolvable restoration problems. It may not fit in your back bedroom, but a lot of fuselages have sat in garages while husband-and-wife teams moved Stearman wing panels into a bedroom to rib-stitch the fabric into place. But if you want small, the PT-22 Ryan is so tiny it fits very nicely into a single-car garage.

The **Yak-11** was a postwar trainer modification of the Russian Yak-9 frontline fighter. This airplane was found, abandoned on Cyprus, by English enthusiast Anthony Hutton, who fought a paperwork war with the Soviet government to clinch his ownership. (Credit: Budd Davisson.)

If you haven't been discouraged from restoring a warbird at this point, but are facing huge talent and financial obstacles, then the liaison grasshoppers will come to your rescue. Even the big old Stinson L-5 fits into a garage and a back yard builder's budget. And the smaller of the grasshoppers, such as the L-2, L-3, and L-4, are downright erector-set simple, and won't even come close to crowding your garage, or even your back bedroom, for that matter.

Can You Fly It?

It's no secret that one of the contributing factors to the ranking on the warbird totem pole is pilot proficiency, imagined or otherwise. The combat superbirds at the top of the totem pole have not earned an enviable reputation in safety, while it's just the opposite for the trainers and the liaison birds. This is to be expected; with 1,500 to 2,000 hp in the nose and weights approaching 10,000 pounds, the combat airplane can't be expected to have the best of manners. It was, after all, supposed to be a prizefighter in a life-or-death arena. The grasshoppers and the trainers, on the other hand, were made to let anybody look and learn.

The flight characteristics of the bigger-engined airplanes are both exhilarating and demanding. This is undoubtedly one of their attractions. They will do what you tell them to do, but first you have to know what language to speak. With thousands of horsepower swinging twelve- and thirteen-foot propellers, the torque generated on takeoff alone is enough to make some pilots decide they would rather take up golf instead.

Everything about the combat fighter or bomber happens quickly. For some it can be a real chore to keep up with the machine mentally, but the price of getting behind can be extremely high. Any fighter or bomber is most unforgiving, if you don't fly it by the numbers. While most airplanes will shudder and shake just before they reach stall speed and then mush gently forward, fighters won't give you that margin. They will fly right up to the edge of stall and then, with absolutely no warning, you can find yourself on your back pointed down. If you throw the power in too hard on takeoff, most fighters will execute a rapid left turn, dragging the wing tip and cartwheeling down the runway, throwing pieces of your beautiful airplane off into the bushes. Misjudge your height and try to land a couple of feet in the air, and the airplane will unceremoniously drop you like a sack of cement and give you the ride of your life.

Don't get the impression that fighters and bombers are totally unflyable—they are definitely not. You must remember that they were flown in combat by nineteen-year-olds with no more than 200 hours of flying time. But these kids had been taught to fly the military way: they flew by the numbers and followed procedures exactly. If this is done, almost anybody can fly a fighter or bomber, but this is a mental attitude that must be trained into the pilot. The characteristics of the airplane must be learned, and getting that kind of knowledge these days isn't easy, since virtually all fighters are single-place airplanes and there are no trainers even remotely resembling them.

The normal route into the cockpit of something like a Wildcat or a P-38 is to buy a lot of flight time in the good old AT-6 Texan. Although the AT-6 can't even begin to approximate the performance of the fighters, it can give a feel for flying heavier military aircraft and let you experience the smells and emotions that live only in a military cockpit. This environmental conditioning is almost as important as the actual flight training, because it allows you to overcome the strangeness and concentrate on manipulating the controls. Also, the Texan's ground handling is demanding enough that once you have mastered the Texan in a crosswind, you are more than ready for a Mustang.

The best of all possible routes into the big warbirds is to fly the Texan for fifteen or twenty hours and then talk your way into one of the few two-place TP-51s still around. Although they are ultra-rare and the owner may or may not be willing to give you

100

training in it, it's worth any amount of money to buy at least an hour of flight time with him. That's the only way you're going to get prior knowledge of the fire and brimstone you find in any warbird cockpit. Also that TP-51 time may satisfy your desires, and you may decide it's not necessary to spend all that time and money on a restoration or an acquisition just to live out a boyhood dream. However, you may find you are willing to sell your house and business just to get an airplane like that; it's happened before.

Flying the Little Ones

The trainers and liaison airplanes can be as demanding as the big ones, but they are much more forgiving of your mistakes, and the results of a mistake are generally not catastrophic. The grasshoppers, for instance, can be flown by virtually anybody with any tail-wheel time. The old saying "It flies like a Cub" means it's easy and docile to fly, and it certainly applies to the grasshoppers, since most of them *are* Cubs. Some of the trainers, such as the Stearman and the PT-22, have a reputation of being ground loopers, but that's not really a factor. They are both two-place trainers, and it's quite simple to find somebody else to teach you how to fly them. Anywhere from five to eight hours of instruction normally prepares almost anybody for the worst situation the airplane can offer, providing, of course, you know how to fly a tail-wheel-equipped airplane in the first place.

The AT-6 Texan is a complicated 650-hp airplane that's a far cry from a grasshopper, but, with the right instructor, learning to fly it can be quite an enjoyable challenge. The AT-6 can be the best of all possible worlds. You sit up front, master of all those Pratt & Whitney horses, with your feet spread wide apart on the rudders and your hands grasping the fighter-type control stick. It's very easy to make believe that you are flying a fighter, and for the dollar and maintenance difference, you can fly an AT-6 for three or four hours for every one you put into a Mustang or a Corsair.

101

Warbirds of America

The EAA's Warbirds of America division is probably the most far-reaching and nationally active of the warbird organizations. While many warbird organizations tend to be regional, the EAA division has a universal appeal; it cooperates with all the other warbird organizations for the betterment of the breed. Because of Warbirds of America's close ties with EAA, it benefits from the interaction between the EAA and the FAA that influences the development of regulations that won't restrict the growth of the movement.

Using the massive headquarters support provided by the parent EAA organization, Warbirds of America publishes its own magazine and generally looks after its own. The stories of the friendly swapping of parts to keep members' airplanes flying are legendary. Warbirds of America, like EAA, has a strong family orientation. Although only one member of a family may be a pilot, the others are usually decked out in matching flight suits or WA hats and shirts. This gives the warbird lineup at Oshkosh a family-reunion atmosphere, as complete clans fly in from all corners of the country for their once-a-year bash.

The Confederate Air Force

In the 1950s there were few individuals who cared much about high-performance warbirds, but as these aircraft began to disappear interest slowly began to build. One day, Lloyd Nolan, a crop duster from Brownsville, Texas, who liked big engines, purchased a Bearcat at a military surplus sale. When he got the airplane home, he suddenly realized that aircraft that only a few years earlier had been plentiful were suddenly extremely rare, and he saw that a

Only two **Bell P-39 Air Cobras** of the thousands built during World War II have survived in flying condition. The airplane is unusual: the engine, mounted behind the pilot, drives the propeller shaft that runs between the pilot's legs. (Credit: Budd Davisson.)

valuable piece of our heritage was slipping away. So Nolan and fellow Texan Lefty Gardner got together and formed the Confederate Air Force. The name was chosen on the premise that since the United States already had an air force, the Confederates should have one, too.

Today, twenty-five years after the CAF first unfurled its flag, they have surpassed their goal of keeping at least one of each U.S. warbird flying, but not without climbing many obstacles, both logistical and financial. The CAF flying inventory includes such rarities as the B-29 Super Fortress, the same airplane as the *Enola Gay*, which dropped the first atom bomb, the rare F-82 twin Mustang, P-38s, Mustangs, Corsairs, P-39 Air Cobras, Spitfires, Messerschmitts, Heinkels, and just about everything else that was in any way available. Over and above the aircraft, they have assembled a small but very creditable museum that houses some extremely interesting artifacts of the period, including the world's leading display of bomber nose art. Apparently some individual working or living around the salvage yards right after the war took a liking to the paintings on the noses of the bombers being destroyed. So, before the aircraft were melted down, he would cut out the part of the fuselage that contained the painting. In a very short time, he had dozens and dozens of spectacular nudes, grinning devils and other wartime expressions of individualism. The CAF found that collection and now has it displayed around their main hangar at Harlingen.

Since the CAF has headquarters just across the Rio Grande from Mexico, it is not exactly conveniently located. For that reason, they have found it to their advantage to form wings in such places as Minnesota and Arizona. Usually, these wings were formed by local warbird enthusiasts to help support or restore a single warbird. The Oklahoma wing, for instance, has restored a Curtiss C-46 Commando twin engine transport. The Arizona wing in Mesa, Arizona, has a B-17, one of the very best flying. The Colorado wing has a C-45 utility transport that they have restored. In this way, the CAF has made it possible for individuals living in areas outside Texas who may not have the financial wherewithal to tackle a large restoration project to play the warbird game. Under the wing plan, they can band together in a clublike atmosphere and pool their finances and talents to get their aerial artifact into the air.

No, it's not World War II—it's air show time, Confederate-style, at the CAF's warbird get-together in Harlingen, Texas. (Credit: Budd Davisson.)

Valiant Air Command

The Valiant Air Command started as a wing of the Confederate Air Force, but, because of philosophical differences, decided to branch out on their own. Located in Titusville, Florida, they have managed to put together a sizable membership in the southeastern United States. While the Confederate Air Force is very formal and everybody wears the same colonel's uniform, the Valiant Air Command has dropped much of the paramilitary trappings of the Confederate Air Force to become an organization with its own original flavor.

The Canadian Warbird Heritage

It's often forgotten that our friends north of the border were very much at war when we were and were actually there first. So, it's only natural that they have enthusiasts who actively support their own aeronautical history. The Canadian organization, the Canadian Warbird Heritage (CWH), has very much the same aim as the CAF: they want to put one each of every aircraft that Canada operated in the war back into the air. This is an even more ambitious project than that of the CAF, because many of the aircraft the Canadians operated are even more rare than those which the United States armed forces used. The CWH has a further disadvantage in that they don't have many Texans as members, and the tax situation is a little different up there. Therefore, it may take some time to restore their Lancaster bomber, although they have made incredible headway on all the rest of their aircraft, which include a Corsair, a TBM Avenger torpedo bomber, an Avro, a

Tudor, and many others. A little over ten years old, the organization has done an excellent job of converting an ex-military field just outside of Hamilton, Ontario, into headquarters of authentic British appearance.

Warbirds Aloft: The Fly-ins and Air Shows

Each major air show or fly-in of any type pulls in at least a few warbirds. For example, although Oshkosh's primary emphasis is not on warbirds, every year there will be more than 160 warbirds, including ten or twenty Mustangs, twenty or thirty T-6s, and several of each of the other surviving types. 1981 was a stellar year: all four of the surviving restored B-17s showed up. However, because of the general sport aviation orientation of the Oshkosh Convention, the nightly air shows vary, and the warbirds don't have center stage as much as the warbird enthusiast might like. For that reason, other air shows have begun to specialize in showing off the high-power hardware of the last big one.

The Confederate Air Force puts on their AirSho (yes, that's how it's spelled) twice a year, with the primary bash held in October. At this time they combine all of the aircraft from their various wings with their own to stage some of the wildest horsepower extravaganzas the world ever sees. The central theme of each CAF show is the reenactment of the highlights of the war, beginning with Pearl Harbor and ending with the *Enola Gay's* mission against Hiroshima.

The show begins with the obligatory replica Japanese Zero making a pass, met by P-40s scrambling off the ground. Then the Doolittle raid is reenacted as several B-25s roar over the runway. Pyrotechnics and ground-bound explosions add realistic plumes of smoke and debris to their bombing runs. As the two-hour war progresses into the Battle of the Coral Sea, the TBM Avengers and the SBD and SB2C Divebombers (the only surviving birds of their breed) take center stage. They hold the crowd's attention, making vertical dives toward the earth, pulling out at the last second.

Somewhere in the early stages of this 'war,' the Battle of Britain is played out with the Messerschmitt and the Spitfire sparring overhead. Later, as the B-29 drones down the runway, its bomb bay doors open, a mushroom cloud erupts out of the field across the runway. The narrator explains that this is a war of man against man and machine against machine, and that both sides suffered mightily. The point is illustrated by the missing man formation— a four-ship flight of fighters that flies down the runway, one aircraft breaking up and away, leaving an empty spot in the formation to symbolize those on either side who never came home.

One of the biggest disadvantages to the CAF's show is that it is so far off the beaten path it's difficult for much of the nation to get to it. This is not the case with either the Valiant Air Command or the Canadian Warbird Heritage show. Since Hamilton is less than 100 miles from Detroit and is easily reached by both air and car, the CWH show deserves to grow to the size and stature of the CAF show. Although they put up as great a variety of aircraft as the CAF does, the CWH does not stage aerial war reenactments. Instead, they have a pleasant mix of high-speed passes and aerobatics with the warbird airplanes front and center, mixed in with various other types of military aircraft, such as the Canadian F101s, T33s, and other current military hardware.

The Valiant Air Command's show is a very relaxed, enjoyable presentation combining warbird acrobatics and normal acrobatic aircraft. One nice thing about the Valiant Air Command show is that many aircraft attend that do not come to even Oshkosh because of the distances involved. You burn so much gasoline in a warbird that if you're going to make a trip of any size, you had better take a bundle of travelers' checks along. And since the Valiant Air Command is only an hour from Disney World, it becomes natural to combine a family vacation with a warbird trip.

The Flying Collections
There is a subtle difference between a warbird that's sitting in a museum and one that's sitting out on the ramp, its hot exhaust crackling as it cools from a flight just completed. One is a vividly alive machine, the other is a static monument, and the emotions stirred by both are entirely different. The excellent static displays of nonflying warbirds, such as those at the National Air and Space Museum, the air force museum at Wright Patterson Air Force Base, and the navy museum at Pensacola, Florida, are very exciting. But these museums don't begin to compare with those few that keep their aircraft ready to go at any time.

The EAA Museum.   Many of the museum's aircraft are kept airworthy and are flown at Oshkosh and other EAA fly-ins. Undoubtedly the crown jewel of the EAA's collection is the North American XP-51, the fourth one built and the first Mustang accepted by the Army Air Corps. Close behind the XP-51 in popularity is the EAA's B-17. The flying warbird collection continues to grow as historic airplanes are added to its flight line. Recently a P-38, a Corsair, and a Spanish-built Messerschmitt 109 were donated to the EAA; they have become part of the EAA's efforts to keep aviation history in the air, where it belongs.

The Confederate Air Force Museum.   Located on Rebel Field in Harlingen, Texas, the Confederate Air Force's Museum is not as large as the Confederate Air Force's membership would indicate, because their aircraft are not all kept on the field at one time. The aircraft likely to be found at any moment include the Heinkel 111, the F-82 Twin Mustang, the P-40, Spitfire, and Messerschmitt 109 (HA-1112). It's only during the air show week that all of the CAF airplanes are on the field at one time.

Planes of Fame Museum.   Ed Maloney's Planes of Fame Museum in Chino, California, due east of the Los Angeles area, is not a museum in the normal sense of the word. Many of the aircraft sit around outside the small hangar, some of them restored, some of them unrestored; some of them are flying, and some of them totally unflyable. Maloney has amassed a unique collection of one-of-a-kind aircraft, including such rarities as a Ryan Fireball, which combines a piston and jet engine, one of the smaller Northrop Flying Wings, a B-17, a SB2C divebomber, a Messerschmitt 262 jet fighter, and many other extremely rare aircraft. The flyable machines include a very rare A-Model Mustang, a Corsair, a Hellcat, a B-25, and, as the star of the collection, the only flying Japanese Zero in existence. The museum also has pre-World War II flying aircraft, including the sole surviving Boeing P12E and a P26A Peashooter.

Champlin Fighter Museum.   Doug Champlin made it a goal some years ago to establish one of the premiere collections of flying aircraft in the world, and he has done exactly that. In his Mesa,

Arizona, museum, on Falcon Field, you will see some of the finest and rarest examples of World War I and World War II aircraft anywhere. Among the rarities are an F2G Goodyear Corsair with the R-4360 'corncob' thirty-six-cylinder engine, an original Focke-Wulf FW 190-D2, the only flyable example in the world, and a Messerschmitt 109 in the original configuration. These are joined by a Corsair, a Wildcat, a Hellcat, and a generous sprinkling of World War I fighters. This museum has the advantage of being located on the same field as the Confederate Air Force Arizona wing and their B-17 *Sentimental Journey*. Falcon Field is also the site of at least one major fire-fighting operation that utilizes B-17s, and there are numerous derelict Lockheed Lodestars (PVs).

The Kalamazoo Aviation History Museum. Pete and Sue Parrish of Kalamazoo, Michigan, have been involved with World War II fighters since he was a cadet in the Army Air Corps and she was a WASP ferrying and testing army trainers. Their immaculate museum at Kalamazoo Municipal Airport lets that long-time love show through. Their attention to detail in both the museum facility and the airplanes makes it one of the premiere flying museums. Their aircraft restorations keep their trophy room overflowing; both their FG-1D Corsair and their F6F Hellcat have been grand champions at Oshkosh. Other aircraft in the collection include a rare F8F-1 Bearcat, a Spanish-built ME-109 (HA-1112), a P-40N Warhawk, one of two Bell P-39 Aircobras still flying, and many other rare aircraft.

4 **The Antiques**

J. R. Nielander hacks away at the tree growing through the cockpit of the remains of a **Ford Tri-Motor** he found in Central America. He subsequently recovered this hulk and shipped it home. (Courtesy of J. R. Nielander.)

The antiquer's interest lies in the world of aviation that was; he is attempting to reconstruct artifacts of eras that have long been nothing more than dog-eared scrapbooks and faded pictures. To the antiquer, the restoration of a fifty- or sixty-year-old airplane is a process in which memories are brought to life in the form of brightly colored biplanes, polished wooden and brass propellers, and anachronistic engines that were developed before the word *reliability* meant anything to a pilot.

The Search

Some years ago, two friends were poking around an abandoned hangar. It was very dark inside because all of the windows had been covered with wood to keep the vandals out. Every inch of

A fly-in lineup of antiques, including an **Aeronca C-3** and a **Ryan STM.** (Credit: Budd Davisson.)

The **DeHavilland Rapide** is hardly a small restoration project, yet several have been restored in the United States and serve their owners admirably as six- to ten-place personal airliners. (Credit: Budd Davisson.)

available floor space was taken up with boxes and decrepit machinery, the typical inhabitants of a large building that has outlived its primary usefulness in an urban area. The airport had been closed for years, and what had once been the hangar was now nothing more than a large storage shed for surrounding industrial plants. One of the fellows, Ben Nihart, paused for a second and played his flashlight on the beams above them. "Look, there it is, see? The old guy was right, it's still up there!" As both of them peered upward they could make out the ragged outline of bare wooden ribs and sagging fabric that had once covered the wing. Even from the floor they could see the large numbers NC1258.

Their flashlights revealed a ladder running up one of the girders. As they scrambled up the rickety ladder to do their tightrope

The **DeHavilland Moth** is a beautiful combination of anachronistic design and enclosed cabin comfort. (Courtesy of Ted Koston/EAA.)

A **Belgian Stampe** awaiting restoration looks out the workshop door at one of its freshly restored French cousins. (Credit: Budd Davisson.)

walk across the rafters of the building, the two men could hardly keep from laughing. They had found something that every antiquer dreams of. They had discovered a treasure that to them was as important and exciting as anything hidden in Tutankhamen's tomb. They had found the long-dead corpse of a 1929 biplane.

This story lives on in many variations in the minds of all antiquers; for them it's the ultimate fantasy.

Antiques Aplenty

Although it would be erroneous to say that the number of antique aircraft yet to be found and restored is unlimited, it can be said with some certainty that the number is significant. From about

Two **Stampes** cavorting over the Bucks County, Pennsylvania, countryside, are fabric embodiments of what fun in the air is supposed to be. (Credit: Budd Davisson.)

1915 to 1945, the span normally considered the antique era, there were thousands of airplanes built by dozens of manufacturers. There are today some 7,000 airplanes that were made before 1942, and that figure doesn't include the thousands that may be still undiscovered.

Another staggering thought is the variety of aircraft built and supposedly still surviving. They range from little 37-hp Aeronca C-3 putt-putts to 1000-hp Vultee V-1A transport-type aircraft. In between are myriad wire-and-tube biplanes, wooden monoplanes, and all-metal, high-speed, retractable-landing-gear corporation planes.

Subdividing the Species

The first thirty or thirty-five years of aircraft production saw a tremendous amount of progress and technological change in aircraft, which was in no way matched in the second thirty-five years of aviation. Because early aircraft changed so radically from one decade to the next, and in even shorter periods, competitions such as those conducted by the EAA at Oshkosh have had to set up a category breakdown that takes technologically similar aircraft and groups them into tidy cubbyholes.

The antique category includes any aircraft built prior to 1945. But it's pretty obvious that comparing a 1941, 200-mph, 450-hp Spartan Executive with a 1917 Curtiss Jenny is hardly fair. So some subdivisions are now recognized. The first few years of aircraft

Just relaxin'. A wing of the **Butler Blackhawk** offers more than shade; it's a glimpse of a corporation's history. Butler now builds steel buildings, but once it manufactured airplanes; this is the sole remaining example. (Courtesy of Ted Koston/EAA.)

The **Spartan Executive,** the forerunner of today's business jet, was designed specifically for high cruise speeds and maximum comfort. (Courtesy of Ted Koston/EAA.)

production, notably those before 1921, are grouped into what is called the Pioneer Age category. These are the rarest of the rare—the Bleriots and Wright Flyers, early Curtisses, and the trainers and combat aircraft of World War I.

The aircraft that fall into the 1921-to-1927 category are generally referred to as Golden Age aircraft. This period saw the formalization of the true aircraft industry, when nearly all modern aircraft manufacturers were established; Cessna and Beechcraft can both trace their beginnings back to those days, and nearly all the big names—such as Boeing and Douglas—started their aircraft building activities.

The period from 1928 to 1932, referred to as the Silver Age, was one of transition. The older airplanes were being phased out

This **Grumman G-32A** was a two-place version of the famous F3F Gulfhawk that was built specifically for the use of Leroy Grumman. (Credit: Budd Davisson.)

Top: The **Bücker Jungmeister** has always been considered the finest example of classic aerobatic performance and genteel handling. (Credit: Budd Davisson.)

114

August afternoon in Iowa. An **Arrow Sport** shows what it used to be like.

The unmistakable lines of a **WACO** cabin biplane at sunset.

Facing page: The **WACO UPF-7** saw service as a military trainer but today it's far better known as a "good old airplane."

Fifty years old, the **J-3 Cub** will outlive us all.

A **Travel Air D4D** and a quiet meadow—how memories are made.

Facing page: The handsome lines of the **Stearman N2S** (PT-17 in the Army) made it world famous and widely popular.

The **Tiger Moth** was England's primary trainer for decades.

Facing page, top: That rarest of birds, a completely stock 85-hp **Swift.**

Facing page, bottom: Takeoff! The **Airmaster** shows how it's done.

The taperwing **WACO** Johnny Livingston used to win the 1929 transcontinental race.

A **Bücker Jungmann** poses in front of a **Junkers JU-52;** both aircraft trace their design lineage back to the early 1930s. (Credit: Budd Davisson.)

This is what the **Jungmeister** pilot sees. (Credit: Budd Davisson.)

This 1929 **Cessna AW** was 1981 grand champion antique at both the EAA Convention in Oshkosh and the Antique Airplane Association's blast at Blakesberg. Gar Williams, its restorer, was the first to garner both awards in the same year since the early 1970s. (Courtesy of Jack Cox.)

in favor of those using newer technology. All-metal aircraft were coming to the fore, and the biplane was finding itself replaced by both high- and low-wing monoplanes.

The Silver Age faded into the Contemporary Age by 1933, and all aircraft produced between 1933 and 1945 fall into that category. The aircraft of that period were, and still are, reliable modes of transportation. In some cases, Contemporary Age birds are as fast and as comfortable as anything produced today. It is during the Contemporary Age that many of the true legends of aviation were produced, such as the Piper Cub and the Staggerwing Beechcraft, both of which will far outlive many so-called modern designs.

The Restoration Process

Restoring a battered, beaten, and neglected antique airplane can in many cases be far more complicated, time-consuming, and painful than building an airplane from scratch. The restoration of a basket case airplane involves healing the damage done by thirty or forty years of aging, which includes rust, rot, and any other type of deterioration that man and the elements can concoct. In many cases, once this deterioration has been removed, it's found that the part is no longer airworthy, and a new part must be either found or manufactured. Although this endless process of cleaning and rebuilding can be aggravating, it can also be a tremendous challenge, and so can the scrounging for parts.

Facing page, bottom: Author Richard Bach made his **Parks biplane** famous in his books. Here its current owner flies past the Antique Airplane Association's Museum and hangar complex in Blakesberg, Iowa. (Credit: Budd Davisson.)

This rare **Fairchild 71 Transport** is part of the AAA's Antique Airpower Museum. (Credit: Budd Davisson.)

A **G Model Staggerwing** breaks ground showing its fine lines. (Courtesy of Ted Koston/EAA.)

Imagine how many hours go into the covering of something like this **Stinson Tri-Motor.** The covering, of course, comes only after thousands of tiny parts within have been faithfully restored. (Credit: Budd Davisson.)

As restoration projects go, this British **SE-5A** in the EAA shop is in far better condition than many. (Credit: Budd Davisson.)

The antique airplane is one clearly defined area in sport aviation where skill and tenacity can substitute for dollars (the all-metal superbirds, such as the Spartan Executive, notwithstanding). It is still quite possible for an individual to spend far less than the price of a high-quality used car on an airframe that may have the makings of a champion. What makes the difference between the way it looks as he pulls it into his garage and the way it looks when it's finished is the money for parts and materials—plus thousands of hours of his own time.

The word *parts* begins to gain new meaning when you're trying to reassemble a fifty-year-old flying machine. In most cases, no more than a few thousand, and in many cases only a few hundred of a given machine were built. So in the fifty years since their

This **Stinson Model A Tri-Motor** was found abandoned at a rural Alaska airport and trucked to Illinois for restoration. Thousands of manhours were expended in manufacturing parts to completely restore the primary structure shown here. (Courtesy of Dick Stouffer/EAA.)

A view into the **Model A Stinson's** flight deck during restoration shows how roomy the airplane is. (Courtesy of Paul Clarke.)

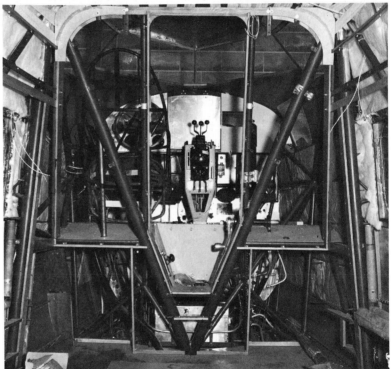

birth, it's entirely possible that many parts have been scattered to the winds or lost completely. But this doesn't prove fatal to a restoration. There are very few parts in a really old airplane that cannot be duplicated today for a reasonable price. Even when it comes to the more complex items, such as engines, restorers are finding that modern industry is coming to their rescue with a veritable supermarket of pistons and bearings, rings and seals. In fact, almost any part can be remanufactured by one process or another.

Antique airplanes suffer from three basic problems: wood problems, steel problems, and fabric problems; skills in those three areas are basically the ones you will need in restoring an antique airplane. Although the skills don't differ substantially from those

Command-Aire was one of the many names that disappeared in the wake of the 1929 stock market crash. It wasn't a winner then, but it takes plenty of prizes now. (Credit: Budd Davisson.)

DeHavilland versus Douglas: The British **DH Dragon** contrasts with its contemporary, the American **DC-3**. (Courtesy of Ted Koston/EAA.)

required to build a home-built airplane, there are a few unique aspects to antique restoration. Among other things, what you'll be doing first is disassembling a badly decayed corpse, and saving the parts you remove to use as patterns for new ones. If some of the parts are reusable, you have a different problem, that of cleaning and restoring the existing parts. Just cleaning something as big as a steel tubing fuselage can be a major undertaking. Although sandblasting is the normal technique used, few home-builders or restorers have adequate sandblasting capability to be able to do an entire fuselage. There are several small sandblasting units available that let you do at least the fittings and the cluster joints, which are the most difficult to clean. It should be pointed out, however, that sandblasting is not an indoor activity. Even when

The enormity of a restoration project: Gar Williams is dwarfed by the one-piece wing of his **Cessna AW**. (Credit: Budd Davisson.)

done outside, sandblasting turns your front yard into Miami Beach in a matter of minutes. It is a dusty, dirty, messy job. But without sandblasting, the restoration of any antique is much more difficult. So, if you're not going to do it yourself, you had better find somebody who can.

One other skill that a restorer absolutely must have is that of making friends with those who can help. Specifically, it would be nice to have a friend with a machine shop, because machining capability will make a night-and-day difference in your ability to regenerate missing or broken parts. Except for the more complex antiques, however, there were very few really complex machined parts used. Where we would use a machined part or a casting today, they used weldments, made up of multitudes of layers of small steel sheets welded together with little ears pointed every which way.

Going Shopping: An Antique Purchasing Guide

There are old antiques and not quite so old antiques; big antiques, little antiques; some with termites, some nearly new. If there's one thing the thirty-five years of aircraft production prior to 1945 produced, it was variety, and variety may be one of the most exciting things about the antique aircraft movement. As with all other aircraft, however, the trick in fitting an airplane to your own needs, talents, and financial wherewithal means doing more than just a little looking around. It requires knowing what has been produced, knowing what you're looking for, and in many cases, being in the right place at the right time.

The Model A Ford engine in the **Pietenpol** offered a way for early homebuilders to have useful horsepower at low cost. (Credit: Budd Davisson.)

The following thumbnail sketches touch briefly on the more popular and more common antiques of all categories. These are certainly not the only ones available, but they are the ones you are most likely to run across and therefore they present the most realistic opportunities for you to join the ranks of the antique buffs.

Travel Air. In the late 1920s the big Travel Air biplanes set the standard for private aircraft. Of traditional construction—a fabric-covered steel tube fuselage with fabric-covered wooden wings— the Travel Airs were built in large enough numbers that some were still being used as crop dusters into the 1960s. The distinctive overlapping ailerons, commonly known as 'elephant ear' ailerons, were a Travel Air trademark in the early models, as was the unique overbalance on the rudder. Usually fitted with radial engines with 200 hp and better, the Travel Air is not a small airplane, and it requires a good-sized working area to rebuild it. Once flying, however, it is one of the more docile, better-mannered biplanes of its day, which may be one reason why it was so popular.

Curtiss Robin. The standard Curtiss Robin was a three-place, high-wing monoplane, generally fitted with a Wright J-5 radial engine. Some of the other variants had four seats or an OX-5 water-cooled V-8, which gave the airplane a distinctive nose. One of the first successful high-wing monoplanes, it was nonetheless one of the last of the Curtiss civilian designs. Although the Curtiss Robin

122

With its unique elephant-ear balances on the ailerons and the extended balance on the rudder, the **Travel Airs** of the 1920s often served as phony Fokkers in the movies, earning them the title "Wichita Fokkers." (Credit: Budd Davisson.)

In the early 1930s, designers used promotional stunts—in particular, endurance flights—to gain popularity for their aircraft. This **Curtiss Robin** held the endurance record for some years at 16 days aloft with aerial refueling. (Credit: Budd Davisson.)

is not a small restoration job, it is simpler than biplanes of its day, if only because it lacks the bottom two wings. It is a slow and somewhat cumbersome airplane that will behave itself on a grass runway, but, as with most airplanes of its day, is not happy landing on pavement with a crosswind. To put it more accurately, the Curtiss Robin *pilot* is not happy in that situation.

The Early WACO Biplanes. WACO aircraft all carry a three-letter designation identifying the airframe size, the engine, and the wing shape. It's one of those codes that nobody understands except those who delve deeply into it. It takes only a casual perusal of history, however, to see that WACO started out with a large, open-cockpit biplane, the WACO 9, and progressed through smaller variations, all of which emphasized improved performance and handling. The famous Taperwing WACOs were some of the fastest of their day, and indeed, Johnny Livingston used one to set a transcontinental record in 1929. There are probably more WACOs extant than any other aircraft of its time, which makes it much easier to become a WACO owner than, say, a Bird or a Swallow owner. Also, the WACO Club of America is a very active association that prides itself on the help it gives its individual members. The WACOs demand the same respect you would give any other high-performance, high-drag biplane; they will ground-loop and bite you only if you let them.

The WACO Cabin Bipes. By the 1930s, WACO saw the writing on the wall and realized that the flying public didn't like having their heads hanging out in the wind. So they designed a four-place cabin variation, which led to an entire line of aircraft that continued through World War II. Although appearing generally similar, the WACO Cabin planes showed a definite evolutionary development, beginning with the chunky little QDC and progressing to the SRE, with its long, slinky fuselage and ready-to-romp 450-hp Pratt & Whitney. As antiques go, they are among the more usable cross-country machines, since most of them cruise in excess of 120 mph. Some of the later ones can really move. All those wings, struts, and big round engines mean more drag, so your fuel mileage isn't anything to brag about. But they are big, comfortable, and relatively easy to fly, once you get used to looking around, under, and over all of the airplane parts obstructing your vision.

The Staggerwing Beech. The Staggerwing Beechcraft is considered by many to be the king, or queen if you will, of the antiques. Some antiquers will dispute that claim, but the shape of the Staggerwing has undoubtedly done more to fire imaginations than any other. In production from 1932 to 1946, the airplane was remarkably sophisticated for its day, considering that it carried two sets of wings. It was produced in such a wide variety of models that you can own one in whatever form your pocketbook allows. The 225-hp early versions are the docile puppies of the litter, while the 450-hp D and G models of later years claim speeds of over 200 mph. As a rebuilding project, the Staggerwing ranks as one of the

The **WACO 9** and **10** series biplanes are popular among restorers, even though their cantankerous OX-5 and OXX engines can be extremely unreliable. (Courtesy of EAA.)

Jonathan Livingston's original seagull? Race pilot Johnny Livingston flew this **WACO Taperwing** in the 1929 Transcontinental Speed Dash, long before author Richard Bach named the *Seagull* after him. (Credit: Budd Davisson.)

most complicated but at the same time most rewarding projects you can get into. It is also one of the best investments in terms of return on the dollar. It is a demanding airplane to fly, but if you treat it the way it expects to be treated, you will have the most fun of your life. If it gets away from you on the runway, you can generally count on the results being fairly spectacular, although seldom fatal.

The Cessna Airmaster. In 1934, when the first Cessna Airmaster rolled off the assembly line, it was considered one of the trimmest, sleekest machines around, and time hasn't diminished that image one bit. One of the very first of the high-performance aircraft for which the design goal was maximum miles per horsepower, its

125

The postwar **G model Staggerwing Beechcraft** is perhaps the best example of classic lines and high performance in an antique airplane. Factory specifications claim that the airplane can cruise at more than 200 mph, a speed seldom seen in actual practice. (Credit: Budd Davisson.)

cramped little cabin could handle four people but not with ease. Later models incorporated bigger engines, wider landing gear to eliminate some earlier handling problems, and even more performance. The only thing that prevents the airplane from being a neat garage-size restoration project is the one-piece wing, which is quite a bit longer than most garages. Unless you are an accomplished restorer or woodworker, don't touch an Airmaster with a bad wing, because just building a new wing is more work than the complete restoration of many other airplanes.

The Monocoupes. Regardless of the year, 1932 or 1982, when you taxi up to the fuel pumps in a Monocoupe, you've earned your status on the airport as a real hot rock: a man with a machine that demands a master and flies masterfully when it gets him. The very early 90 series Monocoupes used a little 90-hp engine and were fast but docile. By 1931 or 1932, however, the race pilots and acrobatics specialists had discovered it, and so the factory began to hang larger engines on it and produce short-wing racing and acrobatic versions. The Monocoupe became the era's favorite for fast, high-spirited, two-place personal transportation. A fellow named Lindbergh had one of the D-145 models. Even today, the later 90 Ls and Fs, which used modern, flat engines, are considered good transportation. As a restoration project, the Monocoupe rates high on the lists of all purists, since it is not a very big airplane, nor is it particularly complicated. Here again, as with the Airmaster, the wing is the primary concern, since it is also a one-piece unit running from tip to tip; a total rebuilding or remanufacturing of it is a major job. In the air, it's a macho ballerina with overtones of a karate boxer; very agile, but very muscular at the same time. On the ground it has a reputation for being quick and extremely demanding, although this is more true of the D-145 series than any of the others.

The Little Ones

In contrast to the major restoration projects described above, many smaller antiques are much simpler, more "do-able," and much more affordable. There are the "pasture airplanes," craft that you would fire up on Sunday morning to go watch the sun rise, or

126

Pugnacious appearance and performance made the 110 **Monocoupe Special** a favorite among early race and aerobatic pilots. (Courtesy of Ted Koston/EAA.)

maybe hop over to the next airport for coffee and donuts. Most will fit nicely into a garage-size workshop and, assuming you get one that hasn't been eaten by corrosion or termites, they're great projects for the first-time builder who has to learn as he goes.

Aeronca C2/C3. The Aeronca bathtub series of airplanes was the first successful attempt at a mass-produced, light aircraft. With the little two-cylinder, 37-hp engine popping away up front, C2/C3s probably taught more people how to fly in the early 1930s than any other type. As a rebuilding project, the little Aeroncas are on a par with big *model* airplanes, assuming, of course, the steel isn't too badly corroded. If the Aeronca has a shortcoming, it's in its engine: parts are almost nonexistent. But don't let that stop you. The engine is simple, and there are enough restorers who have overcome the spare parts problem; you, too, can find yourself up there floating around in what is one of the most minimal airplanes ever mass-produced.

The Cubs. The not-so-mighty but nonetheless legendary Piper Cub was produced from about 1932, (when it was a Taylor Cub) up to 1948. During that time it developed from an open-cockpit, 35-hp contemporary of the Aeronca C-3 into the 65-hp grasshopper of World War II. In between it went through a half dozen different makes of engines, and two or three minor configuration changes. But it was still a Cub. As a flying machine, it is the standard by

127

which all other trainers are judged. It's docile, predictable, and above all, fun to fly. As a restoration project, it's one of the best, if only because parts are plentiful. Even new ones can be had from certain suppliers. The best of the variants is the J-3, which is also the most numerous. And the best of the J-3s are those equipped with the 65-hp Continental, rather than the Lycoming or Franklin engines, both of which are extremely hard to maintain because of parts shortages. Of all antique aircraft, the J-3 Cub is by far the most numerous in ready-to-fly condition. In 1980 dollars, they fall into the $9,000-to-$11,000 bracket.

The Rearwins. Although not particularly well known, the Rearwins are nonetheless one of the best buys in the little antique

The **J-3 Piper Cub** has been subjected to many modifications; a conversion to nose wheel was common in the late 1940s and early 1950s. Since it is inherently unstable in that position, it is normally tied tail-down to keep the wind from blowing it over. (Credit: Budd Davisson.)
Top: The **Aeronca C-3,** affectionately known as the "Flying Bathtub," marks the beginning of light aircraft. (Credit: Budd Davisson.)

Until the **Pitcairn Mailwing** was designed for the purpose, air mail was delivered by whatever aircraft was available. This Mailwing, restored by Jack Rose of Washington state, was owned by Steve McQueen at the time of his death. (Credit: Budd Davisson.)

airplane market. A high-wing monoplane with conventional fabric-covered wood wings and a steel tube fuselage, they have, for no apparent reason, failed to catch the public's eye. As a restoration project, they are slightly more difficult than a Cub, and the radial engines used on some are certainly more difficult to rebuild and maintain than the more modern A-65 Continentals. However, those small radial engines make the Rearwin Cloudster, for example, much more desirable than many of its contemporaries.

The Interstate. The Interstate is another one of those airplanes which, although produced in some numbers, is still virtually unknown in the antique field. Its configuration is basically the same as the Cub's, and it uses the same power plants; the Interstate's

ungainly appearance may have been the reason it never matched the Cub's popularity. It flies very well, with better accommodations for the pilot and passenger than a Cub offers, and today it can be purchased and rebuilt for anywhere from half to two-thirds of the price of a Cub.

Clubs and Organizations. Every conceivable type of airplane, even those that were built in minute numbers, has its own organization. There is the Airmaster Club, the Staggerwing Club (which incidentally has an impressive museum at Tullahoma, Tennessee), the Rearwin Club, the 1932 Widget Association, and heaven knows how many more. Hardly any antiquer need feel alone in a world populated with so many organizations. The best way to locate the one that appeals to you is to contact the EAA's Antique/Classic Division or the Antique Airplane Association in Blakesburg, Iowa.

The Howard DGA (Damned Good Airplanes) series culminated in this 450-hp **DGA-15P**. An outgrowth of the prewar Mr. Mulligan racer, the Howards soldiered through the war as navigation trainers and continued to earn their keep as bush planes in the north country. (Credit: Budd Davisson.)

What better place to watch an airshow from than the top wing of your favorite biplane? (Credit: Budd Davisson.)

Many fly-ins offer the unparalleled opportunity to turn back the clock in the open cockpit of a biplane such as this **Stearman.** (Credit: Budd Davisson.)

5 Classic Forms

It's amazing what time does to the value of mechanical things. Who would ever have thought that today we would see $10,000 1965 Ford Mustang convertibles or '55 Thunderbirds selling for more than $20,000? It's been interesting to watch '57 Chevrolets evolve from grocery hack status, to used car, to junker, to hot rod, to super classic. This progression has been paralleled exactly by aircraft of postwar vintage.

They're now called *classics*, those aircraft designed and built between 1945 and 1955, but in 1960, they were simply used airplanes. By 1970 many of them were regarded as junk; they sat around airports with weeds growing up around their tires and mice leaping around inside their wings, eating the rib-stitching. As recently as the mid-1970s, every airport had at least a few so-called

The cowling grill and triple exhaust identify this plane as a true rarity: a nearly unmodified **Swift**. However, the one-piece windshield and modified quarter windows show even this one didn't escape the hot-rodder's touch. (Credit: Budd Davisson.)

132

The **Aeronca Champion,** along with the Piper Cub, was the backbone of practically every postwar flight school. Docile and forgiving, the Champ is a perfect Sunday afternoon mount for cruising the back country. (Credit: Budd Davisson.)

classics sitting on the back row, leaning to one side as tires went flat and the landing gear got tired. At about that time, these airplanes from the postwar boom hit bottom and began to bounce back; today their used-car-lot image has vanished as their eminent practicality as low-cost, entry-level airplanes has become apparent. It was Jack Cox, now editor of EAA's *Sport Aviation,* who first proposed that this group of homeless airplanes be given their own category and gave them a name.

Why So Many?

The tremendous numbers of classic aircraft can, like the baby boom, be blamed on the war, and a massive marketing miscalculation. The experts with the narrow lapels reasoned that the war had given America a taste of something it had never had before—flight for the masses. Hundreds of thousands of pilots had been trained and turned loose in the skies, some of them in a kill-or-be-killed atmosphere, but many more in utilitarian jobs transporting people and freight in quantities never before believed possible. The ivory tower experts reasoned that these pilots, both men and women, wouldn't want to give up their wings and return to a mundane, ground-bound way of life. The popular theory was that America had finally taken to the air and planned on staying there.

The war had also created an industry that was capable of cranking out hundreds of airplanes a day. Where design and production of flying machines only five years earlier had occupied a few individuals and even fewer companies, 1946 saw an aviation industry bulging with talent and production capabilities. Companies such as Republic, which had been hammering out the P-47 Thunderbolt, armed with six .50-caliber machine guns, decided that the promised aviation boom was going to demand an airplane that could land on both water and land. So they began production of the SeeBee, their personal amphibian. Stinson didn't even slow down its grasshopper lines, and they started turning out the fabulous 108 series—including the Stationwagon and others.

The majority of companies took advantage of their wartime experience and changed their manufacturing techniques to use what they had learned during the war, such as high-performance airframes and sheet metal construction. In some cases, this created strange dichotomies, in which prewar civilian production lines were reopened to produce 1939 designs, while at the same time, brand new production lines were banging out sophisticated, state-of-the-art machines. At Beechcraft, for instance, there was a time when the ancient Staggerwing fabric biplane was being produced right alongside the all metal V-tailed superbird, the Bonanza, a machine that is still in production thirty-five years later.

In late 1946, when the industrial wheels of war had stopped turning completely, the wheels of the aviation industry had just started rolling, and for the next several years manufacturers seemed to ignore the fact that they were producing machines nobody was buying. By the time another war (this one called a police action) had closed in on us, the industry finally realized that the boom had been inaudible and America was really not ready for an airplane in every garage.

Overpopulation as a Plus

The marketing mistakes of three decades ago have turned out to be a mighty boon to today's sport aviator in the form of a treasure trove of classic airplanes. Not only is there variety, but there is also a massive oversupply that has gone a long way toward keeping prices down.

Today, the demand has never been greater for aircraft of the postwar era, and the reason is obvious: dollar for dollar, you get more airplane in a classic than in any other type of airplane. If you buy a 1950 Cessna 170, for instance, you get a thirty-year-old, four-place airplane with very nearly the same utility as its replacement descendant, the Skyhawk, but at one-fifth the price. More important, in the Cessna 170 you have an airplane with classic lines and classic behavior.

Restoration Sometimes Isn't

While no airplane restoration project can be described as easy, the restoration of a classic is getting close. At least half of the classics had outgrown rag and steel tube construction, so tubing rot is a problem in only the Stinson, Piper, and a few other designs. Of course, instead of tubing rust, you may find aluminum corrosion,

134

There were many variations of Luscombes, but none rarer than this **T8F Observer.** Several were built with tandem, rather than side-by-side, seating, to win a government contract; they lost the bid. (Credit: Budd Davisson.)

and while that's still a challenge, you can't really compare the restoration of a Luscombe, for instance, with that of a Monocoupe of the same basic size.

One of the most improved areas of restoration in the postwar classics is that space between the propeller and the firewall—the engine. Although most of the engines used in the smaller aircraft have been long out of production, they were produced in such huge quantities to supply the military version of the same airplane that parts aren't nearly the problem they are for prewar engines. To be certain, you don't go down to your local garage to pick up a couple of 65-hp Continental cylinders, but it generally takes only one phone call to get them sent to you from one of the many houses that specialize in such engines. The same thing is true of just about all of the airframe parts, from windshields to interiors, instrument panels to brakes; there is somebody, somewhere who specializes in the parts for nearly all of the classic era airplanes. Besides, we're not too far from the time when the classics were new airplanes, so wrecking yards across the country all have parts for at least some of these not-quite-so-old birds.

Type Organizations

Name the classic, and you won't have to look very hard to find a club or association that puts that particular aircraft on a pedestal as some sort of a winged idol. In most cases, it's not religion that brings the owners of one type of classic aircraft together; it's a

135

combination of love for a machine, and the help fellow members can give each other in restoring and maintaining their aircraft.

Almost all classic aircraft associations publish a monthly or bimonthly newsletter that can be the single most useful tool to have when it comes to restoring a classic airplane. It's the medium through which information is exchanged concerning parts problems, sales of parts, or completed aircraft, as well as those tips on how to do a particular job better at a lower price. It's also through the newsletter that interest can be built up among a group of individuals who need a particular part remanufactured. One man with a Cessna 170, for instance, can't afford to have instrument panel covers made specifically for his airplane, but if he can get another 100 owners to chip in, it becomes practical for everybody.

Undoubtedly the extreme to which an association will go to protect its own breed is the ultra-active Swift Association. The Swift is one of the aircraft for which Univair Aircraft Corporation of Denver, Colorado, purchased the standard type certificate and manufacturing rights for all parts from the original manufacturer and for years a small manufacturing facility produced parts for the Swift. At one point, however, it appeared that those parts and rights were going to be sold to a foreign government, a thought that curdled the blood of loyal Swift Association members. A cry went out through the land, "Save our bird!" Charlie Nelson, head guru of the Swiftites, beat the drum loud, long, and successfully: the Swift Association now owns the type certificates for the Swift aircraft and all the parts, so the association is now the central repository for all Swift knowledge and expertise.

The **Taylorcraft BC-12**, originally built in 1936, was reintroduced after the war, and is still in limited production. Whether you call it an antique, classic, or modern airplane, its fabric-covered steel bones are an eternal favorite. (Courtesy of Ted Koston/EAA.)

Before You Buy

Before you run out to the garage and start throwing bicycles and croquet mallets out into the driveway to make room for your classic restoration project, you should realize that there are other routes to go. It's not necessary to skin knuckles and bury your weekends just to own a classic airplane. One good way to begin is to join the EAA's Antique/Classic Division and start reading its magazine, *Vintage Airplane.* It will help you decide which airplane to own and give you hints on what restoring will be entailed.

The large number of classics and the supermarket variety that's available means that in many cases you might be as well off to go to the bank and get the backing to *buy* a classic, because you wouldn't save much rebuilding one. That, of course, depends on several considerations.

- Are you buying a classic to fly it or to rebuild it?
- Are you willing to settle for a nice, clean airplane, or do you want a gem that shines so bright it sets the grass on fire at fly-ins?
- Does your financial situation force you into going at an airplane a piece at a time, or can you jump in all at once with one big check?

Unless you want an absolutely pristine example of the breed, and you are not willing or able to drop a bundle on an award-winning restoration, you will find that buying a flying airplane is the best route.

If you pay market value for a classic airplane, it's all but impossible to lose money on it. It's been proven time and again that a plain, well-maintained classic always sells for more than its purchase price, and you can fly it for years and years and still wind up with a net investment that includes nothing but the cost of gas and oil. It's a mistake, however, to buy a bottom-of-the-market airplane if you intend to restore it. The difference between a ratty but flying airplane and a top-notch specimen of the same type may be no more than a couple thousand dollars, but it will cost you far more than that to make your turkey into the peacock that you imagine. In other words, if you're going to restore an airplane, it's always better financially to get your hands on the cheapest air-

Luscombe's entry in the post-war four-place market was the **Luscombe Sedan.** Produced in limited numbers, it is loved by the few who own it. (Courtesy of Ted Koston/EAA.)

plane you can find. But, if you want the airplane just to fly it, you should buy the best that you can afford. Don't stop anywhere in between, because it will wind up costing you more in the long run.

You cannot buy a bottom-of-the-market flying airplane, over-haul the engine, and then expect to have anything less than a very expensive airplane. For example: a postwar Luscombe, which will soon need a frontal lobotomy on the engine, may fall into the $6,000-to-$7,000 bracket, while one that has just had an overhaul may run only $8,000 or $9,000. But for you to have that engine overhauled and reinstalled is going to cost a minimum of $3,500. Add that to the cost of your bargain-basement airplane and you'll find it's no longer a bargain. You'll end up spending more than if

The classic **Luscombes** were produced with 65-, 75-, 85-, and 90-hp engines; all offer spritely handling, phone booth visibility, and surprising speed for their power. (Credit: Budd Davisson.)

you had bought a top-of-the-market airplane. Besides that, most aircraft that have been flown long enough to need an engine overhaul probably need attention in other areas, too. But it's seldom that anyone overhauls the engine in a classic without doing other work as well; buying a classic with a freshly overhauled engine means other parts of the airplane are also freshly refurbished. Boiled down to the simplest terms, this means you should buy the best one you can get your hands on.

What Is "Best"?

If you're going to kick tires and poke fabric while your mind is all afire to buy an airplane, it's a good idea to get somebody to hold your checkbook while you consider the following points that apply to buying classics, as well as any other used aircraft.

Power Plant. Unless you're looking at one of the few classics with a radial engine, such as a Cessna 195, the chances are that no matter what you pick it's going to have a Continental, a Lycoming, or, in lesser numbers, a Franklin engine. These are all four- or six-cylinder, flat opposed, air-cooled engines identical to those still being used today. They strike a midpoint between being state-of-the-art and archaic and, with the exception of the Franklin, parts are still readily available for all of them. However, make sure the logbooks show that the engine has something less than 500 hours on it, since 300 hours following a major overhaul (SMOH) is preferable. Unless it's extremely cheap, never buy a classic with an engine in the 900-to-1,000-hour bracket. Although the time allowed between overhauls (TBO) may be advertised as 1,500 hours, most classics generally suffer from lack of exercise; they just aren't flown enough, and they sit around for long periods between flights. This inactivity hurts the engines and shortens their TBO by some unquantifiable amount. The 1,200- to 1,500-hour figure that's quoted for a given engine should be regarded as fiction, at best. Have your mechanic do a compression test and a compression bleed-down test on the engine; these will reveal the general condition of both the rings and valves. At the same time, have a sample of oil analyzed. The printout you get back on the oil analysis will tell you exactly what kind of metals are being worn away; this gives a clear picture of what shape the engine is in.

139

Airframe. Don't trust the logbooks to show you every bit of damage the aircraft may have sustained. In the thirty or thirty-five years those aircraft were going through their junk-aircraft stage of evolution, a lot of shade tree mechanics and less-than-legal owners might have covered up minor damage and not entered it in the log. Theoretically, all work on the aircraft shows up in a log, but don't count on it. A thorough inspection will tell you what is, not what's claimed to be.

Look for deterioration: corrosion on all-metal airplanes, rust and rot in steel tube and wood airplanes. Unfortunately, most of these problems occur in some of the most insidious, difficult-to-reach areas, those tiny niches and crannies an airplane is loaded with. In the case of a fabric-covered airplane, check the log to see whether the plane is covered with a synthetic covering, such as dacron or fiberglass cloth, or a natural fiber; cotton or linen won't last more than four to six years in the open. The actual epidermal condition of the covering can be checked by the licensed airplane mechanic (whom you wisely brought along), who simply pushes a meter against the fabric and tells you whether it's flyable or not. The cost of labor and materials has driven the price of a new suit of fabric clothes for even the smallest classic close to $3,000, so it's imperative that the airplane's wardrobe be checked carefully.

Since the interiors of most small, classic aircraft are rudimentary and easily replaced, their condition shouldn't be a primary factor in the purchasing decision. However, a pilot who has let the interior of his airplane get dirty and disheveled may be cutting the same kind of maintenance corners elsewhere in the airplane where they're much more important.

Radios. One of the nice things about the smaller classics, the Cubs, the Luscombes, the Taylorcrafts, and so on, is that they're usually not purchased for running in and out of O'Hare Field. They are around-the-patch, personal-amazement machines. But, with the ever-tightening web of regulations and airport controls, you may find the availability of a radio and the quality of the equipment installed worth noting. On larger classics, such as the Navion and the Cessna 195 that are used for cross-country work, the radio equipment becomes a primary factor. The bottom line in evaluating radios is this: replacing radios isn't cheap, and repairing them isn't much better. Besides that, radio technology changed drastically in the 1970s, when the old tube-type radios were replaced with solid-state models. Today, many avionics shops aren't even equipped to work on tube-type radios, regardless of how well they may be working or how efficient they may be. So it's axiomatic that the newer the radios and the more useful they are, the more expensive they are. With even the most simple navigational radio running $2,000 to $3,000, plus installation, it's quite easy today to put more than the price of the airplane itself into the holes in the instrument panel.

Instrument Panel. The instrument panel holds a lot of dials, switches, and gadgets, which, if the classic has not been restored, will be yellowed with age and decades of mishandling. If you like an instrument panel that's clean and neat, with the numbers and needles so white they jump out at you, you should take the panel's condition into careful consideration when buying a classic, because it will cost you $80 to $100 a hole to replace the instruments.

Paint. Depending on the airplane, it now costs between $2,000 and $3,000 to lay a simply trimmed coat of paint on a normal-sized classic, but that new paint job will go a long way toward making the airplane tug at your heartstrings. You know that and the seller knows that, so you should buy the airplane that's underneath the paint, and try to get the price down to the point where you can afford to have it painted, should you not like its present complexion. Unless you have a workshop and a family who are much more acclimated to the smell of paint than most, don't even think of trying to paint it yourself. It's the one thing that can make an airplane look good or bad, and it's best left to a professional. You can do a lot of the stripping, sanding, and cleaning yourself, but let the pros do the final prep and shooting. Incidentally, be suspicious of an airplane that has a nice shiny paint job but otherwise has all the earmarks of a dog—ratty interior, dirty engine compartment, and dinged-up skin. When you're three or four thou-

The two-place **Cessna 120/140** series was the standard all-metal trainer of the early 1950s. With only 90 hp, it cruises in excess of 100 mph—a very usable mode of transportation. (Courtesy of EAA.)

sand feet in the air, beauty is a whole lot more than skin deep, and a paint job does nothing to keep you up there.

A Few Favorites

The classic airplane category can almost be considered crowded and, at the very least, confusing. For one thing, the classics overlap some prewar antiques; some of the prewar airplanes, such as Cubs, Taylorcrafts, and Luscombes, were reintroduced after the war, sometimes by the same company, sometimes by another. Then there were dozens of new designs that showed up after the war. This creates cranial chaos for anyone trying to sort out each model and make, although it is a fun kind of confusion. Even more confusing is the fact that the postwar designs were supposed to capitalize on the coming aviation boom, so the variety of training and utility airplanes is enormous. There are all sorts of little around-the-patch two-placers/trainers, medium-speed four-place airplanes, and high-speed, four-place airplanes. Some major manufacturers put out five or six different types, while other manufacturers hatched only one. Rather than trying to describe the entire classic category plane-by-plane, we'll run down a partial list that is organized the way the EAA does it—by horsepower. Category I is 80 hp and less; Category II, 150 hp and less; and in Category III the sky's the limit.

The 80-Hp Putt-Putts.

After the war, the prevailing theory was that if an airplane were available that was not much more expensive than a car, all those ex-service pilots would buy one. This imagined need for an aerial Volkswagon was met with a vengeance by dozens of manufacturers.

Piper Aircraft Corporation responded to the postwar non-boom by stretching, shortening, and widening their popular Piper Cub and generally using whatever existing parts they could to produce an entirely different line of aircraft for the serviceman and his new wife. The Vagabond series (PA-15 and PA-17) went from idea to runway in exactly eighty-eight days. The original PA-15 used a 65-hp Lycoming and was so rudimentary that the landing gear was rigid; it depended on balloon tires to absorb landing shock. The PA-17 added another control stick, sprung the wheels, and went to a Continental engine. These little machines then metamor-

A trio of **Tri-Pacers.** Not exactly the glamor gal of the classic set, the Tri-Pacer is nevertheless an extremely useful airplane that can be bought for $6,000 to $7,000. (Credit: Budd Davisson.)

phosed into the Clipper of 1949, and eventually into the four-place Pacer of 1950. Of the 600 or so Vagabonds built, a majority of them are flying or in the process of being restored. Cruising at about 100 mph on four gallons of gas an hour, a Vagabond is one of the more economical two-place airplanes available. It's fabric and steel tube, of course, just like the old Cub, but it's a relatively small airplane and easy to maintain or restore.

Over at Cessna, they too figured that there would be a lot of ex-military pilots buying airplanes and a lot of ex-servicemen learning to fly; so they developed the C-120, a two-place trainer/sport airplane, later to become the C-140. With an all-metal structure (the earlier airplane has fabric wings; the later one has metal wings), the 120 and 140 became fantastically popular with those flying schools that were affluent enough not to have to base their entire living on Piper Cubs. Thousands of the little 85-hp machines were built, and they are still one of the very best two-place airplanes that you can buy. Although there are some required modifications to watch for, such as extended gear legs on the 120s to cure a ground-handling problem, they are such a numerous breed that you have plenty to pick and choose from.

The prewar Luscombe design may look a little like the 120/140 Cessna, but it is an entirely different airplane in almost all respects. With engines in 65-, 75-, 85-, and 90-hp variations, they can cruise at well over 100 mph, some as fast as 110 mph, and all are mildly acrobatic. They are less forgiving of mistakes on landings and takeoffs, although this fits right in with their sporting

143

Since the **Ercoupe** came with no rudder pedals, you drive it like a car. It produced 110-mph speeds on less than 85 hp, with docile flying characteristics. (Credit: Budd Davisson.)

As America moved into the tricycle-gear era in the 1950s, Aeronca tried to meet the market by putting a nose gear on the Champion and calling it a **Tri-Traveler.** Unfortunately, in windy areas the airplane spent more time on its back than on its feet. (Credit: Budd Davisson.)

image. Their zippy performance and appearance have made the Luscombe one of the favorites of those seeking to restore an award-winning classic to take to airshows and fly-ins.

Taylorcraft brought back their old BC series in a slightly upgraded BC-12D of 1946. The BC-12D is one of the fastest in the 65-hp category; with the optional wing tanks, it is capable of 400- and 500-mile cross-country flights. It still wears its prewar costume of grade A fabric over tubing and wood, and, oddly enough, it was produced well into the 1980s by several manufacturers.

The Ercoupe was a prewar design that was totally spin-proof and, therefore, theoretically much safer than conventional aircraft. With its low wing, tricycle gear and twin tail, it was one of the most distinctive in appearance of the low-horsepower two-placers

For years the Swift Association faithful gathered at Kentucky Dam State Park in Paducah (above). Nowadays, some 200 of them make the pilgrimage to Athens, Tennessee. (Credit: Budd Davisson.)

The military cousin of the Swift was the **Temco T-35 Buckaroo.** The few that were built are highly prized by their owners today. (Credit: Budd Davisson.)

then around. Most Ercoupes had a unique control system as well: the control wheel is linked directly to both the rudders and the ailerons, so there are no rudder pedals on the floor. You steer it on the ground and in the air just like a car. The Ercoupe was another one of those designs produced by three or four companies well into the 1960s, but in all but the very final version, it was still a twin-tailed, all-metal airplane with fabric covered wings.

More Horses, More Class. As you move up the horsepower scale, you enter the area where true fanaticism regarding airplane types reigns. Take the Globe/Temco Swift, for instance. There are many enthusiasts who claim the Swift is the uncontested king of the classic airplanes, and when you look at one, it's hard to disagree.

A perky little all-metal private fighter, it began life with 85 hp, but most available versions have 125-hp or 145-hp engines. Since it looks like a fighter, many owners have decided to make it into a fighter by installing bigger engines, the most common being the 180-hp Lycoming or a 210-hp Continental.

Whether the Swift is the king of the classics can be debated, but what cannot be questioned is the fact that the Swift is the aerial version of the two-place sports car. Its controls are very light and quick, and it dearly loves to go zipping around corners, tucking into a playful barrel roll now and then. But, as with any sports car, you must learn to work with both the good and bad parts of its personality to enjoy it truly. In gentle, knowing hands, the Swift is a joy machine of the very finest order. But to a ham-handed pilot, it can become a real handful and bite at the least provocation. Considering its size, the Swift is a sophisticated airplane. The larger stock engines (the 125s and 145s) have six cylinders, and this, along with the retractable landing gear, adds to the maintenance of the machine. Also, since the airplane is quite clean, with no external supporting struts or wires, the consequences of unnoticed corrosion in the wings can be much more severe than in many other aircraft.

It's extremely rare to find a 100 percent stock Swift. Since they have such an aerodynamically clean airframe, they've become the '57 Chevy of the classics set—everybody loves to modify it, and installing big engines isn't the only method. There are STCs (Supplemental Type Certificates) that let you replace the control wheels with regular fighter-type control sticks, STCs for faster-acting gear motors, for different windshields, different canopies, different wing tips. You name it, and they've modified it.

While the Swift is the hot rod of the classic crowd, the Cessna 170 appears to be the family grocery hack for the same people. Cessna 170s are seldom modified or hopped up; rather, they're restored, refurbished, and shined to perfection. With enough seats to carry a family of four, the 170 of 1947 in one form or another is still with us today, especially in the metal persona of the 172 Skyhawk. The primary difference between the two is that the 170 sits with its not-so-sexy tail on the ground. Still, the 170, with its 145-hp, six-cylinder Continental engine, responds admirably to elbow grease and interior stitchery. At 120 to 125 mph, it won't set

A pair of WACOs—A **YOC** in the background and a **VKS** up front.

The pilot's hat and cigar, and the **Cessna Airmaster's** classic form set the calendar back to 1937.

Wings over mid-America. A **Ryan SCW.**

Fun in the air and on the water is what ultralights are all about.

Pterodactyls can be led around by the nose.

The **Mohawk** shows how ultralights are developing into the true airplanes of a new category—Aircraft Recreational Vehicles.

The **Swallow** hides its Cuyuna two-cylinder engine under a fiberglass cowl.

The **Invader**—a new ultralight design shown at Sun 'n Fun 1982.

The **Swallow** rolls over and dives away, showing the maneuverability
true ailerons provide.

The postwar **Stinson 108** series was one of the most comfortable and delightful airplanes of the era. Time hasn't changed those qualities. (Credit: Budd Davisson.)

Top: Cessna's first all-metal airplane was the **170** of 1948. Today, it's being built with a nosewheel and a myriad small changes. (Courtesy of Ted Koston/EAA.)

the world on fire, but it will carry your family to a far distant vacation or fly-in with comfort and style.

In terms of utility, the old Stinson 108 series is almost a duplicate of the Cessna 170. But in terms of hardware, the Stinsons are another story altogether. All of the 108s are *post*war designs executed with *pre*war technologies. The fuselage is fabric with a maze of steel tubing running around inside to protect the occupants. The airplane's pugnacious stance on the ground, the large tail surfaces, and the prewar Buick interior give the Stinson a character totally different from anything we know today. The Stinson has something else that the 170 Cessna does not have: a general feeling of heft and solidity like the old Buicks and Packards. The doors slam with that same refrigerator clunk, the seats are overstuffed couches, and the machine sits solidly on her landing gear, not rocking in the wind like a bandy-legged rooster. In the air, she's just as solid, although her controls are surprisingly light, due to the fact that roller and needle bearings are used liberally throughout the control system. She will cruise all day long at 120 mph, but her 150-hp or 165-hp Franklin engine can be a problem to maintain. Also, some of the early engines have a disconcerting tendency to crack their crankcases, which is why later engines are referred to as "heavy case" models.

Classical Heavyweights.   What's a classic? Something that stands the test of time, visually and functionally. Something that says "yesterday," but somehow manages to fit right in with today. Another way to say this might be "Cessna 195," because, as surely as there are flying classics, the indelible lines of the Cessna 195 represent the best of the old and the new. Here was a 1947 airplane with state-of-the-art sheet metal construction and almost unmatched interior appointments, combined with a radial engine and the ageless tail-dragger configuration. Carrying Jacobs radial engines varying from 245 to 300 hp (330-hp Jakes in the Military UC-126s, and 240-hp Continentals in the C-190), the five-place 195 could step along at 160 mph and, as the saying goes, carry anything you could get through the door.

The 195 has certain idiosyncracies that set it apart from other classic aircraft. The Jacobs engine, for instance, with its seven cylinders and miles of rubber tubing, almost always leaks; the larger 275-hp and 300-hp engines, even when equipped with two oil radiators, still have a tendency to heat up on the ramp. Also, the windshield that looks tiny from the outside is all but non-existent from the inside. For this reason, the 195 has an undeserved reputation for extreme blindness on the ground. Actually, by crowding up against the side of the cockpit, you can look ahead and see the center line of the runway, fifty or sixty feet in front of you. Taxiing, however, is something else. Off to your right there's a blind spot big enough to hide an average sized hangar; some 195 owners mount a small convex mirror on the right wing root so they can see what's out there. Also, in flight the wing is even with your head, so you can't look directly out to the sides. People who haven't flown 195s imagine you can't see anything in a turn, but

It's hard to believe the **Beech-craft Bonanza** qualifies as a classic, but this 1947 model proves that a classic shape is timeless. (Courtesy of Gene Chase/EAA.)

that's not the case. As soon as you drop the inside wing to turn, you can look up over the top of it through the top of the windshield. However, it's that same large expanse of glass on the top that can give the pilot a severe sunburn if he's not careful. That's why many 195 owners have installed sliding sunscreens on the top part of the windshield.

In its original configuration, the instrument panel of a 195, with its collection of archaic flat switches and patterned plastic, looks a lot like a Wurlitzer jukebox of the same era. But the instrument panel is so large that many owners have completely redesigned it to accept modern radios and instrumentation. Another popular modification is to install a 350-hp turbocharged Jacobs engine, which pushes the cruising speed at altitude to over 200 mph, a worthwhile, albeit somewhat expensive, increase in performance.

When Cessna brought out its 1947 classic heavyweight, which is blunt and just a little old-fashioned, Beechcraft went in the opposite direction and introduced an airplane that, for 1947, might as well have been a space ship—the famous V-tailed Bonanza. With its retractable tricycle gear and so-called butterfly V-tail, the Bonanza very quickly became *the* airplane to own, and this hasn't changed; the Bonanza is still one of the best-selling aircraft in production. If you purchase an early 35 series Bonanza, however, keep in mind that several airworthiness directives (AD) have been written against the old series because of their distressing habit of shedding wings. This problem was traced to fatigue failures in the

tubular steel center section which was highly modified in the later series Bonanzas. Like the Swift, the early series Bonanza is an airframe that hot-rodders love to modify to match their aerial fantasies. Therefore, it's seldom that you see a series 35 Bonanza running around without a different engine, or without new teardrop windows added behind the old blunt square ones.

The North American Corporation's Navion, along with the 195 and the Bonanza, is a favorite of a select and fanatical few. Designed for the military as a high-performance liaison airplane, the all-metal Navion (most of which were built by Ryan) is built like a tank and stands tall on landing gear designed to use dirt roads for runways. With its wing nearly shoulder high, it towers over all other classics. To a Navion owner there is no other airplane. It has one of the largest, most comfortable cockpits, and its unique sliding canopy provides tremendous visibility, especially when modified with the later wraparound windows. Like most airplanes designed for the military, the Navion carries around a great deal of extra metal that a pure civilian craft wouldn't have. It has the strength, but, equipped with the original engine, it didn't have enough power to perform well with all that weight, and one of the most common modifications is to haul out the old engine and put in a 260-hp or larger Lycoming, so it'll be at least as fast as it looks.

Navions come in all colors and flavors; they all stand tall, with an unmistakable solid feel. Originally designed as a liaison military bird, they have always seen much more action as civilians. (Courtesy of Ted Koston/EAA.)

6

The Ultralights:
First Steps in a New Direction

Into the sunset: the ultralight pilot's favorite journey. (Credit: Budd Davisson.)

The first person to gain lasting fame in the bird imitation contest was Icarus, the mythical hero who built wings of feathers and wax to escape his island prison, but soared so close to the sun that the wax melted and he plunged into the sea. Was Icarus the first to attempt ultralight flight?

John Moody Versus Icarus

John Moody, from Milwaukee, Wisconsin, is universally regarded as the man who did Icarus one better. Moody and Icarus came to the same conclusion from two different directions. Icarus was trying for flight in any form, which, for him necessarily meant the simplest form. John Moody, a child of present-day technology, was trying to escape from the island of over-complexity by stripping flight down to its bare minimum: in so doing, he, like so many of his contemporaries, passed through the world of the hang glider.

In the early 1970s, Monarch butterflies must have felt they were being invaded by giants from another planet, as every cliff and hillside sprouted a cloud of multicolored man-made butterflies. These fragile-looking creations came in all possible shapes, from the kite-like Rogallo wing to the three-axis-control Volmer to John Moody's Icarus II, a tailless biplane named after his aerial ancestor. But none of these hang gliders produced a solution for the problem of gravity. No matter how gossamer light, all hang gliders had one basic requirement: If you were going to glide *down*, you had to be *up* to begin with. This meant that hang gliding

151

required you first of all to fling your frail body and your equally frail machine off a cliff or hillside, which made for some very interesting first-flight experiences. This basic requirement also ensured that there were many parts of the country with billiard-table topography where hang gliding never had a chance.

In 1975, John Moody came to the rescue of all those seeking to escape gravity: he bolted a propeller on a go-cart engine and then bolted the entire unit to the back of his Icarus II. With less than 10 hp blatting away behind him, he took two or three short steps for mankind, leaped into the air, and forever changed the concepts of what minimum flight could be.

The Ultralight Kaleidoscope

When John Moody powered up his Icarus hang glider he could not have imagined what effect his actions were going to have on sport aviation. It was as if he opened the floodgates on a dam that had been holding back an enormous amount of interest and energy; enthusiasm has accelerated so rapidly in the few years since Moody's first powered flight that the ultralights, as powered hang gliders are known, have become one of the strongest segments of aviation and certainly the most active. The ultralight gold rush made quite a few millionaires almost overnight, and in a year or two there were nearly twenty-five full-fledged manufacturers of ultra-light aircraft, the majority of which attained multi-million-dollar status in a few months. An all-out marketing war erupted, along with a nose-to-nose battle of the designers.

Because the ultralights are so incredibly simple, the gestation period of a new design could be a matter of only weeks, or even days for the more prolific designers. You could sketch a new idea on the back of an envelope, run out to the shop, and have it fully articulated in three-dimensional form long before your enthusiasm was eaten up by the tedium of building. It's this quick-to-build aspect that has made ultralights so popular and inexpensive. It has also led to a lot of very dubious designs.

The early years of the ultralight were also marked by design philosophies that were still closely tied to their hang glider origins. The fuselage structure, if you could call it that, was often nothing

This ultralight sports a zip-up canopy enclosure that requires no structural modification. (Credit: Budd Davisson.)

but half a dozen lengths of lightweight aluminum tubing cross-drilled and bolted together. The wings were more aluminum tubing with a limp sail of nylon cloth draped over it; the sail depended upon air pressure to pull it into a shape vaguely resembling a wing. The entire system was held together by hundreds of feet of stranded wire cable that crisscrossed in every direction giving the structure stability and strength.

EAA and the Ultralight

Since John Moody was from Milwaukee, it was only natural that Oshkosh was the place the public got its first glimpse of ultralight flight. The EAA, always in the vanguard of anything that's new in aviation, immediately recognized the potential of the ultralight movement and, as the movement gained momentum, eventually formed a separate Ultralight Division. This division, in cooperation with other ultralight organizations has helped the FAA develop a regulation package that will give the ultralight pilot the freedom he seeks and still give the government the control it requires. The division's magazine, *Ultralight*, is an important channel of communication within the ultralight community.

Regulations

To say that the population of ultralight aircraft exploded is a gross understatement. It grew so rapidly that at the beginning there were four or five machines in the air, and barely twenty-four months later there were dozens of companies building thousands of them a year. The Federal Aviation Administration stood in the middle of this turmoil, scratching its head, trying to find the best way to control a beast that flew but somehow didn't fit into the rule books as an airplane. They didn't see it as a threat to the public health and welfare, but the numbers were getting so huge that they knew they were losing control. They had not been thinking about 150-pound, 10-hp kites when they had written the regulations.

After taking a careful look at the ultralight population, and conferring with the EAA and other groups, the FAA realized that, for the most part, ultralight pilots preferred to fly off farm fields rather than airfields. They preferred to be out in the country rather

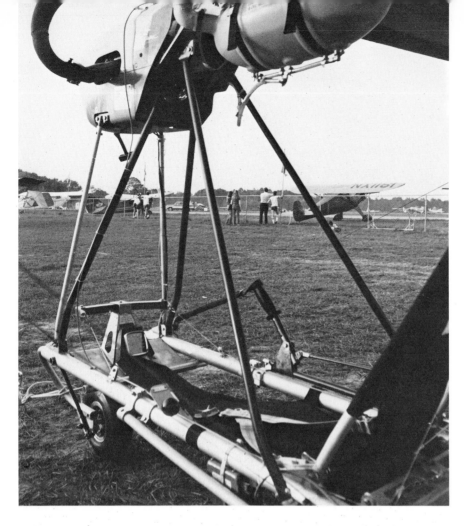

The flight deck of a **Swallow Aeroplane,** a second-generation ultralight, contains aircraft-type controls, such as a stick-and-rudder arrangement. (Credit: Budd Davisson.)

than in population centers, and close to the ground, rarely getting much more than 1,000 feet up. Thus, the ultralights had created their own area of operations and were staying in it. So the FAA picked the most logical and, as it turns out, the most effective form of regulation; they defined the ultralight as a non-airplane and therefore outside of their regulations. They defined what an ultralight is and what it isn't, and set up those areas in which it could not operate, formalizing what already existed. Drawing from the ultralights' hang glider heritage, the FAA said that even though the machine usually had landing gears, to be classed as an ultralight it must be capable of being "foot launched." This means you have to carry it like a hang glider and launch it by running with it. That requirement was supposed to limit the weights and power packages. However, manufacturers got around that by employing at least one Goliath on the staff who could foot-launch a DC-3, so they could prove their airplane was an ultralight.

The primary reason that ultralight manufacturers, then and now, want their products to remain defined as ultralights and not airplanes, is that an ultralight has absolutely no licensing requirements. Since it is a non-airplane, you need no license to fly it, mechanics don't have to inspect it, and the bird itself requires no licensing by the FAA. As far as the FAA is concerned, an ultralight is nothing more than a bicycle with vertical capabilities.

Problems began to surface in the late 1970s as designers closed the gap between ultralights and true airplanes. They were using bigger engines, multiple engines, and much better-designed and

Put all the parts in the foreground together and you'll have what's in the background, excluding the pilot. (Courtesy of Eipper Performance.)

therefore heavier airframes. In general, they were trying to cater to the desires of regular airplane pilots who sought less expensive ways of flying. The aviation associations and the FAA were happy to see this happening: it meant that ultralights were no longer being wafted around like maple seeds in the wind. They had much more control and therefore were much less dangerous. The problem was they were also much heavier. While an average man can pick up a 150-pound machine and run with it, the average man can *not* pick up an 200-or 225-pound machine and safely launch it into the air. And, besides the population of ultralights continued to expand as though they were self-propagating outside the factories. All of this forced the FAA to face yet another decision: they were going to have to come up with a better, tighter definition of an ultralight, without producing a definition so restrictive that it produced machines of unsafe design.

When this book went to press, the FAA was still wrestling with the problem. When does a machine stop being an ultralight and become an airplane? They published their ideas in a Notice of Proposed Rule Making (NPRM), which limits ultralights to 153 pounds and eliminates the foot-launching requirement. The ultralight associations and the EAA replied that they'd feel more comfortable designing aircraft up to 220 pounds, which would allow the designers to take advantage of better, stronger materials, and more powerful, reliable engines. The extra fifty pounds would narrow the gap between ultralights and airplanes from a safety and performance point of view, but still have a non-airplane machine.

155

The **CGS Hawk,** awarded the Best New Concept award at Sun 'n Fun 1982, illustrates the clear trend towards regular airplane features, including strut-braced wings, aircraft-type landing gear, and no wire bracing. (Credit: Budd Davisson.)

Like everything else in the ultralight arena, regulations are in a state of flux and are not likely to settle down for some time to come.

Construction

It's dangerous to make generalizations in a rapidly changing technological environment, but let's make one anyway: the general trend appears to be away from structures that fold up and fit into a bag for transporting like a hang glider, and toward a more rigid structure that requires a trailer, like a folding-wing airplane. Also, virtually all ultralights have sprouted landing gears rather than relying on a pair of size 10D sneakers for takeoff and landing.

All of this has produced a greatly improved structure, but, if you're looking at an ultralight with the idea of buying it, you must still pay attention to the small details of the structure. Begin investigating an ultralight's structure at the places where bolts go through tubing. Are the holes simply drilled through, or are there small tube bushings pushed into the holes so the bolts can be pulled down tight without crushing the tubing? At the points where the bolts go through, has the tubing been strengthened in any way? It should be, especially in high stress areas such as strut and boom attach points and control surface hinges.

If the airplane has controls (don't laugh!), you should examine the materials and construction used in the control system very closely. For instance, if it uses pulleys, are they in direct line with the control cables? Do they have guards to keep the cables from jumping off the pulleys? Is the control stick mounting system adequately engineered, or is it only a bolt that runs through the stick and a frame tube? If you hold the elevator in your hands and somebody else moves the stick, is there movement of the stick caused either by slack in the linkage or by flexing of some of the fuselage tubes? If the machine fails any of these tests, think twice about buying that design.

Wings are another component that show a tremendous variation in construction techniques. For instance, the very early Rogallo hang gliders with engines on them really didn't have a wing structure; their "wings" consisted of a large, triangular sail with a hold-down strap across the middle and wires to the corners; not

The **Waspair Tomcat's** outline is unmistakable in the sky. A canard design with airfoiled support structure, it swings one of the biggest propellers of any ultralight. (Credit: Budd Davisson.)

much structure there! The most common current wing structure has small pockets sewn chord-wise into a wing covering bag, which is slipped over a tubing framework. Small tubes, bent into an airfoil shape, are inserted into these pockets, giving the wing its curve. Some manufacturers have become adept at building a very stiff airfoil by this method. At the same time, however, many of the designs don't incorporate drag/antidrag (forces which move the wing forward and backward) structures inside the wing. This drag/antidrag structure, which can be in the form of crossed wires or diagonal pieces of tubing, adds greatly to the stability and strength of the wing.

As time passes, and more and more manufacturers realize that it makes a significant difference to pay attention to detail, the quality of workmanship is improving. We are seeing fewer hacksaw marks in tubing, cleaner fittings, more aircraft quality hardware, and less hardware-store nuts and bolts. Thus the gap between ultralights and airplanes is being closed.

Power Plants

Ultralight power plants are as varied as their airframes and wing designs. When you consider that an ultralight seldom needs more than 10 to 25 hp, it's easy to understand the wild variations of engines chosen, since engines of that power are available in nearly ready-to-use form from a thousand sources. The original ultralight engines were almost exclusively go-cart or chain saw engines, and

157

The two-stroke engines on most ultralights are refugees from chainsaws, go-carts, and snowmobiles; they give a surprising amount of power in a small package. (Credit: Budd Davisson.)

The **Invader** debuted at Sun 'n Fun 1982 where its clean foam-and-wood structure and hide-nothing mylar covering drew plenty of attention. (Credit: Budd Davisson.)

to this day they are all two-stroke engines, which require mixing oil with the fuel. The reason for the popularity of the two-stroke, or two-cycle, engine is that it has none of the normal intake and exhaust valving of the four-stroke engine and is therefore much lighter and cheaper.

One of the biggest problems of the small two-stroke engine is that to develop horsepower they must be screaming like banshees, often in the 8,000- to 10,000-rpm range. This is a problem because propeller tips cannot exceed the speed of sound or the resultant shock waves destroy nearly all of the propeller's effectiveness. So, the higher the rpm, the smaller the diameter of the propeller and the less efficient it is. Some of the ultralights, such as the Lazair, got around the rpm/propeller problem by using two

Where ultralights began: tiny engines bolted onto hang gliders. Seldom weighing more than 130 pounds, such craft can be launched by taking two or three steps forward. (Credit: Budd Davisson.)

small engines turning extremely small propellers at very high speeds. In fact, there are many model airplanes using propellers bigger than the Lazair's. The opposite approach, taken by an increasing number of ultralights, is to reduce the rpm of the propeller shaft through a pulley-and-belt arrangement. This allows them to use a propeller that is much larger in diameter, which is not only much more efficient, but also much quieter.

A new generation of specialty engines, many with their roots in the snowmobile industry, use two cylinders and are of a much higher power output, generally in the 20- to 30-hp bracket. But these engines are still two-stroke units, since no four-stroke can compete for weight and cost. However, the reliability of two-stroke engines cannot compare to that of four-stroke designs.

Control Systems

That the ultralight clan is dedicated to reenacting the post-Wright decade is nowhere more visible than in the control systems they are using. Today, eighty years into the age of the airplane, there are no arguments that the standard aileron/rudder/elevator control system works quite well, and that system was standardized in airplanes by 1915. However, many ultralight designers still seem intent on doing it their way.

A conventional aircraft control system, whether using a control wheel or a stick, utilizes a fore and aft movement of the stick or control wheel to move the elevators up and down. The pedals

No, it's not 1910; the ultralight movement has simply come full circle in terms of design. If Orville and Wilbur could see us now! (Credit: Budd Davisson.)

The ultralight pilot sits suspended from his craft's framework; he controls the airplane by shifting his weight, thus altering the craft's center of gravity and making it do his bidding. (Credit: Budd Davisson.)

Chest-pack parachute and helmet prepare this ultralight pilot for any eventuality. His aircraft illustrates how hang gliders are upgraded to ultralights by suspending a power package and landing gear from the glider structure in a trike arrangement. (Credit: Budd Davisson.)

In the weight-shift control system, the pilot's seat is suspended by straps; the pilot moves fore and aft and side to side to change flight direction. Note the motorcycle-type twist-grip throttle on the cabane tubing. (Credit: Budd Davisson.)

Well, the FAA says you don't need a license. (Credit: Budd Davisson.)

on the floor always operate the rudder. Moving the wheel or the stick from side to side moves the ailerons. With very few exceptions, this is the way all aircraft are controlled today. The significant word in that statement is *aircraft*, because ultralights haven't come close to standardizing control systems.

The reason ultralights are caught in the dark ages of control design has to do, partly, with their hang glider heritage. Nearly all hang gliders are controlled by weight shift, meaning the pilot, who hangs suspended in a sling-like seat, grasps a bar to push himself forward and back, right and left. In this way, he shifts the center of gravity of the aircraft, making it go where he wants. It may sound crude, but it's surprisingly effective in hang gliders and featherweight ultralights.

One step away from the weight-shift control system is the *two-axis* control system. The two-axis system doesn't use ailerons on the wings, but does have an elevator and a rudder, which may or may not be controlled in the normal manner. The fore-and-aft movement of the control stick controls the pitch of the aircraft in a normal fashion. An increasing number of ultralights do use a *three-axis* control system, in which roll, pitch, and yaw controls

162

Flying ultralights off of water breeds its own salty excitement, but it does complicate foot launching. (Credit: Budd Davisson.)

are independent of each other. That shouldn't be construed, however, to mean that these aircraft are controlled like the garden variety Cessna. Here, too, there's a tremendous amount of variety. Yet another system has drag rudders on the tips of the wings, which are turned sideways in the wind by the control stick, thereby slowing down that wing and causing the airplane to turn toward it. This system may sound like an invention of Rube Goldberg, but at such slow speeds, it apparently works just fine.

The pilot really doesn't care what's out there on the wing, so long as it is controlled by something in the cockpit that he can easily master. That's why, in the long run, regardless of what they use on the wing and the tail, the ultralights will eventually come around to using normal stick and rudder controls in the cockpit. Also, if a standard control system is used, it will be much easier for pilots to shift from airplanes to ultralights.

How Do They Fly?

The first sight of a number of ultralights buzzing around usually elicits one of two responses from the observer: "They all must be crazy," or, at the other extreme, "I'd love to be up there with them." But both sorts usually ask: "What's it like to fly an ultralight? Do they fly like airplanes, or do they fly like kites?"

It's difficult to make one definitive statement about how ultralights fly, though, because, like all airplanes, each one of them flies differently. However, what would otherwise be an indiscernible difference in control response, wing loading, or some other factor can assume massive proportions in an ultralight because they are all operating with such low horsepower and at minimal speeds. Also, you can't compare one of the early ultralights, such as a powered Rogallo wing, to some of the later, more sophisticated rigid-wing machines with three-axis controls.

All ultralights, regardless of size, weight, power, or generation, do share some common characteristics produced by their light weight, low horsepower, and open-framework construction. For instance, the combination of their extremely light weight, in relationship to their size, and the drag caused by their open framework gives them all the general aerodynamic characteristics of a whiffle ball. Most of them are affected by wind of any magnitude, and for that reason, the majority of ultralights must be flown in the early morning or the late afternoon when the winds have died down. The low-weight, high-drag combination gives the machines the penetration of a feather so they can't work their way through gusts. This is most noticeable on final approach.

The trend toward enclosed cockpit areas reaches down to the most rudimentary ultralights. Note the FAA registration number, which indicates that under prior rules this airplane wasn't foot launchable and therefore had to have aircraft registration papers. (Credit: Budd Davisson.)

All ultralights, regardless of size, weight, power, or generation, do share some common characteristics produced by their light weight, low horsepower, and open-framework construction. For instance, the combination of their extremely light weight, in relationship to their size, and the drag caused by their open framework gives them all the general aerodynamic characteristics of a whiffle ball. Most of them are affected by wind of any magnitude, and for that reason, the majority of ultralights must be flown in the early morning or the late afternoon when the winds have died down. The low-weight, high-drag combination gives the machines the penetration of a feather so they can't work their way through gusts. This is most noticeable on final approach.

Another characteristic most ultralights share is relatively low control response, especially in roll. This low roll response coupled with the lack of penetration means that many of the ultralights really don't like flying in anything approaching turbulent gusty weather. Only a few designs—such as the Lazair and the Swallow—can handle rough air with any degree of exactitude.

Earlier hang glider-derived ultralights are the lightest of the breed and almost always depend upon weight shift for control. They absolutely *must* be flown in calm air. At the same time, they are the ones most capable of soaring on thermals.

Tailless designs have an unearned reputation for longitudinal instability. In fact, a tailless airplane can be designed to be as stable longitudinally as one with a tail. However, one or two of the very early tailless ultralights exhibited a disconcerting willingness to tumble end over end, and the public has assumed that all tailless designs have that trait. Some of the very latest designs, such as the Mitchell Wing or the Kasper, show absolutely no tendency to give their pilots a roller coaster ride.

What can be more fun than sharing the sky with a friend—especially in an Eipper **Double Quick!** (Credit: Budd Davisson.)

Ultralight Trends

The general trend in ultralight design had been toward heavier, airplane-like machines, usually equipped with ailerons, as well as the normal rudder and elevator combination. However, the FAA's Notice of Proposed Rule Making (NPRM) slowed that trend because it was unclear what weight limitation would finally be placed in the definition of *ultralight*. If the final rules adhere to the 153-pound maximum empty weight proposal, then most ultralight aircraft will revert to the hang glider stage, while a much heavier class of licensed ultralights will then be developed. If, however, the 220-pound limit suggested by the EAA and the Professional Ultralight Manufacturers Association (PUMA) is adopted, then the present trend toward heavier, more controllable ultralights will continue. The later designs, especially the heavier ones with three-axis controls, such as the Swallow Aeroplane or the Mitchell B-10, are, for all intents and purposes, small aircraft, and must be licensed as homebuilt experimental aircraft. Their control responses are quick and positive, and their heavier wing loadings give them slightly better penetration in rough air. Also, these later aircraft use more powerful engines, in the 30-hp bracket, giving them a better power response that lets the pilot power out of a bad situation, unlike underpowered ultralights.

Flight Training

The amount and type of training required to fly an ultralight depend not only on the individual and his flight background, but also on the type of ultralight he's learning to fly.

Just because you're already a pilot, don't assume that flying an ultralight is a no-sweat operation. For instance, in many of the weight-shift ultralights, the controls are exactly the *opposite* of those in a real airplane. To bring the nose up in a conventional

165

airplane, you pull the wheel back. But in a weight-shift ultralight, you have to move your own weight back, which means you are pushing forward with your hands, doing what seems to be the opposite of a regular airplane. Also, a simple thing like nose-wheel steering can be a problem, since it is direct on an ultralight—just the opposite from a normal airplane. A normal airplane turns toward the rudder pedal that is depressed, both on the ground and in the air. An ultralight, however, often turns in the direction *opposite* the depressed pedal when on the ground.

So, even a rated pilot should try to find an ultralight training school or, at the very least, a high-time ultralight pilot who has taught a number of individuals to fly in ultralights. Their advice will be absolutely invaluable.

Since most ultralights are single-seat craft, it goes without saying that once you're off the ground, you're on your own, pilot or not, and your instructor must stay on the ground. This is one place where a CB radio comes in handy. Nearly all of the schools have CB radios mounted in their ultralights, so that the instructors can talk directly to the fledgling ultralight pilot. If you're not at a school so equipped, it is quite easy to jerry-rig an installation with a battery and a normal CB radio.

If you're a nonpilot who has never flown an airplane, you should ferret out the local flight training school for real airplanes, and take ten or twelve hours of instruction, so you can solo in a Cessna 150 or, preferably, an old Piper Cub. This will give you a base of experience to draw on when the ultralight instructor begins talking. Also, if you tell your flight instructor you are getting ready to fly an ultralight, he may be able to help you in preparing your own thought processes. In a Cessna 150, for instance, if you fly the landing approaches with full flaps all the time, you get a feel for an airplane which is very much dependent upon power and which loses speed as soon as the nose is brought up; very like an ultralight. Although many nonpilots have flown ultralights without the benefit of prior experience in an airplane, such experience is guaranteed to help.

Most of the reputable ultralight manufacturers provide a flight manual for their aircraft which not only describes their bird's basic flight characteristics and peculiarities but also gives you a thumbnail guide on how to fly for the first time. If you can't make it to

Touchdown! (Credit: Budd Davisson.)

an ultralight flight training center, the manual will tell you when to pull, when to push, when to laugh, and when to duck.

Most ultralight instructors recommend taxiing around in the aircraft to get a feeling for the operation of the controls on the ground. They may recommend taking short hops down the runway. Give the airplane full power, get it off the ground a foot or so, and then bring the power back and let the aircraft settle down. There are good and bad things to say about this short-hop routine: it makes the airplane stay in the critical stages of flight—just after takeoff and just before landing—entirely too long. On the other hand, this method confines mistakes to a much lower altitude, where there's little chance of personal injury.

Your first flight in an ultralight is an experience you will remember forever. As you blat down the runway, sounding like an enraged chain saw, and waft gently into the air, you suddenly understand the true meaning of the words *freedom* and *nakedness.* There is nothing between you and flight except the face plate on your helmet and the billowing polyester on the wing framework. You will be extremely conscious of the ground falling away as soon as you lift off, and for every foot the aircraft gains in altitude, your mind gains ten. Five hundred feet, initially, looks like five thousand. For the first several minutes you will probably keep your eyes riveted on the far horizon, trying to gauge your pitch angle and your relationship to the ground. At least that's what your mind tells you you're doing. In reality, you may be a little afraid to look back at the small group of people standing at your takeoff point, where they are watching you, the newborn bird, circling in your element. They can't hear the thoughts that are racing through your mind; they don't know the exhilaration and the excitement you are feeling.

Going Shopping

Although jumping into any other area of sport aviation may be confusing, getting started with ultralights is bound to cause utter cranial chaos. Every other area has been around long enough to become reasonably settled, but that's not the case with ultralights. The ultralights' Kitty Hawk occurred in 1975, and the field is more unsettled now than at any time since.

American Aerolites, one of the largest manufacturers of ultra-lights, entered its **Falcon** in the registered ultralight category. (Credit: Budd Davisson.)

The ultralight spectrum presents severe dichotomies, in terms of quality, design, and performance. There are a few designs that are downright marginal, and some of the kit manufacturers define quality in a way that leaves very much to be desired. On the other hand, some designs are extremely innovative and of high quality, and they also offer performance and safety that you would expect in a real airplane. Although only one or two kit manufacturers have come up with genuine aerospace quality in their manufacturing, there is a definite trend toward higher quality kits and the use of aircraft-certified material.

Fortunately for the newcomer to the ultralight scene, the entire movement has been publicized by all the news media, making it very easy to gain access to the most detailed information for nearly any ultralight.

There are several monthly tabloids devoted entirely to the ultralight movement. These include *Glider Rider*, *Ultralight Flyer*, and the EAA's magazine, *Ultralight*, all of which take a relatively objective view of designs and problems, as well as presenting the most up-to-date news on developments and ideas. Timeliness is extremely important when investigating the ultralight movement, and normal newsstand periodicals have a very difficult time keeping up with it because of their three- to four-month printing lead time. Four months can cover the development, testing, and flight of an entirely new, revolutionary design. At the same time, however, all media, including magazines and tabloids, depend upon advertisers for their income; therefore they are not likely to label a junk design for what it is. As a general rule, they are as objective as possible without stepping on any advertisers' toes. However, only your first-hand investigation of a design will bring any secrets or problems out of the closet.

As with any other form of sport aviation, your best decision-making process involves borrowing upon the experiences of people you meet along the way, and the best way to meet those people is to join the EAA's Ultralight Association. If you do, the EAA will automatically let you know where the ultralight events are taking place and give you a chance to become part of the crowd.

Although the ultralights have their own special events from time to time, these have not grown in stature to match the other less specialized events. However, both Sun 'n Fun (held at Lake-

Using Pterodactyl Ultralights' own brand of spelling, this scene would be captioned: "Ptwo Pterodactyls ptraveling and ptenting." (Courtesy of Pterodactyl.)

land, Florida, in March) and Oshkosh (held the first week in August in Oshkosh, Wisconsin) have large gatherings of ultralights. They are, in fact, better attended than many of the pure ultralight events. Additionally, at both Oshkosh and Sun 'n Fun, the manufacturers are all there, wooing the public with their latest hardware. This is where you can see each manufacturer's goods side by side and can make the most accurate appraisal.

Once you've homed in on two or three designs, it's time to go find the fellows that are flying them and discover what their experiences have been. At the same time, check out their backgrounds as pilots to see if they resemble yours. Don't hesitate to talk to owners of other designs.

Kits: Quality and Completeness

While the home-built aircraft generally begins as a set of plans from the designer, and the kits from other vendors, the ultralight movement is centered entirely around kit production. Few, if any, of the manufacturers will sell only the plans for their aircraft. However, the twenty-five or thirty manufacturers all seem to have different definitions of what comprises a kit. It's important, before jumping into an ultralight project, to evaluate the kits closely. The following general guidelines can point you in the right direction, when evaluating a kit and/or a design:

Percentage of Completion. Look carefully at the parts in the kit to evaluate how much more work you'll have to do on them to

169

assemble the airplane. For instance, are the holes finished, drilled in all the pieces of tubing, or are you simply receiving a quantity of tubing cut to length in which you will have to align and drill the holes? This can be extremely time-consuming, and it's an area where it's easy to make mistakes. The same thing is true of the cables. Since the majority of ultralights use hundreds of feet of cable, all of which must be cut and attached to the proper fittings, if that work is not done for you, you can count on spending many hours doing nothing but that. Also, the proper method of attaching cables involves pulling the cable around a preformed thimble and looping it back through a specially designed collar that holds the cable loop tight. In most cases this requires a special NicoPress tool that is not found in the normal workshop.

Completeness. It's difficult to tell in advance whether a kit is complete. You only know that for sure late on Sunday afternoon when you find you're short the three bolts you need to finish putting it together. The more reputable kit manufacturers do guarantee that their kit is complete. However, it is necessary to ask them exactly what *complete* means. Does that mean every last little bolt, nut and cotter pin? Or does that mean you receive the major components but have to supply your own attaching hardware? Some kits, incidentally, include the necessary drilling jigs and/or Nicopress tool to allow you to finish components.

Quality. Quality of design is a difficult thing to evaluate, because you're talking about some relatively sophisticated aerodynamic and structural concepts. However, the quality of a kit is not at all difficult to ascertain. Look at the edges of one of the fittings to see if there are tooling marks still in evidence; this is never permitted on a fitting. An inspection will tell you a lot about the manufacturer's attitudes, because any kind of mark left on the edge of a fitting serves as a stress riser that can lead to fatigue cracks. The edges of all the fittings should be smooth and very slightly rounded. The same is true with all the holes: there should be no jagged edges anywhere, and they should be very slightly deburred and chamfered. All of the bolts should use either self-locking nuts with nylon inserts or castellated nuts with cotter pins to prevent them from working loose. Because of the high vibration of the two-stroke engines, it's absolutely essential that there are

The **ATV Jetwing** is the successful marriage of a self-contained powerpack and landing gear to a pre-existing hang glider. (Courtesy of Flight Designs.)

no hardware-store-type bolt-and-nut arrangements that can easily unscrew under vibrations. The ends of all the tubing should be cut smoothly, again with no burrs or sharp edges; major high-stress points should have extra sleeves pushed over the ends.

Assembly Directions.   Assembly directions for the kits vary more than the kits do. A few of them look like manuals generated for the space shuttle by NASA, and a few of them are almost comical with their crude drawings and hand-lettered notations. Most assembly directions, however, fall somewhere between the two extremes. The more drawings and photos which are included, the easier time you will have assembling the machine.

Safety

The earlier phases of the ultralight movement were marred by many accidents, some of which were pure pilot error, while a few were design failures brought about by either untested radical designs or simple structural failures. Today, however, the safety record is greatly improved because the machines themselves are greatly improved. There are still safety aspects which must be evaluated before choosing a design, however.

Engine and pilot location are two primary prerequisites for crash survivability: Ultralights that have the engines up front invariably must compensate by having the pilot sit a little aft in the airframe. This arrangement naturally places more structure between the pilot and the ground, should he have an accident. Just

The Eipper **Quicksilver MX** enjoys true freedom in flight. Roll is controlled by spoilers mounted on top of the single-surface wings. (Courtesy of Eipper Performance.)

Top: JFK isn't the only place where traffic gets backed up; the taxiway at Sun 'n Fun. (Credit: Budd Davisson.)

the opposite is true of the aircraft that mount the engine in back. In these cases, the pilot is generally sitting further forward in the aircraft, and has less protection. Also, in many of those designs, the engine is so positioned that, in a serious accident, it will move forward, striking the pilot from the rear. Although crash survivability is not a pleasant subject to contemplate, it is something that must be worked into the decision-making process.

A crash helmet is an absolute necessity for flight. Obviously, it protects you in the event of an accident, and a full coverage helmet with a face plate acts as a windscreen and does a much better job than goggles of reducing the effect of the slipstream on your vision and your skin. This is especially true in northern climates where even late autumn or early spring flying can produce cheeks with a distinct bluish tinge. Another benefit of wearing a crash helmet is that it quiets the noise from the high-rpm engines and the slipstream.

Ultralight Profiles

At the end of the book there is a complete, detailed directory of the ultralights currently being manufactured. Bear in mind that this list changes almost daily, as manufacturers bring out new models and manufacturers enter and leave the scene.

Since there is such a wide variation, in both concept and performance, it might be interesting to describe and compare some of the front-runners.

Weedhopper. The Weedhopper is one of the front-runners in terms of the most units sold. This success is primarily the result of an effective public relations and marketing campaign. The Weedhopper is also unique: it's the only design that uses an engine designed especially for the aircraft. Since the late John Chotia first brought the airplane out in late 1978, it has sold an estimated 10,000 units. The aircraft uses a two-axis control system in which the rudder is used to skid the airplane in the direction of the turn, thereby causing a bank. The wings utilize a single-surface construction. The Weedhopper is also unusual in that it has strut-braced wings, as opposed to the standard wire-braced concept used by all but a few of the other ultralights.

Eipper Quicksilver. The Eipper Quicksilver has a lot of hang glider in its construction. It is extremely light, but at the same time it uses one of the larger engines available, a Cayuna 30-hp engine, which is an ex-snowmobile engine with proven reliability. The different versions of the Quicksilver use different control systems. The earlier models, and still the least expensive ones, use weight shift for control, while the later ones, notably the MX, offer three-axis control. However, the controls are not arranged in a standard aircraft configuration. Roll is controlled by wing spoilers, which are activated by pedals, allowing you to deploy them one at a time for turns, or deploy them both to steepen an approach descent. The rudder itself is on the control wheel, and the elevator is standard. The Quicksilver kits are among the better kits on the market.

The **Lazair** (first in line) sports a see-through aluminum-and-foam wing and minimal structure elsewhere. A labor-intensive design to build, it gives outstanding performance on low horsepower. (Credit: Budd Davisson.)

American Aerolite Eagle. The American Aerolite Eagle has two distinct claims to fame: first, it was the one chosen by a major beer manufacturer to use as a promotional item for their distributors, and second, its designer and builder is Larry Newman, a member of the balloon crews that crossed both the Atlantic and the Pacific Oceans. The Eagle shows yet another variation in controls. Its canard configuration, with the elevator out in front, uses a combination of weight shift and elevator deflection in which the pilot's sling is hooked to the surface by cables. Turning is accomplished with drag rudders out on the wing tips: one of them is turned obliquely to the direction of flight, causing that wing to slow down and the airplane to skid around. The extremely simple construction of the Eagle allows it to be broken down and put into a bag about ten inches in diameter and twelve feet long, which fits very nicely on top of a car. This is also true of a number of the other ultralights, but the Eagle has it down pat. The Eagle is also one of the few powered ultralights that weighs less than the FAA's proposed limit of 153 pounds. So, regardless of what happens to the Notice of Proposed Rule Making, the pilot's license will not be required to fly the Eagle, nor will it have to be inspected by the FAA.

Lazair. The Lazair is an entirely different approach to ultralight flight: it uses a combination of extremely light metal and foam to build a wing that is much more akin to a regular aircraft than most of the other ultralights. Although the wing is labor-intensive

174

The **Aerolite Eagle,** one of the most popular foot-launchable designs, uses a combination of weight-shift and movable surfaces for control. (Credit: Budd Davisson.)

and takes a while to put together, when you complete it, the aircraft is much more maneuverable and airplane-like than most of the rest. The Lazair is one of the more agile, responsive ultralights, although its low horsepower does keep its climb rate somewhat below average.

Mitchell Wing. The entire Mitchell series of aircraft steps out of the normal ultralight mold, especially the B-10 Wing. The construction of the Wing itself is not unlike that of a real airplane, although the materials used are much lighter and the pieces much smaller. The deep section of the Wing allows it to contain all its structure internally, so there are few external drag-producing members. This results in an aircraft that can run at twice the speed of most ultralights. It is, however, a much longer building project. The company reports that approximately 100 hours are required to construct it; this estimate may or may not be on the conservative side.

7 Odds and Ends

As in any field, there are a few sport aviation mavericks that don't fit into convenient cubby holes. Some machines don't fit any recognized category for the simple reason that they are unique. Others that appear to be special breeds are actually trend setters that will eventually develop into an entirely new category. And other aircraft stand alone simply because of their specialized uses; they may be homebuilt aerobatic airplanes or factory-built racing airplanes, but in the lexicon of sport aviation, their specialized uses set them apart from the crowd.

John Monnett's **Moni** design is a forerunner of the aircraft recreational vehicle concept, in which the cost and ease of the ultralight are mated with the design and performance of regular aircraft. (Courtesy of Monnett Experimental Aircraft.)

The Trend Setters—ARVs

Five or six years ago, ultralight aircraft were the mavericks of sport aviation; but they were also the true trend setters. Today they're part of the establishment, a recognized category. But the pressures that initially produced the ultralight—namely the never-ending pursuit of personal amazement and the high cost of aircraft and fuel—are stimulating another new development, the ARV, or aircraft recreational vehicle, a term coined by Paul Poberezny.

The ARVs occupy that narrow gap between the ultralights and the very light true airplanes that used to be filled by such little airplanes as the C-3 Aeronca and the E-2 Cub. Although an exact definition of the ARVs has yet to be written, it's generally accepted that these machines fit into the 350-pound category, and are much more airplane than ultralight. An ARV is, in fact, the logical extension of an ultralight with an enclosed cabin, a much more sophisticated structure, and possibly a four-stroke engine in place of the high-revving two-strokes found on true ultralights.

John Monnett's Designs

There are only a few airplanes that presently fit the ARV classification. Three of these are John Monnett's designs: the Moni, the Monex and the Monerai.

Moni. The Moni falls somewhere between a power glider and a normal aircraft. Using all-metal aluminum construction combined with space-age adhesives for skin bonding, the Moni can in no way be confused with an ultralight. Its structure, appearance, and its unique V-shaped tail put it in a class of its own. There is a long-wing version with a sailplane-like single wheel in the middle of the fuselage, outriggers on the wing tip. There's also the mini Moni, which looks like it's missing a wheel or two.

The standard power plant for both Monis is the Italian-built 25-hp KFM 107 two-cylinder two-stroke engine. Monnett would love to install a four-stroke engine, but there is none of the right horsepower and weight to service his designs or any other ARVs.

The long-wing Moni is designed to fly like an airplane but still retains some sailplane characteristics—thus the long wings and the outrigger landing gear. The only unusual flying characteristic is its ground handling: It taxies along with one wing tip on the ground at all times. However, once you're in the middle of the runway and apply full power, that wing tip is easily picked up with the aileron. Once airborne, the long-wing Moni can be flown as a glider, riding thermals upward without the help of the engine.

177

Monex. The Monex predates the Moni, but developmental problems and a lack of a suitable engine forced it to sit on the back burner while work on the Moni continued. Using the same basic fuselage structure and butterfly tail as the Moni, the perky little Monex sits on its tail-dragger landing gear, a striking example of what can be done with a straight line and clever plexiglass forming. Aside from the blown canopy, there are no compound curves in the airplane's fuselage, yet it gives the impression of being extremely sleek and well formed. Monnett has flown the Monex with either the KFM 107 or a Volkswagen conversion; both performed well, but neither produced the ideal package. As four-stroke 40- to 50-hp engines are developed in the coming years, the Monex will take its place as one of the first high-performance ARVs.

The French-designed **Cri-Cri** (translated "Cricket") is a tiny 160-lb. package that demonstrates unbelievable maneuverability and speed. The Cricket team amazed the Oshkosh audience with a 1981 debut performance featuring inverted formation passes. (Courtesy of Ted Kosten/EAA.)

178

The **Monerai** powered sail-plane can launch itself off the ground and then maintain soaring flight with the engine shut down. (Credit: Budd Davisson.)

Monerai. Monnett mated a KFM 107 engine with his Monarized sailplane and came up with a self-launching sailplane that is also part ARV. The airplane is capable of true, sailplane-like performance with an L/D, or glide ratio, of 28 to 1. Although not the only powered sailplane in sport aviation, it is one of the few available in kit form, using an aluminum structure with a fiberglass fuselage pod. This machine doesn't need a tow plane to get up to altitude as a sailplane does, but once you're there, you can shut off the noisy two-stroke and float along in the blissfully tranquil world of the sailplane pilot, who shares his thermals with an occasional hawk.

To most pilots, just getting off the ground is something special. But to a small percentage of the sport aviation population, the idea of flight means something very specialized. These pilots demand finely tuned machines for special uses, especially racing and aerobatics. These private worlds, existing parallel to but separate from mainstream aviation, are extremely small when compared to the rest of sport aviation, but they engage in such high profile activities that almost everyone else watches them with envy.

The Speed Merchants

Airplane races have recently divided into two separate categories. The first is the traditional closed-course pylon races in which aircraft that meet specific design parameters chase each other around a course marked with checkered pylons, an arrangement much like Indianapolis or any other two-dimensional race course. The second type, which has gained popularity recently, is the handicapped efficiency race. In this style, aircraft of different designs are assigned to several categories; planes in each group are issued a specific amount of fuel to cover a given distance; thus it becomes a matter of who gets there the first and burns the least.

Pylon Racing

When pylon racing was revived after the war, the basic styles and types of aircraft used were set, and they have changed little since. However, at least two categories have been added to increase both the number of contestants and spectator interest.

Sailplane champion A. J. Smith's custom-built racer blew the doors off everything else in the 1981 LBF efficiency rates. Averaging nearly 234 mph over a 500-mile course, it burned only 20 gallons of fuel. (Courtesy of Ted Koston/EAA.)

Unlimiteds. Unlimited means anything goes—any size engine, any size airplane. However, virtually all unlimited racers are highly-modified World War II fighters, because they already have the strength, the aerodynamics, and the horsepower to go fast. Unfortunately, modifying these airplanes means reducing a valuable piece of history to a special-interest racing machine. Many people feel that racing rare machines such as World War II fighters is akin to taking a Duesenberg out to run a quarter-mile oval: It's a waste of a beautiful machine. There are a number of homebuilt unlimited projects underway, but until the cash purses for the races become generous enough, there is little inducement for an individual to build an unlimited airplane from scratch.

T-6 Category. The T-6 racing category puts six or seven 100 percent stock North American AT-6 Texans on the race course at one time. The thing that makes this type of racing interesting to the spectator also makes it dangerous to the pilot. Since all the aircraft are of similar speeds, they remain very close to one another. This increases the possibility of mid-air collisions—something that is virtually impossible in unlimited racing where the aircraft fly widely spread apart.

Formula I. Formula I racers are tiny single-place machines that must use an engine of 200 cubic inches or less—which is another way of saying they all use the Continental O-200 engine. In this class the benefits of fine tuning both the airplane and the engine are readily apparent, and it's not unusual to have airplanes on the course with a differential in speed of 30 to 40 mph. The winners generally fall into the 230-mph class. Many aircraft of earlier Formula I races, such as the Cassutt, the Midget Mustang, and the Shoestring, are available in plans for the homebuilt market.

The **Christen Eagle** springs from the most sophisticated aircraft kits available anywhere in the world. A superb aerobatic machine, the Eagle comes packed as boxes full of shrink wrapped parts, carefully annotated for final assembly, along with a complete set of assembly manuals. (Courtesy of Dick Stouffer/ EAA.)

Biplane Racers.   The biplane category was originally intended for individuals of limited means who could become race pilots flying a Pitts Special or a Mong Sport. In the beginning it worked that way, but now there are many highly sophisticated biplanes that bear little or no resemblance to the garden-variety Pitts Special. A good example is the Burt Rutan-designed Amsoil racer, which though technically a biplane bears an eerie resemblance to the homebuilt canard designs of the Quickie and Quickie II.

Efficiency Races

Until 1981, when the sailplane champion A. J. Smith fielded a specially designed racer for the Oshkosh 500 (also called the Lowers, Baker, Falck race), all the efficiency racers had been normal homebuilt machines with ultra-fine-tuned aerodynamics. The net result of efficiency races, such as the CAFE 400, the LBF race, and the Pazmany race, has been designs that achieved unbelievable fuel economy. The final placing in such races is determined by a formula that takes into account the airplane's speed, the people on board, and the amount of fuel burned. At the same time, the airplane must take off in a given distance to climb over a string barrier so as to ensure that takeoff performances don't deteriorate in the interest of speed.

It's efficiency races above all that produce technological fall-out beneficial to all forms of aviation. The manufacturers of kits covet the prestige that is gained by winning one of these races, so they go all-out to produce airplanes that will put their name before the public in big, bright lights. Since brute horsepower won't win the race, the designers are forced to do the very thing our energy-conscious society demands: go the fastest and the farthest while burning the least amount of fuel possible.

Aerobatics

Aerobatic competitions have existed on an informal scale since the days when Andre Pegoud did the first loop-the-loop in France and Lincoln Beachey followed shortly thereafter in this country. Contests were arranged between countries in the 1930s, but it wasn't until the 1960s that international competition was placed on a formal basis paralleling the Olympic games.

Aerobatics on an informal basis have long been the backbone of sport aviation, gaining great public recognition in air shows; this has given rise to two divergent views of aerobatics—one, the familiar air-show type; the other, the competition pilot who views aerobatics as three-dimensional gymnastics in which precision of line and form is paramount.

Before the Pitts Special became popular in the late 1950s, virtually all aerobatics were performed in antique biplanes or highly modified specials, such as clipped-wing Cubs. But the homebuilt Pitts Special brought blazing aerobatic performance within reach of everyone. This was especially important since there were no aerobatically certified commercial airplanes produced between World War II and the mid-1960s. The trend toward high-performance acrobatic airplanes has accelerated, however, to the point where every nation, including the United States, has in production at least one truly competitive aerobatic airplane. In the United States, naturally, it is the Pitts Special, both in single and two place form. Thus today you'll find two kinds of Pitts Specials: the homebuilt version, and the factory built.

Many homebuilt aircraft available today include aerobatics as part of their fun potential; some of them, such as the Stephens Acro, exist solely for aerobatics. But it's up to the individual pilot to determine where he falls in the aerobatic spectrum. Is he simply out to have a good time, or is he going to challenge the big boys in the three-dimensional arena of competition aerobatics?

In competition aerobatics, all maneuvers must be performed within the tight confines of an imaginary box. In addition, each maneuver is assigned a difficulty factor that, along with the performance rating, determines an individual's score.

As in figure skating or gymnastic floor exercises, aerobatic contestants must perform three, and in some cases four, different types of sequences. There are the *compulsory known* sequences, in which all competitors know well in advance what the maneuvers are and in what order they come. Then there are the *compulsory unknown* sequences, in which the competitors are each given different sequences only on the evening before they must fly them. The third type includes the *freestyle* sequences, in which the competitor jams a great many difficult maneuvers into a free-flowing sequence of his own design. Finally, there is the recent

182

Up and over the top: **Pitts Special** pilot Glenn Giere finds a new perspective of the world at the top of a loop. (Credit: Budd Davisson.)

addition, the *air show* sequence, in which pizzazz and show business appeal are also deciding factors.

Naturally, competitors have different levels of skill—there are supermen and there are rank beginners. This has led to a four-category breakdown at competitions. The sportsman category is an entry level for those just beginning to develop a taste for high Gs and spinning horizons; although the maneuvers are basic and the sequences few, the competition is extremely fierce. The same holds true for the other categories—intermediate, advanced, and unlimited. From the last, which is the highest group, the nation's finest men and women pilots are chosen for the U.S. aerobatic team which does battle every two years with similar teams from other nations in Olympic-level competitions.

Although the U.S. teams are at a distinct disadvantage when it comes to competition aerobatics, they have done themselves proud. The disadvantage is that most Soviet-bloc countries subsidize their aerobatic teams by giving them airplanes, fuel, and time to practice. American contestants must build their own airplanes, pay for them, and pay for the transportation to the contest site, whether it's in the Soviet Union, Czechoslovakia, Spain, or anywhere else; this requires a massive fund-raising effort to cover as much of the costs as possible. The first American World Champion was Charlie Hillard in 1972; in 1980 Leo Loudenslager, five-time National Champion, repeated the feat.

The **RotorWay Scorpion** helicopter, a rare bird because of its cost and complexity, offers vertical capabilities unmatched by any other homebuilt. (Credit: Budd Davisson.)

Ken Brock's **Gyroplane:** Unlike a helicopter, it has no power to the main rotor. Forward motion induced by the rear propeller causes the rotor to turn, which then lifts the craft off the ground. (Courtesy of Brock Enterprises.)

Rotor Craft

Although there is at least one true helicopter available to the homebuilder, the RotorWay Scorpion, these are vastly outnumbered by the simpler and much less understood rotor craft. The terms Gyroplane, Auto Giro, and Gyrocopter are all trademarked names for the same animal: a light-weight airframe with a small motor in the rear or the front driving a normal aircraft propeller, and a large helicopter-like rotor fixed to the top. But don't confuse this machine with a helicopter; in a helicopter the engine delivers power directly to the main rotor, driving it up to speed while the helicopter stands still; this produces instantaneous lift, allowing vertical takeoffs. In the Gyroplane (the newest name) the main rotor is totally free-swinging, with no power whatever applied to

Ken Brock pushes his **Gyroplane** to the flight line for another aerial demonstration. (Credit: Budd Davisson.)

Homebuilders always find a better way to do things: witness this highly customized **Gyroplane** with Volkswagen power. (Courtesy of Jack Cox/EAA.)

make it turn; the rotor is nothing more than a very long, skinny wing that's pivoted in the middle. What makes it work is the forward motion imparted by the small drone engine driving the normal propeller, which in the Ken Brock's Gyroplanes is a 90-hp McCulloch drone engine, or in some cases a Volkswagen conversion. As the drone engine accelerates the fragile-looking framework forward, the main rotor begins to turn and instantly develops lift, yanking the Gyroplane off the ground in 30 to 50 feet, depending on the head wind. The pilot controls the Gyroplane as he would a normal airplane: with stick, rudder, and throttle.

The Gyroplane can come down like a helicopter if the engine quits. Once the rotor starts spinning, any amount of forward motion will keep it going and generating lift; this allows the pilot to glide almost vertically down to a perfectly safe landing in a power-off situation.

Although the Gyroplane is a true aircraft recreational vehicle, Brock stresses the fact that it has some usable applications; to demonstrate this, he flew one from Los Angeles to Kitty Hawk, North Carolina. That's certainly a long time to be hanging out in the breeze.

Epilogue

By now it should be clear that sport aviation is a combination of simplicity and complexity, visionary leaps forward and a reactionary longing for times long past. More important, over the past 30 years this rapidly expanding, dynamically changing activity has continually attracted larger numbers of America's more dedicated and interesting people. For this reason alone, it is next to impossible to draw a portrait of the sport and have it remain accurate for any length of time.

Today it is obvious that many changes are just over the horizon, some of them only a few weeks away; there will be great regulatory changes affecting the ultralights; by 1983 there will be new engines and new designs that will greatly change the ultralight field. Aerial recreational vehicles, just broken out of their shell, stand on the same exciting threshold ultralights did only five or six years ago. Even in a supposedly static division such as Warbirds or Antiques, where the activities and the hardware are totally pre-determined by what happened in the past, there is good news along with bad. The bad news is that more and more warbirds are being acquired by local Air Force bases for display on poles, which terminates their flying career and limits their ability to survive the elements. At the same time, hardly a month goes by without news flashing through the warbird movement about another airplane found somewhere, possibly one that was thought to be extinct. And every so often a cache of parts turns up, like a hoard of pirate gold, which allows one breed of airplane to continue flying a little longer. The same thing holds true for the antiques: Each year another long-lost flying machine appears on the air show circuit as a monument to one person's dedication to making the past live in the present. Logic dictates that only a finite number of warbirds and antiques remain to be found and refurbished, but somehow they keep turning up.

The homebuilt movement is as open-ended as man's imagination. Although the homebuilder was once dependent upon the aircraft industry for technology and ideas, exactly the reverse is now true. Homebuilders are pioneering the techniques that the rest of aviation appears to be watching closely. While traditional designs and traditional constructions will always be with us, the trend is towards new, efficient structures and airframe designs;

sport aviation technology will accomplish more in the next ten years than it has in the past thirty-five.

In the past decade, the entire aviation community has increasingly looked to the EAA for technological advances and for leadership, especially in representing the cause of sport aviation in Washington, D.C. The local EAA chapters have become integral parts of local aviation; their activities reflect flying enthusiasts' interests and concerns everywhere.

Sport aviation exists for only one end—namely, the enjoyment of flight. However, just as in the space program, sport aviation seems to be sprinkling a beneficial fallout over the rest of the aviation community. Beside the obvious technological fallout, sport aviation has given birth to a colorful and highly visible part of aviation, which not only serves to attract people to the field, but at the same time continually creates entry-level aircraft and activities, injecting new life into the roots of the aviation tree. Industry regulations, high-priced technology, and inflation have all but eliminated any way for an interested person to get into commercial aviation on a reasonable price level. Sport aviation has rectified this by building its own ladder of progression, beginning with ultralights on the lowest cost level and going up through homebuilts, classics, antiques, and warbirds. It seems logical that many people who come into sport aviation will branch out from sport aircraft into commercial machines for business purposes; thus, aircraft manufacturers will benefit from the interest generated by sport aviation.

To those already in the movement, the only thing that need be said is, Hang on—we're in for a wild, exciting, enjoyable ride. To those contemplating making the leap, all we can say is, Come on in; it's a decision you'll never regret.

Survey of Experimental Aircraft Plans and Kits

Harvey R. Swack

Disclaimer: The technical data contained in this Survey were furnished by the designers and/or vendors of the aircraft, plans, and kits described. All efforts have been made to ensure accuracy; nevertheless, the publisher assumes no liability for the accuracy of the information given here. Inclusion in this Survey implies no warranty whatever on the part of the publisher as to the availability, reliability, or airworthiness of the aircraft described.

The United States leads all other countries in the total number of amateur aircraft builders, experimental aircraft completed, and hours flown by these aircraft. This survey describes the plans and kits for experimental aircraft that are currently available in this country or are advertised in periodicals addressed to the amateur builder. Complete technical data and description for nearly 200 homebuilts have been organized in these categories: fixed-wing powered aircraft, gliders, rotary-wing aircraft, ultralight powered aircraft, and "In the Wings," a section for projects still in the design and testing stages.

A survey similar to this one was made fifteen years ago, and apparently has never been updated in a similar form. Surprisingly, many of the plans presented in the first survey are still being sold, and these aircraft continue to be popular with builders. There are more designers now who supply complete materials kits, welded parts, and many finished components. There is also a new approach to selling plans and kits: Some designers supply partial plans that enable a builder to complete the aircraft only with the kit furnished by the designer. In this way the designer retains complete control of the materials furnished.

How to Use This Survey

The information presented here can be used in three ways:

1. Anyone involved in selecting a design to build can narrow the choice of aircraft by studying the scope, availability, and specifications of the aircraft plans and kits listed.
2. People interested in designing their own aircraft can analyze these data to establish guidelines and reference points for their own work.
3. Those who have built any of the aircraft described here can compare their own performance figures with those of other aircraft of similar configurations and powerplants.

A word of caution: All the data listed were furnished by the designer or the distributor of the plans. This does not imply that these figures aren't true or that a prototype hasn't demonstrated the performance figures stated. However, over the years amateur builders have often been heard to complain that the aircraft they built can't match the published performance figures. Whenever I hear this complaint, I ask the builder a few pointed questions; the answers invariably reveal that the original plans were not followed to the letter. Many amateurs make what they call "tiny changes" in the specifications; these often substantially alter the final performance figures. Often an aircraft that doesn't perform as expected is 10 percent or more overweight. The reasons include too much paint, extra structural members to increase strength, extra instruments that are not needed, and excess radio and navigation gear that were not included in the designer's equipment list, among others. Perhaps the most widespread fault is failing to use the propeller recommended by the designer. Apparently, wrong-size props often end up on amateur-built airplanes because they are cheap or no longer needed by another builder. Cut-down metal props invariably cause poor performance; they thrash a lot of air but have insufficient effective blade area.

If you aren't satisfied with the performance of your aircraft, take a look at the true specifications of the machine; perhaps the reasons just mentioned explain your disappointment.

From the designer's point of view, it's a heavy responsibility to handle when someone crashes and gets hurt flying one of your planes. Most concerned designers would agree that the point cannot be made too emphatically: if you build an airplane from plans, stick to them and do not make any change unless the designer approves. If you make changes, you will then have a different experimental airplane, with many new surprises; in all probability, these surprises won't be pleasant.

How This Survey Was Compiled

This survey includes only those aircraft that have satisfied the FAA minimum requirements in the experimental-built category. They have all demonstrated the performance parameters listed and have had the FAA operations limitations amended to permit flight outside of the test area. This requirement does not apply to the ultralights, since they are not usually licensed aircraft. New aircraft designs that have yet to be flight tested or are in some stage of development are listed at the end of the survey under the heading "In the Wings." The performance figures in this section are estimates, and the specifications are subject to change before the design is made available to the public. Paul Poberezny will shortly make two contributions: a new ultralight and a new version of his popular Acro II. His new two-place airplane will be lighter in weight and designed to perform well on an O-200 Continental or 108/115 Lycoming engine.

Several designs were omitted from the survey; this was not by design (pun intended). John Thorp's T-18 was excluded at his own request; other designers did not respond for their own reasons. It is unfortunately true that designers sometimes wear out after a lifetime of heavy correspondence devoted to selling plans. If a designer did not reply to the request for information, his model does not appear in the survey. It is of vital importance that the kind of information given here be current and accurate; the only place to get that information is from the original source.

Standards for Experimental Aircraft

How can you pick a well-engineered design? Not all of the aircraft listed were designed by aeronautical engineers. This isn't a drawback, as long as the primary structure has been thoroughly tested, either by actual testing or by engineering analysis. The need for testing designs and reviewing available plans to determine their conformity to good design practices led to the formation of the National Association of Sport Aircraft Designers (NASAD) ten years ago. Since then, this independent, non-profit organization has made significant contributions to the amateur movement by reviewing aircraft designs, kits, and automotive engines converted to aircraft use. NASAD was organized by a group of dedicated aircraft designers and enthusiasts to help the amateur aircraft builder achieve success with a project and avoid disappointments.

The essence of the organization is contained in its standards of quality and its approved list. Professional aeronautical engineers, none of whom is involved in commercial sales to amateur builders, have set up the standards under five categories: (1) general specifications, (2) plans and drawings, (3) manuals, (4) history of experience, and (5) parts and kits. A designer may submit plans for approval in one of three classes. Class 1 includes plans and kits for aircraft designs that have been built and flown in the advertised configuration for at least 150 hours. Class 1 plans are for the average amateur. Class 2 is for the experienced amateur; completed aircraft must also have flown 150 hours. Class 3 is for the very experienced experimenter who can build an aircraft from good, three-dimensional scale drawings, stress test it, and fly the finished product. Aircraft in Class 3 must have flown at least five hours, during which time basic tests were performed.

A compliance board of engineers reviews all plans and kits submitted to NASAD, and, if they meet the standards, issues a certificate of approval and a seal of quality. The product then is added to the approved list; all aircraft included in this survey that meet the standards are identified as "NASAD approved." Even the most professional designers need not be embarrassed to seek NASAD approval for their designs if they intend to sell them to others. For example, Paul Poberezny's designs have all been submitted and approved. Burt Rutan also submits his designs for review.

All members of NASAD have adopted a code of ethical standards that states that it is unethical to offer for sale plans or kits of one class to builders not qualified for that class. It is also unethical to sell plans for aircraft that have not flown. You may sell information about a new design, but you may not sell plans until the basic flight requirements are met. There are a few experienced designers who sell drawings for aircraft that have not flown; they make no bones about telling you this. Building and flying these aircraft involves some risk. Normally these designers are particular about whom they will permit to build the aircraft; sometimes they delay delivering the balance of the drawings until the test flying has been finished.

Membership in NASAD costs $25 and is open to anyone. The *Standards of Quality for Aircraft and Engines,* which costs $15, can be obtained from the NASAD secretary, 1756 Hanover Street, Cuyahoga Falls, Ohio 44121.

A new organization called PUMA (Professional Ultralight Manufacturer's Association) has been formed to carry out objectives similar to NASAD's in the ultralight field. PUMA has set up sweeping programs to establish standards of airworthiness, product-testing procedures, and pilot training for ultralights. Although NASAD has not attempted to go this far, the two organizations could learn a great deal from each other that could aid the entire sport aviation field.

Choosing a Design

Many amateur builders forget that there is more to performance than the way an airplane looks. If you are serious about building your own aircraft, be honest about what you intend to use it for and what you can afford to spend. There is no point in building a good cross-country airplane when you will only fly to local fly-ins. If fun and local flying are what you want, pick a design that will provide your kind of flying pleasure.

The question of the kind of construction to choose also deserves careful thought. The new composite aircraft are neat, but don't turn up your nose at the traditional wood and welded steel-tube structures. There is a great deal of education and recreation in acquiring and using these skills.

If you're interested in learning about designs that have been around for many years, there are several places you can turn to for information. The Pietenpol Air Camper, for example, has been popular since 1930. Today it still excites those with nostalgia for old aircraft. The plans for this aircraft appeared in the well-known *Flying and Glider Manual* of 1931, which has been reprinted by the EAA. Many old designs were first printed in *Modern Mechanics* magazine in the early 1930s. The EAA reprints most of these; they are available at a modest price. The EAA Antique/Classic Division publishes *The Vintage Airplane* monthly, which also reprints old designs. Builders interested in old glider and sailplane drawings will find a good selection available from the Vintage Sailplane Association, 3103 Tudor Road, Waldorf, Maryland 20601.

Finally, when you've made up your mind about the aircraft you wish to build, send for the information packet, study it carefully, and then order the plans and kits. Plan your project and set to work; perhaps you will finish your airplane in time to attend the annual EAA Fly-in at Oshkosh in 198?.

The following abbreviations appear throughout the survey on pages 194–237.

Cont.	Continental	**Revm**	Revmaster
L/D	Lift over drag	**sbs**	Side by side
Lyc.	Lycoming	**sl**	Sea level
max.	Maximum	**tand.**	Tandem
McCul	McCulloch	**3-ax.**	Three-axis
NA	Not available	**Var.**	Varies
NC	No charge	**VW**	Volkswagen

Fixed-Wing Powered Aircraft

Publisher or Distributor	Aircraft Name and model number	Configuration	Type of Construction	Engine(s)	Specifications									
					Wingspan (ft.-in.)	Length (ft.-in.)	Height (ft.-in.)	Wing Area (sq. ft.)	Number of Seats	Load factor +/−	Gross Weight (lbs.)	Useful Load (lbs.)	Empty Weight (lbs.)
Ace Aircraft Mfg. Co. 106 Arthur Road Asheville, NC 28806 (704) 252–4325	Baby Ace Model D	Parasol	Tube/ wood/ fabric	Cont. A-65 65 hp.	26-5	17-8¾	6-7¾	112.3	1	8.3	950	375	575
	Baby Ace Model E	Parasol	Same	65–100 hp.	26-5	17-8¾	6-7¾	112.3	2 sbs	9.3	1,050	409	641
Acro Sport Inc. P.O. Box 462 Hales Corners, WI 53130	Pober Pixie	Parasol	Tube/ wood/ fabric	VW 40 hp.	29-10	17-3	6-2	134.2	1	NA	900	373	527
Gerald M. Bakeng 19025-92 Avenue W. Edmonds, WA 98020	Bakeng Duce	Parasol	Tube/ wood/ fabric	75–150 hp.	30-4	20-9	7	NA	2 tand.	NA	1,450	552	898
Eric Clutton 92 Newlands St. Stoke-on-Trent England ST4 RRF	Fred	Parasol	Wood/ fabric	VW 1,500 cc 40 hp.; Cont. 65 hp.	23-6	16	6-3	110	1	3.5/ 1.5	800	200	540
John Grega 355 Grand Boulevard Bedford, OH 44146	GN–1 Air Camper	Parasol	Mostly wood and fabric	Cont. 65 hp.	29	18	6-9	150	2 tand.		1,129	NA	699
John Powell 4 Donald Drive Middletown, RI 02840 (401) 846–6757	Acey-Deucy Model P-70	Parasol	Tube/ wood/ fabric	Cont. 65–100 hp.	32-6	20-9	6-9	135	2 tand.	NA	1,275	525	750
Stewart Aircraft Corp. 11420 State Rt. 165 Salem, OH 44460	Stewart Headwind	Parasol	Tube/ wood/ fabric	VW 32–85 hp.	28-3	17-9	5-6	111	1	NA	700	267	433

Fuel Capacity (gal.)	Baggage (lbs.)	Performance								Price Data				Comments
		Top Speed (mph)	Cruising Speed (mph)	Initial Climb (sl) (fpm)	Stall Speed (mph)	Take-off Run (ft.)	Landing Run (ft.)	Service Ceiling (ft.)	Range (miles)	Information Packet	Plan Price per Set	Materials Kit	Time to build (hrs.)	
16.8	25	110	90	1,200	44	NA	NA	16,000	350	$3	$50	Yes	600	A proven design with a 55-year history.
16.8	NA	115	90–95	800	54	NA	NA	12,000	350	$3	$65	Yes	600	A proven design; performance varies with engine and prop used.
12.3	20	130	85	700	30	NA	NA	12,500	290	$4	$47	Yes	NA	Designed by EAA President Paul Poberezny as economical, easy-to-build plane. *NASAD approved.*
30	NA	140	120	1,500	36	150/ NA	NA	17,000	NA	$5	$60	No	NA	Won the Outstanding Design award at Oshkosh in 1971; parts are available.
12	10	80	60–70	50	Won't stall	250–400	300	NA	200	$4	$38	No	NA	Very cheap to build and operate; performance depends on engine used.
12	NA	115	90	500	35	250	200	11,000	400	$1	$25	No	1,200	Drawings show modernization details only; uses several stock J-3 parts.
14	25	98–104	87–90	2–450 1–650	25–27	250–300	300	10,000	270	$1	$27	No	1,500	This aircraft is larger than most homebuilts; performance with 65 hp. *NASAD approved.*
5	None	85	75	650	35	300	400	10,300	195	$5	$35	Yes	1,000	Basic construction techniques; no complicated tools or tooling.

Fixed-Wing Powered Aircraft continued

Publisher or Distributor	Aircraft Name and model number	Configuration	Type of Construction	Engine(s)	Wingspan (ft.-in.)	Length (ft.-in.)	Height (ft.-in.)	Wing Area (sq. ft.)	Number of Seats	Load factor +/-	Gross Weight (lbs.)	Useful Load (lbs.)	Empty Weight (lbs.)
Aircraft Specialties Co. Box 1074 Canyon Country, CA 91350 (805) 252–5054	Hovey Beta Bird	High wing pusher	Wood/ alum. tube/ fabric	VW 1,385 cc 45 hp.	25-6	16-9	6	87	1	6	630	180	405
Headberg Aviation 265 Needles Trail Longwood, FL 32750 (305) 788–0431	Flaglor Scooter	High wing	Wood/ fabric	VW 1,500 cc 50 hp.	28	15-6	NA	115	1	NA	625	NA	390
K-Meyer Aero, Inc. 21211 125th Street, E. Sumner, WA 98390	K-Meyer Model A	High wing	Tube/ fabric	Cont. 0–200 100 hp.	25	20	5-2	125	2 sbs	NA	1,450	600	857
O'Neill Airplane Co. 791 Livingston Carlyle, IL 62231 (618) 594–2081	O'Neill Jake	High wing	Tubing/ sheet alum.	Jacobs R755 350 hp. turbo	30	23-4	8-2	156	6	8	3,580	1,580	2,080
Richard Szaraz 1000 Aspen Lane Mansfield, TX 76063	Daphne SD-1A	High wing	Tubing/ fabric/ plywood	Cont. 85–100 hp	26-3	19-7	5-10	130	2 sbs	7	1,350	385	825
Molt Taylor Box 1171 Longview, WA 98632 (206) 423–8260	Mini-Imp	High wing Pusher	Metal	Rev-master 2100D 65 hp.	25	16	4	75	1	6	950	300	650
	Micro-Imp	High wing Pusher	Fiber-glass/re-inforced paper	Citroen 2GV 25 hp.	27	15	4	81	1	6	650	300	350
Wag-Aero, Inc. 1216 North Road Lyons, WI 53148	CUBy	High wing	Tubing/ wood/ fabric	65–125 hp.	35-2½	22-2¾	6-8	178.5	2 tand.	NA	1,400	680	720

Fuel Capacity (gal.)	Baggage (lbs.)	Performance								Price Data				Comments
		Top Speed (mph)	Cruising Speed (mph)	Initial Climb (sl) (fpm)	Stall Speed (mph)	Take-off Run (ft.)	Landing Run (ft.)	Service Ceiling (ft.)	Range (miles)	Information Packet	Plan Price per Set	Materials Kit	Time to build (hrs.)	
7.8	0	85	75	400	45	250	NA	NA	175	$5	$60	No	600	Rugged construction for ranch-hand operation; excellent handling controls.
5	0	80	65–70	600	35	250	NA	NA	175	$5	$45	Yes	NA	All-wood construction except for motor mount, center section, and fittings.
20	60	140	125	800	48	900	900	15,500	400	$10	NA	Yes	800	Drawings provided with kits, strong for bush operations.
55	Var.	175	160	NA	NA	NA	NA	20,000	NA	$5	$100	Yes	2,000	Flight tests in progress; very large cabin; probably the largest home-built.
21	45	149	130	NA	45	300	300	NA	NA	$5	$75	No	1,200	Simple plywood ribs; excellent short-field performance; 2nd place winner, 1970 Oshkosh efficiency contest.
30	60	200	180	1,300	50	800	750	20,000	750	$5	$200	Yes	700	Extremely clean design; excellent visability.
7	50	125	115	600	45	800	700	15,000	650	$6	$250		700	Extreme fuel economy and low construction costs.
12, 26 aux.		102	94	490	39	375	375	12,000	220, 455 with aux.	$3	$65	Yes	1,230	Can be built in four versions, including regular J-3 cub.

Fixed-Wing Powered Aircraft continued

Publisher or Distributor	Aircraft Name and model number	Configuration	Type of Construction	Engine(s)	Wingspan (ft.-in.)	Length (ft.-in.)	Height (ft.-in.)	Wing Area (sq. ft.)	Number of Seats	Load factor +/−	Gross Weight (lbs.)	Useful Load (lbs.)	Empty Weight (lbs.)
				Specifications									
Wag-Aero, Inc. (*cont.*)	Wag-A-Bond	High wing	Tubing/wood/fabric	65–125 hp.	29-3	18-7	6	147.5	2 sbs	NA	1,250	610	640
	Wag-A-Bond Traveler	High wing	Same	Lyc. 108–115 hp.	29–3	18-7	6	147.5	2 sbs	NA	1,450	725	725
S.J. Wittman Box 2762 Oshkosh, WI 54901	Tailwind	High wing	Tubing/wood/fabric	85–140 hp.	22-6	19-3	5-6	90	2 sbs	NA	1,400	NA	700
Taylor Aero Industries, Inc. 5231 Stratford Avenue Westminster, CA 92683	Taylor Bird #1	Mid-wing	Alum./fiber-glass	Subaru 1,400, 1,600, 1,800 cc	26	18	5-6	110	2	NA	1,160	460	700
Brokaw Aviation, Inc. 2625 Johnson Point Leesburg, FL 32748 (904) 787–2329	Brokaw Bullet BJ–520	Low wing	Metal	Cont. TS10–520 310 hp.	22-6	286.3	106.0	84.3	2 tand.	NA	3,042	1,109	1,933
Darrell Brown 3040 South Star Lake Rd. Auburn, WA 98002	Edelweiss RD–02	Low wing	Metal	90/100 hp.	28-11	21-2	7-8½	118.5	2 tand.	NA	1,430	NA	840
	RD–03	Low wing	Metal	125–150 hp.	28-11	22-7	same	118.5	4	NA	1,630	NA	937
Peter M. Bowers 10458 16th Ave. Seattle, WA 98168	Bowers Fly Baby 1–A	Low wing	Wood/fabric	Cont. 65–100 hp.	28	18-10	6½-11	120	1	5	925	320	605
Busby Aircraft, Inc. Rt. #1, Box 13A Minooka, IL 60447 (815) 467–2346	Midget Mustang M–1	Low wing	Metal	65–150 hp.	18-6	16-5	4-6	68	1	9/9	900	300	550

Fuel Capacity (gal.)	Baggage (lbs.)	Top Speed (mph)	Cruising Speed (mph)	Initial Climb (sl) (fpm)	Stall Speed (mph)	Take-off Run (ft.)	Landing Run (ft.)	Service Ceiling (ft.)	Range (miles)	Information Packet	Plan Price per Set	Materials Kit	Time to build (hrs.)	Comments
				Performance							**Price Data**			
12	40	105	95	625	45	NA	NA	NA	NA	$4	$89	Yes	1,175	A replica of the original Vaga-bond.
26	60	136	124	850	45	380	700	NA	500	$4	$89	Yes	1,175	Sleeping compartment on ground; long range.
25	65	165	150	900	55	800	600	17,000	600	$1	$125	No	NA	High-speed cross-country airplane; straight-forward building methods.
15	NA	130	115	NA	25	Est. 300	Est. 200	NA	450	$5	$165	Yes	NA	Catalogue available for $25; wings fold for easy transport to and from airport and for home storage.
92	40	200	185	1,400	74	1,500	1,500	20,000	880	$7.50	$750	No	NA	Range depends upon power setting; performance varies with engines used. Sophisticated aircraft with outstanding performance.
22	NA	158	145	650	49.5	NA	NA	15,000	560	$7	$300	No	NA	Many have been built and are flying in Europe. Sophisticated, well-designed.
33	NA	173	157.5	1,200	51.5	NA	NA	16,500	510	$7	$325	No	NA	
12–16	Up to 75	120	95–115	850–1,100	45	200	NA	15,000	300	$3	$50	No	720–1,000	Very flexible design; available in biplane version; provision for external baggage; 375–400 built.
16–32	20	245	240 at 7,000 ft.	2,400	57	300	500	25,000	1,100	$5	$85	Yes	1,200	Simplified metal construction; no rigs or machining; no compound curves.

Publisher or Distributor	Aircraft Name and model number	Configuration	Type of Construction	Engine(s)	Wingspan (ft.-in.)	Length (ft.-in.)	Height (ft.-in.)	Wing Area (sq. ft.)	Number of Seats	Load factor +/−	Gross Weight (lbs.)	Useful Load (lbs.)	Empty Weight (lbs.)
Busby Aircraft, Inc. (cont.)	Mustang II M–II	Low wing	Metal	125–180 hp.	24-4	19-5	5-3	97.1	2 sbs	9/9	1,600	600	1,000
Anton Cvjetkovic P.O. Box 323 Newbury Park, CA 91320	CA–65 Skyfly	Low wing	Wood	Lyc. 125 hp.	25	19	7-4	109	2 sbs	9/6	1,500	NA	900
H.L. Moore 231 Washington South Attleboro, ME 02703 (617) 761–8189	Davis DA–2A	Low wing	Metal	Cont. 65–100 hp.	20-7	17-10	5-5	87.5	2 sbs	NA	1,175	540	635
Dyke Aircraft 2890 Old Yellow Springs Road Fairborne, OH 45324	Dyke Delta JDII	Low wing	Steel tube/composite	Lyc. 0–360 AIA 180 hp.	22	19-6	6	173	4	6	1,950	910	1,040
Evans A.C. Box 744 LaJolla, CA 92037	VP–1	Low wing	Wood/fabric	VW 1,600 cc	24	18	6+	100	1	3.8/1.5	650	210	440
	VP–2	Low wing	Wood/fabric	VW 2,100 cc	27	19-3	6+	130	2 sbs	3.8/1.5	1,040	400	640
Hapi Engines, Inc. #1, Box 1000 Eloy, AZ 85231 (602) 466–9244	Corby Starlet CV–1	Low wing	Wood/fabric	VW 30–60 hp.	18-6	14-9	NA	68.5	1	6.7	650	240	410
John O. Isaacs 23 Linden Grove Chandlers Ford, Hants. England 50 S05 ILE	Isaacs Spitfire	Low wing	Wood	Cont. 100 hp. 0–200	22-1½	19-3	5-8	87	1	9/4½	1,100	295	805

Fuel Capacity (gal.)	Baggage (lbs.)	Top Speed (mph)	Cruising Speed (mph)	Initial Climb (sl) (fpm)	Stall Speed (mph)	Take-off Run (ft.)	Landing Run (ft.)	Service Ceiling (ft.)	Range (miles)	Information Packet	Plan Price per Set	Materials Kit	Time to build (hrs.)	Comments
						Performance				**Price Data**				
25–35	80	245	220	2,400	61	400	600	20,000	600	$5	$150	Yes	2,000	Both well tested and proven designs. Both *NASAD approved.*
28	70	180	155	1,000	55	450	600	15,000	500	$3	$125	No	1,500	This design is also available in an all-metal version. Wood aircraft has folding wings; both have retractable gears.
20	75	150	115	NA	60	800	700	NA	450	$2	$100	Yes	NA	Simple and inexpensive to build; mostly made from flat stock aluminum; the 2B is slimmer and faster.
41	Var.	210	185	2,000	Partial 70	400 light	1,600	15,000	700	$5	$150	No	2,000	Designed for high performance and as a practical, towable, "keep at home" aircraft; wings fold.
8	NA	95	75	600	40	NA	NA	NA	NA	$3.50	$85	Yes	NA	Simplest wood one- and two-place aircraft; many built; designed by a professional engineer.
14	NA	100	75	500	40	NA	NA	NA	NA	$3.50	$85	Yes	NA	
8	40	135	125	800	47.1	300	400	NA	200+	$7.50	$110	Yes	1,000	First flown 15 years ago; 30 flying today; used in aerobatic competition in Australia.
13	0	150	134	1,100	47	600	450	15,000	250	$6	$200	NA	3,000	Based on ⁶⁄₁₀-scale Spitfire.

Publisher or Distributor	Aircraft Name and model number	Configuration	Type of Construction	Engine(s)	Wingspan (ft.-in.)	Length (ft.-in.)	Height (ft.-in.)	Wing Area (sq. ft.)	Number of Seats	Load factor +/−	Gross Weight (lbs.)	Useful Load (lbs.)	Empty Weight (lbs.)
Monnett Experimental Aircraft, Inc. 895 W. 20th Avenue, Box 2984 Oshkosh, WI 54903 (414) 426–1212	Moni-A.R.V. Motor Glider	Low wing	Steel tube/alum.	KFM 107 45 hp.	27-6	14-7½	4	75	1	6/4	500	240	260
	Sonerai IIL	Low wing	Steel tube/alum.	VW 1700 cc–2180 cc	18-8	18-10	5-10	84	2 tand.	4/4	950	450	500
	Sonerai I	Low wing	Steel tube/alum.	VW 1700 cc–2180 cc	16-8	16-8	5-5	75	1	6/6	750	300	450
	Sonerai II	Low wing	Steel tube/alum.	VW 1700 cc–2180 cc	18-8	18-10	5-10	84	2 tand.	4/4	950	450	500
Option Air Reno Box 20085 Reno, NV 89515	Acapella 200 L	Low wing	All metal alum.	Lyc. 10–360 180 hp.	26	16	5-6	65	1	NA	1,340	399	941
Pazmany Aircraft Corp. Box 80051 San Diego, CA 92138	PL–2	Low wing	All sheet alum.	Lyc. 025 or 0320	28-6	19-4	7-8	116	2 sbs	6/3	1,445	340	900
	PL–4	Low wing	All sheet alum.	VW 1,600 cc	26-8	16-8	NA	89	1	6/6	850	175	578
Polliwagen, Inc. 8782 Hewitt Pl. Garden Grove, CA 92644	Polliwagen	Low wing	Composite	Revm. 2,100 cc turbo	26	16	5-7	90	2 sbs	9/6	1,250	650	600
Sequoia Aircraft Corp. 900 West Franklin St. Richmond, VA 23226	F8L Falco	Low wing	Wood	Lyc. 150–160 hp.	26-3	21-4	7-6	107.5	2 sbs	6/3	1,808	596	1,212
Rand/Robinson Engineering, Inc. 5842 K McFadden Ave. Huntington Beach, CA 92649	KR–1	Low wing	Wood/foam	VW 1,700 cc	17	12-9	3-6	62	1	9/9	750	375	375
	KR–2	Low wing	Wood/foam	VW 2,100 cc	20-8	14-6	4-10	80	2 sbs	7/7	900	420	480

Fuel Capacity (gal.)	Baggage (lbs.)	Performance								Price Data		Materials Kit	Time to build (hrs.)	Comments
		Top Speed (mph)	Cruising Speed (mph)	Initial Climb (sl) (fpm)	Stall Speed (mph)	Take-off Run (ft.)	Landing Run (ft.)	Service Ceiling (ft.)	Range (miles)	Information Packet	Plan Price per Set			
4	0	120	110	700	38	300	500	NA	300	$5	NA	Yes	300	Wings easily removable; trailers home.
10	30	175	155	800	44	700	1,000	15,000	350	$5	$90	Yes	750	Folding wing; self-trailering
10	0	180	155	1,000	40	600	1,000	16,000	350	$5	$50	Yes	700	Folding wing; self-trailering
10	30	175	155	800	44	700	1,000	15,000	350	$5	$75	Yes	750	Folding wing; self-trailering. *NASAD approved.*
34	0	245	214	3,000	81	1,000	1,200	26,500	670	$15	NA	Yes	3,000	Alternative engine 0–235 Lyc.; very complete kit.
25	40	156	132	1,500	54	550	775	18,000	486	$5	$180	No	3,500	Only amateur design used as military trainer; safe design; wings fold. *NASAD approved.*
12	20	120	97	650	46	563	436	15,000	400	$5	$140	No	1,500	
19	50	200	170	800	51	500	500	19,000	1,100	$6	$75	Yes	750	High performance for 75 hp.; uses newest building materials.
40	88	212	190	1,140	62	570	750	19,000	870	$10	$400	Yes	1,200-1,500	Retractable tricycle gear; sophisticated aircraft.
8–30	20	200	180	1,200	52	350	900	15,000	500–1,400	$6	$55	Yes	800	Low-cost airframe kits; easy to fly for medium-size pilots; removable wings; several hundred KR–1s and KR–2s flying.
12–35	35	200	180	1,200	52	350	900	15,000	500–1,600	$6	$55	Yes	800	

Publisher or Distributor	Aircraft Name and model number	Configuration	Type of Construction	Engine(s)	Wingspan (ft.-in.)	Length (ft.-in.)	Height (ft.-in.)	Wing Area (sq. ft.)	Number of Seats	Load factor +/-	Gross Weight (lbs.)	Useful Load (lbs.)	Empty Weight (lbs.)
Sindlinger Aircraft 37030 204th Street, S.E. Auburn, WA 98002 (206) 939–3857	Hawker Hurricane (5/8 scale)	Low wing	All wood	135–180 hp.	25-1	19-8	5-10	102	1	4.4	1,375	391	984
Sport Aircraft Box 1 Trout Dale, OR 97060 (503) 666–6485	Mini Coupe	Low wing	Sheet alum.	VW 1600	22-4	16-4	NA	NA	1	NA	825	331	494
Stoddard Hamilton Aircraft, Inc. Box 1222 Issaquah, WA 98027	Glasair	Low wing	Composite	Lyc. 160 hp.	23-3	18-11	NA	80	2 sbs	NA	1,500	600	900
T.M. Aircraft Box 570, R.D. #1 Furlong, PA 18925	TM–5	Low wing	Alum. & bonded	Cont. 65–100 hp.	25	18-3	5-6	100	2 tand.	6/6	1,400	478	826
Turner Aircraft 5803 Waterview Drive Arlington, TX 76016 (817) 457–5081	Turner T–40	Low wing	Stressed skin/ wood	Cont. C–85	23-3	19-3	5-5	78	1	4.4	1,060	310	750
	Turner T–40A	Low wing	Stressed skin/ wood	Lyc. 125 hp.	27-8	19-9	6-10	92.2	2 sbs	3.75	1,586	536	1,050
Mrs. John F. Taylor 25 Chesterfield Cr. Leigh-on-Sea, Essex England	Taylor Monoplane	Low wing	Wood/ fabric	30–90 hp.	21	15	4-10	76	1	9/9	620	210	410
	Taylor Titch	Low wing	Wood/ fabric	40–100 hp.	18-9	16-1½	4-8	68	1	9/9	710	255	455
Van's Aircraft P.O. Box 160 North Plains, OR 97133 (503) 647–5117	RV–3	Low wing	Alum.	Lyc. 108–160 hp.	20	19	NA	90	1	6/6	1,100	350	750
	RV–4	Low wing	Alum.	Lyc. 150 hp.	23	20-4	NA	110	2 sbs	6/6	1,500	610	890

Fuel Capacity (gal.)	Baggage (lbs.)	Top Speed (mph)	Cruising Speed (mph)	Initial Climb (sl) (fpm)	Stall Speed (mph)	Take-off Run (ft.)	Landing Run (ft.)	Service Ceiling (ft.)	Range (miles)	Information Packet	Plan Price per Set	Materials Kit	Time to build (hrs.)	Comments
						Performance					**Price Data**			
32	44	198	175	1,800	62	490	550	21,000	500	$5	$125	No	NA	Looks and flies like its big brother.
13	NA	105	90	700	43	400	500	NA	300	n/c	$55	Yes	750	Rugged and stable; parts preformed.
36	80	230	224	1,600	60	450	700	20,000	1,000	$7.50	NA	Yes	1,000-1,200	Winner of seven outstanding design awards; tricycle retractable gear version "in the wings."
14	0	150	120–140	1,200	52	NA	NA	NA	300	$10	$200	No	2,300	Wings detach for trailering; terrific visibility and flying qualities.
18.5	20	170	145	1,100	49	600	400	15,000	525	$6	$100	No	2,400	Folding wing; stores in single car garage; *NASAD approved.*
24	30	170	147	1,400	52	1,250	1,200	15,000	475	$6	$175	No	3,000	
9.7	NA	105	90	950	38	NA	NA	NA	230	c.$2	c.$45	No	NA	Popular design; docile flight characteristics; performance figures with 40 hp.
9.7	NA	200	150–160	1500+	59	NA	NA	NA	250	c.$2	c.$55	No	NA	Designed as midget racer; high performance; many footnotes on plans to aid builder.
24	30	195	185	1,900	48	250	300	23,000	525	$3	$85	Yes	1,500	Aerobatic; STOL; light control responses; excellent visibility.
32	32	202	186	1,650	54	450	425	19,500	800	$5	$165	Yes	1,500	

Fixed-Wing Powered Aircraft continued

Publisher or Distributor	Aircraft Name and model number	Configuration	Type of Construction	Engine(s)	Wingspan (ft.-in.)	Length (ft.-in.)	Height (ft.-in.)	Wing Area (sq. ft.)	Number of Seats	Load factor +/-	Gross Weight (lbs.)	Useful Load (lbs.)	Empty Weight (lbs.)
								Specifications					
Western Aircraft Supplies 623 Markerville Rd., N.E. Calgary, Alberta Canada	PKG–1 Hirondelle	Low wing	All wood	Lyc. 0235 115 hp.	26	20-7	7-6	117	2 sbs	4.4	1,475	542	933
Wicks Aircraft Supply 410 Pine Highland, IL 62249 (618) 654–7447	Barracuda	Low wing	All wood	150–300 hp.	24-9	21-6	NA	120	2 sbs	NA	2,200	705	1,495
	Sidewinder	Low wing	Sheet alum./ steel tube	Lyc. 125 hp.	24-10	19-4	5-6	96	2 sbs	NA	1,450	583	867
Zenair 236 Richmond Hill Ontario L4C 3Y8 Canada (416) 859–4556	Mono Zenith CH 100	Low wing	All metal	VW 1,600 cc 115 hp.	22	19-6	6-6	91	1	9/9	980	330	580-650
	Acro Zenith	Low wing	All metal	Lyc. 150 hp.	20-3	20-3	5	84	1	12/12	970	240	730
	Zenith CH 200/250	Low wing	All metal	100–150 hp.	23	20-6	6-10	105	2 sbs	9/9	1,500	500	950
	Tri-Zenith CH300	Low wing	All metal	130–180 hp.	26-8	22-6	6-10	130	2 sbs	5.7/ 5.7	1,850	750	1,100
	Cricket MC12	Low wing	Metal/ foam	2 Valmet 12 hp.	16	12-10	4-8	34	1	9/NA	380	220	160

Fuel Capacity (gal.)	Baggage (lbs.)	Top Speed (mph)	Cruising Speed (mph)	Initial Climb (sl) (fpm)	Stall Speed (mph)	Take-off Run (ft.)	Landing Run (ft.)	Service Ceiling (ft.)	Range (miles)	Information Packet	Plan Price per Set	Materials Kit	Time to build (hrs.)	Comments
						Performance					**Price Data**			
23 Imp.	44	150	145	900	54	750	850	12,000	600	$6	$150	Yes	1,200	Fully enclosed cabin; fuel tanks in wings; very responsive controls.
44	40	218	200	2,000	65	NA	NA	NA	NA	$5	$150	Yes	2,000	Highest-performing amateur-built wood aircraft.
17.5	60	175	160	900	55	800	1,200	18,500	425	$6	$150	Yes	1,500–2,500	Very efficient aircraft; winner of 1969 EAA Best Design Award.
15	30	118–150	105–135	600–1,500	48	350/750	600	14,000	420	$8	$130	Yes	600	Removable wings, roomy cockpit. *NASAD approved.*
14	NA	175	160	2,200	55	300	400	16,000	760 with aux. tank	$8	NA	Yes	700	High performance aerobatic trainer. Low price. *NASAD approved design and kits.*
25–60	50	147–167	130–152	800–1,700	53	600–850	700	14,000	600	$8	$170–210	Yes	600	A strong cross-country airplane; excellent cruise and handling. *NASAD approved design and kits.*
68	80	150–170	140–150	800–1,400	53	650–800	700	12,000	530	$8	$250	Yes	800	A load-carrying family or business aircraft; excellent handling and performing. *NASAD approved design and kits.*
6	6	127	110	850	42	480	400	12,000	330	$10	$180	Yes	400	Removable wings and hangar trailer; single-engine rating needed to fly this aerobatic twin.

Publisher or Distributor	Aircraft Name and model number	Configuration	Type of Construction	Engine(s)	Wingspan (ft.-in.)	Length (ft.-in.)	Height (ft.-in.)	Wing Area (sq. ft.)	Number of Seats	Load factor +/–	Gross Weight (lbs.)	Useful Load (lbs.)	Empty Weight (lbs.)
Acro Sport Inc. Box 462 Hales Corners, WI 53130	Acro Sport I	Biplane	Tube/ wood/ fabric	100–200 hp.	19-7	17-6	6	NA	1	NA	1,200		733
	Acro Sport II	Biplane	Tube/ wood/ fabric	Lyc. 115–200 hp.	21-8	18-10¼	6-6¾	152	2 tand.	NA	1,520		875
Aerosport, Inc. Box 278 Holly Springs, NC 27540 (919) 552–6375	Scamp	Biplane	All sheet alum.	VW 1834 64 hp.	17-6	14	5-6½	105	1	6/3	768/798	245	520/ 550
Aerotech Rt #1, Box 27A Hastings, FL 32045 (904) 692–1639	Boeing F4B/P–12 8/10 scale	Biplane	Wood/ tube/ fabric	Jacobs 245 hp.	24	18	6-10	161.4	1	6/3	2,150	630	1,520
Christen Industries, Inc. 1048 Santa Ana Valley Rd. Hollister, CA 95023 (408) 637-7405	Christen Eagle II	Biplane	Tube/ wood/ fabric	Lyc. 200 hp. AE10–360A–10	19-11	18-6	6-6	125	2 tand.	7/5	1,600	575	1,025
Nick D'Apuzzo 1029 Blue Rock Lane Blue Bell, PA 19422 (215) 646–4792	Sportwing D–201	Biplane	Tube/ wood/ fabric	Lyc. 160 hp.	27	25-9½	7-7½	181	2 tand.	9/6	1,900	598	1,302
Durand Assoc., Inc. 84th and McKinley Omaha, NB 68122 (402) 571-7060	Durand Mark V	Biplane/ nega- tive stagger	All metal	Lyc. 150–160 hp.	24-6	20-3	6-8	144	2 sbs	5.7/ 2.28	1,840	630	1,210
Flight Level Six Zero, Inc. Box 9980 Colorado Springs, CO 80932	Der Kricket DK–1	Biplane	All metal/ pop riveted	VW 1,500 cc or larger	16	15	5-2	96	1	6/6	750	250	500

Fuel Capacity (gal.)	Baggage (lbs.)	Top Speed (mph)	Cruising Speed (mph)	Initial Climb (sl) (fpm)	Stall Speed (mph)	Take-off Run (ft.)	Landing Run (ft.)	Service Ceiling (ft.)	Range (miles)	Information Packet	Plan Price per Set	Materials Kit	Time to build (hrs.)	Comments
						Performance					**Price Data**			
20	25	152	130	3,500	50	150/ 280	800	20,000	350	$5	$60	Yes	2,500	Excellent aerobatic capability; designed by Paul Poberezny; performs with 180 hp. *NASAD approved designs.*
26	30	NA	123	NA	NA	NA	NA	NA	400	$5	$85	Yes	2,500	
8	0	105	90	750	45	350	400	10,500	175	$5	$65	Yes	650– 800	Good aircraft for low-time pilot; *NASAD approved design and kit.*
40	50	165	130	2,600	60	NA	NA	NA	390	$5	$150	No	NA	Design covers F4B–2,3,4 and P–12C,D and E. Can also use W670 or Lycoming R–680 engines.
25	30	184	165	2,120	58	900	1,375	22,200	390	$20	NA	Yes	NA	Classiest kit available; for competition-class aerobatic flying.
30	40	132	122	1,050	47	420	550	19,000	360	$5	$300	Yes	2,500	Aircraft is suitable for 125–200 hp.; information pack has complete details.
24.5 or 32.5	128	135	Var.	1,200	Nonstall	550	450	15,000	400 or 520	$5	$175	No	NA	Full-span flaps; spoiler roll control; requires no machining; good visibility.
8.5	0	110	90	700	52	700	500	11,500	200	$6	$60	No	1,000	Full-size plans; designed for first-time builder.

Fixed-Wing Powered Aircraft continued

| Publisher or Distributor | Aircraft Name and model number | Configuration | Type of Construction | Engine(s) | Specifications | | | | | | | | |
					Wingspan (ft.-in.)	Length (ft.-in.)	Height (ft.-in.)	Wing Area (sq. ft.)	Number of Seats	Load factor +/-	Gross Weight (lbs.)	Useful Load (lbs.)	Empty Weight (lbs.)
John O. Isaacs 23 Linden Grove Chandlers Ford, Hants. England SO5 ILE	Isaacs Fury	Biplane	Wood/ fabric	100–125 hp.	21	19-3	7-1	123.8	1	9/4¼	1,000	290	710
Javelin Aircraft Co. Box 18486 Wichita, KS 67218 (316) 733–1011	Wichawk	Biplane	Steel tube/ wood/ fabric	Lyc. 180 hp.	24	19-3	7-2	185	2 or 3	12	2,400	1,170	1,230
Dudley Kelly Rt. #4 McGee Lane Versailles, KY 40383 (606) 873–5253	HAT2 CB–1	Biplane	Steel tube/ wood/ fabric	Cont. 0–200 100 hp.	25-4	19	7-10	178	2 tand.	5/3	1,400	550	850
	Kelly-D	Biplane	Steel tube/ wood/ fabric	Lyc. 0–235 115 hp.	24-4	19-3	7-8	200	2 tand.	NA	1,500	575	925
Laco Box 415 Desert Hot Springs, CA 92240 (714) 329–0955	Laco 125 04 145	Biplane	Steel tube/ wood/ fabric	Cont. 125–145 hp.	22-8.7	19-6	7-2	150	2 tand.	NA	1,400	380	860
Meyer Aircraft 5706 Abby Drive Corpus Christi, TX 78413	Little Toot	Biplane	Steel tube/ wood/ fabric	Cont. 90 hp.	19	16	7	123	1	10	230		914
Barney Oldfield Aircraft Co., Inc. Box 83	Baby Lakes	Biplane	Steel tube/ wood/ fabric	Cont. 65–100 hp.	16-8	13-9	4-6	86	1	9/9	850	375	475
Gates Mills, OH 44040 (216) 423–3816	Super Baby Lakes	Biplane	Steel tube/ wood/ fabric	Lyc. 108–125 hp.	16-8	13-9	4-6	86	1	9/9	850	340	510

Fuel Capacity (gal.)	Baggage (lbs.)	Top Speed (mph)	Cruising Speed (mph)	Initial Climb (sl) (fpm)	Stall Speed (mph)	Take-off Run (ft.)	Landing Run (ft.)	Service Ceiling (ft.)	Range (miles)	Information Packet	Plan Price per Set	Materials Kit	Time to build (hrs.)	Comments
						Performance					**Price Data**			
12	20	115	100	1,600	42	150	100	NA	150	$6	$85	No	1,500	Based on 7/10-scale Hawker Fury Interceptor used by RAF in early 1930s.
40	120	140	127	1,700	52	300	300	15,000	500	$5	$125	No	2,000	Designer lists 26 engines that can be used. Builders manual has 110 photos. *NASAD approved design.*
18	0	NA	80	NA	40	NA	NA	NA	200+	$3	$125	No	NA	A good two-place, open-cockpit biplane using moderate power.
22	40	105	90	800	45	300	400	NA	275	$3	$150	No	4,000	A lightweight two-place biplane with roomy cockpits, simpler construction.
24	Var.	124	113	900	50	NA	NA	NA	325	$5	$150	No	2,000	A sport biplane that is very agile yet possesses forgiving flying characteristics.
18	25	127	110	55	1,000	500	500	16,500	300	$2	$100	No	NA	Aircraft never has had a reported structural failure; built from plans; can take up to 200 hp.
12 or 21	0	135	118	2,000	50	300	400	17,000	250	$5	$100	Yes	800	Unbelievable champagne aerobatic performance on a beer pocketbook. *NASAD approved designs.*
12 or 21	0	155	135	3,000	50	300	400	17,000	250	$5	$125	Yes	800	

Publisher or Distributor	Aircraft Name and model number	Configuration	Type of Construction	Engine(s)	Wingspan (ft.-in.)	Length (ft.-in.)	Height (ft.-in.)	Wing Area (sq. ft.)	Number of Seats	Load factor +/-	Gross Weight (lbs.)	Useful Load (lbs.)	Empty Weight (lbs.)
										Specifications			
Pitts Aerobatics Box 547 Afton, WY 83110 (307) 886–3151	Pitts S–1S	Biplane	Steel tube/wood/fabric	Lyc. 360-B4A 180 hp.	17-4	15-6	6-4	98	1	9/6	1,150	350	800
	Pitts S–1T	Biplane	Steel tube/wood/fabric	Lyc. 360-A1E 200 hp.	17-4	15-6	6-4	98	1	9/6	1,150	300	850
	Pitts S–2E	Biplane	Steel tube/wood/fabric	180–200 hp.	20	17-9	6-8	125	2 tand.	9/6	1,500	475	1,025
	Pitts S–2S	Biplane	Steel tube/wood/fabric	180–200 hp.	20	17-4	6-8	125	1	9/6	1,500	400	1,100
Quickie Aircraft Corp. Hangar 68 Mojave Airport Mojave, CA 93501 (805) 824–4313 or 824–4626	Quickie	Tandem wing canard	Composite	18 or 20 hp. Onan	16-8	17	NA	53	1	4.4	520	280	240
	Q2	Tandem wing canard	Composite	Revm. 64 hp.	16-8	17-8	NA	67	2 sbs	4.4	1,000	525	475
Redfern & Sons, Inc. Rt. 1 Athol, ID 83801	Fokker DRI	Triplane	Steel tube/wood/fabric	Warner 145 hp.	23-7	19	9-8	202	1	8.3	1,455	343	1,112
	Nieuport 24 Bis or 17	Biplane	Steel tube/wood/fabric	Warner 145 hp.	26-11	18-10	7-8½	161.6	1	6	1,278.5	274.5	1,004
Replica Plans 307-8680 Fremlin St. Vancouver, B.C., Canada V6P 3X3	SE–5A Replica	Biplane	Wood/fabric	Cont. C–85 85 hp.	23-4	18-2	7-8	146	1	6/3	1,150	320	830
Rutan Aircraft Factory, Inc. Building 13, Airport Mojave, CA 93501 (805) 824–2645	Long-EZ	Tandem canard	Composite foam/fiberglass	Lyc. 0–235 118 hp.	26-2	16-9	6-2	94.8	2 tand.	4.4	1,425	575	850

Fuel Capacity (gal.)	Baggage (lbs.)	Top Speed (mph)	Cruising Speed (mph)	Initial Climb (sl) (fpm)	Stall Speed (mph)	Take-off Run (ft.)	Landing Run (ft.)	Service Ceiling (ft.)	Range (miles)	Information Packet	Plan Price per Set	Materials Kit	Time to build (hrs.)	Comments
20	20	147	143	2,600	64	NA	NA	NA	300	$7	$200	Yes	1,600	World's most popular aerobatic biplane.
20	20	185	175	2,800	64	NA	NA	NA	350	$7	$300	Yes	1,600	Smaller unlimited competition machine.
24	20	165	160	1,900	58	NA	NA	NA	300	$7	NA	Yes	1,800	For sport aerobatic competition.
35	20	187	175	2,800	58	NA	NA	NA	450	$7	NA	Yes	1,800	Larger unlimited competition machine.
8	20	140	132	550	53	450	600	15,000	760	$10	$150	Yes	400	Plans intended for use with kit; fun to fly and easy to build.
20	30	180	170	800	64	610	700	15,000	1,025	$10	$190	Yes	500	World's most efficient, fast, economical aircraft; winner 1981 CAFE 250 contest.
30	0	120	100	2,000	40	150	300	20,000	300	$4	$60	No	2,500	True replica of WW I German fighter.
30	0	120	105	1,550	45	100–150	350	18,000	300	$5	$100	No	2,000	True replica of WW I French fighter.
18	30	95	85	600	35	200	200	10,000	250	$5	$100	No	1,200-1,500	Replica of WW I English figher.
52	40	191	184	1,200	59	1,000	600	20,000	1,400	$5	$198.50	Yes	1,000	Kits sold by others. Outstanding designs using latest materials and technology. *NASAD approved.*

Publisher or Distributor	Aircraft Name and model number	Configuration	Type of Construction	Engine(s)	Wingspan (ft.-in.)	Length (ft.-in.)	Height (ft.-in.)	Wing Area (sq. ft.)	Number of Seats	Load factor +/−	Gross Weight (lbs.)	Useful Load (lbs.)	Empty Weight (lbs.)
								Specifications					
Rutan Aircraft Factory, Inc. (*cont.*)	VariViggen	Tandem canard	Wood/composite	Lyc. 0–320 or 360	19	20	6	119	2 tand.	4.4	1,860	760	1,000
Mrs. Frank Smith 3502 Sunny Hills Drive Norco, CA 91706	DSA–1 Mini Plane	Biplane	Steel tube/ wood/ fabric	Lyc. 0–235 115 hp.	17	15-1	5	100	1		1,000	384	616
Steen Aero Labs 15623 DeGaul Circle Brighton, CO 80601 (303) 659–7182	Skybolt	Biplane	Steel tube/ wood/ fabric	Lyc. 180–250 hp.	24	19	7	155	2 tand.	8/5	1,650	570	1,080
Don Stewart 11420 Rt. 165 Salem, OH 44460 (216) 332–0865	Foo Fighter	Biplane	Steel tube/ wood/ fabric	Lyc. 0–320 150 hp.	20-3	18-9	7	135	1	4.4	1,100	350	750
Sorrell Aviation 16525 Tilley Road So. Tenino, WA 98589 (206) 264–2866	Guppy SNS–2	Biplane	Wood	R–800 25 hp.	21-3	15-5	5-3½	129	1	NA	600	260	340
	Hiperbipe SNS–7	Biplane/ negative stagger	Steel tube/ wood/ fabric	Lyc. 10–360 180 hp.	22-10	20-10	5-10¼	150	2 sbs	6/4	1,911	675	1,236
Skycote Aeromarine, Ltd. Box 808 Clark, CO 80428 (303) 879–3823	Skycote	Biplane	Steel tube/ alum/ fabric	Cont. 85–100 Lyc. 118 hp.	20	16	6-8	123	1	9/6	895	302	593
Stolp Starduster Corp. 4301 Twining Street Riverside, CA 92509 (714) 686–7943	Starduster TOO	Biplane	Steel tube/ wood/ fabric	150–300 hp.	24	20-6	7-4	165	2 sbs	6/6	1,700	700	1,000

Fuel Capacity (gal.)	Baggage (lbs.)	Performance								Price Data				
		Top Speed (mph)	Cruising Speed (mph)	Initial Climb (sl) (fpm)	Stall Speed (mph)	Take-off Run (ft.)	Landing Run (ft.)	Service Ceiling (ft.)	Range (miles)	Information Packet	Plan Price per Set	Materials Kit	Time to build (hrs.)	Comments
38	100	172	162	1,000	60	800	650	14,000	650	$5	$165	No	3,000	Earlier Rutan design using larger engines; canard pusher. *NASAD approved designs.*
17	60	125	117	1,250	54	425	NA	14,500	300	$1	$26	No	1,500-2,000	A sweet, stable little biplane stressed for aerobatics. Use 65–125 hp.
29	40	145	130	2,500	50	400	NA	16,500	400	$5	$50	Yes	2,000	Very popular two-place home-built; used for sport and competition flying.
19	10	145	115	1,200	45	350	550	19,000	260	$3	$50	No	NA	Uses basic construction techniques; no complicated tools or tooling.
6.5/ 1.8	0	85	75	500	30	275	200	10,000	270	$5	$50	Yes	400 kit	Plans are Mike Kimbrel's with Sorrell updates. Flies out of any field.
39	80	170+	160	1,500	49 with flaps	400	595	NA	625	$7.50	NA	Yes	1,500-2,000	High performance; aerobatic; excellent cross-country; enclosed cabin.
12	20	120	110	1,500	42	250	350	16,500	220	$2	$275	Yes	3,000	Super control response; hydro-formed heat-treated ribs; STOL capabilities
41	30	148	130	1,500	56	500	750	12,000	450	$3	$85	Yes	2,000	Not complicated to build or fly. Satisfies the sport biplane pilot's desires.

Publisher or Distributor	Aircraft Name and model number	Configuration	Type of Construction	Engine(s)	Specifications Wingspan (ft.-in.)	Length (ft.-in.)	Height (ft.-in.)	Wing Area (sq. ft.)	Number of Seats	Load factor +/−	Gross Weight (lbs.)	Useful Load (lbs.)	Empty Weight (lbs.)
Stolp Starduster Corp. (*cont.*)	Aeroduster TOO	Biplane	Steel tube/ wood/ fabric	Lyc. 180–260	21-5	18-6	6-10	130	2 sbs	6/6	1,800	750	1,050
Viking Aircraft 5825 Grang Lagoon Boulevard Pensacola, FL 32507	Dragonfly	Tandem wing canard	Foam/ fiber/ carbon fiber	VW 1600 cc 45–60 hp.	22	20	4-6	97	2 sbs	4.4/2	1,075	475	600
Donald S. Wolf 17 Chestnut Street Huntington, NY 11743	WOLF W–11 Boredom Fighter	Biplane	Wood/ fabric	Cont. A–65 65 hp.	20	15-7	6	93.5	1	9.1/ 7.1	770	207	473

Seaplanes and Amphibians

Publisher or Distributor	Aircraft Name and model number	Configuration	Type of Construction	Engine(s)	Wingspan (ft.-in.)	Length (ft.-in.)	Height (ft.-in.)	Wing Area (sq. ft.)	Number of Seats	Load factor +/−	Gross Weight (lbs.)	Useful Load (lbs.)	Empty Weight (lbs.)
Osprey Aircraft 3741 El Ricon Way Sacramento, CA 95828 (916) 483–3009	Osprey 1	Mid-wing	Wood/ fabric	65–100 hp.	23	17-3	5-3	97	1	4.5	900	300	600
	Osprey II	Mid-wing amphib-ian	Wood/ foam/ fabric	Lyc. 150–160 hp.	26	21	5-8	130	2 sbs	4.5/ 3.5	1,570	600	960
Spencer Amphibian 12780 Pierce Street Pacoima, CA 91331 (213) 899–1010	Spencer Air Car	High wing amphib-ian	Wood/ fiber-glass /tubing	Lyc. 260 hp.	37	26	10-10	184	4	NA	3,100	NA	2,050
	Spencer S–14	High wing	Wood/ fiber-glass/ tubing	Lyc. 150–160 hp.	33	23	7	165	2 sbs	4/2	800	650	1,150
Spratt Co., Inc. Box 351 Media, PA 19063	Control wing Model 107	Parasol sea-plane	Plastic	Mercury out-board	24	16-8	4-6	96	2 sbs	NA	1,000	NA	450

Fuel Capacity (gal.)	Baggage (lbs.)	Performance								Price Data				Comments
		Top Speed (mph)	Cruising Speed (mph)	Initial Climb (sl) (fpm)	Stall Speed (mph)	Take-off Run (ft.)	Landing Run (ft.)	Service Ceiling (ft.)	Range (miles)	Information Packet	Plan Price per Set	Materials Kit	Time to build (hrs.)	
41	30	160	140	2,100	65	700	1,200	12,000	500	$3	$85	Yes	2,000	Hottest performer in Starduster line. 200 hp. version can be used for advanced competition.
15	30	180	165	1,050	45	450	1,000	18,000	500+	$7.50	$175	Yes	750	Winner outstanding design at 1980 EAA Oshkosh; designed for first-time builder.
15	8	120	110	1,400	42	150	350	16,000	500	$3	$125	No	1,500	Excellent short-field performance; exquisite handling.
14	NA	NA	118	2,000	NA	210	350	21,000	380	$3	$65	No	1,300	A flying boat with folding wings; plans for trailer included.
38	75	140	130	1,300	63	400	680	NA	NA	$6	$165	Yes	2,200	Water take off 600 ft. and landing 800 ft. *NASAD approved.*
90	Var.	150	135	860	48	NA	750	15,000	700	$5	$195	Yes	NA	Designed for home builder by designer of the famous SeeBee. *NASAD approved.* Folding-wing amphibian; can be towed.
52	40	120	110	650	38	400	400	12,000	660	$5	$125	Yes	1,800	
NA	NA	NA	75	NA	40	NA	NA	NA	NA	N/C	$125	No	NA	Unusual seaplane. There is a land version; excellent opportunity for experimenter.

Fixed-Wing Powered Aircraft continued

Publisher or Distributor	Aircraft Name and model number	Configuration	Type of Construction	Engine(s)	Wingspan (ft.-in.)	Length (ft.-in.)	Height (ft.-in.)	Wing Area (sq. ft.)	Number of Seats	Load factor +/−	Gross Weight (lbs.)	Useful Load (lbs.)	Empty Weight (lbs.)
			Specifications										
Molt Taylor Box 1171 Louquiew, WA 98632 (206) 423–8260	Taylor Coot-A	Shoulder wing amphibian	Wood/fiberglass	Franklin 180 hp.	36	22	8	180	2 sbs	6	1,950	650	1,300
Volmer Aircraft Box 5222 Glendale, CA 92101	Volmer VJ–22 Sportsman	High wing amphibian pusher	Wood/fiberglass	Cont. 85–100 hp.	36-6	24	8	NA	2 sbs	NA	1,500	500	1,000

Gliders

Publisher or Distributor	Aircraft Name and Model Number	Configuration	Type of construction	Wingspan (ft.-in.)	Length (ft.-in.)	Height (ft.-in.)	Wing area (sq. ft.)	Aspect Ratio	Design Ultimate Load Factor	Max. Gross Weight (lbs.)	Empty Weight (lbs.)	Number of Seats
			Specifications									
Bensen Aircraft Corp. Box 31047 Raleigh, NC 27622 (919) 787–4224	Gyro-Glider Model B–8	Rotary wing	Metal/wood	21-8	11-4	7-3	NA	NA	9	600	125	1 or 2
Bryan Aircraft, Inc. Williams County Airport Bryan, OH 43506 (419) 636–3184	HP–18	High wing	Alum.	49-2	23-2	4	113	21.4	12	970	470	1
	RS–15	High wing	Alum.	49-2	22	4	113	21.4	12	950	450	1
D.S.K. Aircraft Corp. 13161 Sherman Way North Hollywood, CA 91605 (213) 787–6600	Duster	Shoulder wing	Wood/fabric	42-6	19-10	3-3	103	17.5	6	580	335	1
Harlan Experimental Aircraft 2118 Kansas Street Carson City, NV 89701 (702) 882–8954	Skip-Air Model +7	High wing	Wood/fabric	31-2	20	5-8	128	NA	NA	580	410	1

Fuel Capacity (gal.)	Baggage (lbs.)	Performance								Price Data				Comments
		Top Speed (mph)	Cruising Speed (mph)	Initial Climb (sl) (fpm)	Stall Speed (mph)	Take-off Run (ft.)	Landing Run (ft.)	Service Ceiling (ft.)	Range (miles)	Information Packet	Plan Price per Set	Materials Kit	Time to build (hrs.)	
48	100	140	120	1,000	50	200	250	15,000	450	$5	$150	Yes	1,500	Extremely short water take-off runs. *NASAD approved.*
20	NA	NA	85	600	45	NA	NA	13,000	300	$10	$200	No	NA	Volmer says he would not change a thing if he built another—except for visibility.

Performance									Price Data				Comments
Top Speed (mph)	Cruising Speed (mph)	Auto Tow Speed (mph)	Airplane Tow Speed (mph)	Stall speed (mph)	Min. Sink Speed (mph)	Min. Sink Rate (fps)	Set Up Time (Min.)	L/D Max.	Information Packet	Plan Price per Set	Materials Kit	Time to Build	
85	45	35	NA	0	40	15	15	4/1	$5	$50	Yes	50–100	Can be used as a two-seat rotorcraft pilot trainer; can be converted into a gyrocopter by adding an engine.
150	45–150	90	120	40	46	2	10	40	$5	$150	Yes	1,000	A sailplane designed by R.E. (Dick) Schreder offering the home builder the opportunity to build and fly a high-performance aircraft at reasonable cost. *NASAD approved plans and kits.*
150	45–150	90	120	40	45	2	10	40	$5	$150	Yes	950	
135	54	65	90	42	NA	NA	20	NA	$2	$110	Yes	NA	Sailplane to check out in easily and fly safely.
55	38	38	NA	31	NA	NA	NA	NA	$5	$25	No	250–300	Designed to be converted to power with addition of engine and second wing.

Publisher or Distributor	Aircraft Name and Model Number	Configuration	Type of construction	Wingspan (ft.-in.)	Length (ft.-in.)	Height (ft.-in.)	Wing area (sq. ft.)	Aspect Ratio	Design Ultimate Load Factor	Max. Gross Weight (lbs.)	Empty Weight (lbs.)	Number of Seats
Manta Pro 1647 East 14th Street Oakland, CA 94606 (415) 536–1500	Fledge 3	Flying rigid wing	Alum./Dacron	32-5	9	9	152	NA	NA	NA	NA	1
Jim Maupin Box 5127 San Pedro, CA 90733	Woodstock	High wing	Wood/fiberglass	39	20	4-3	104	14	7.5	450	235	1
Marske Aircraft Corp. 130 Crestwood Dr. Michigan City, IN 46360 (219) 879–7039	Monarch Model D	High wing	Wood/fiberglass	42	11-10	NA	185	9.5	8	450	220	1
Monnett Experimental Aircraft, Inc. Box 2984 Oshkosh, WI 54903	Monerai S	Mid-wing	Bonded alum./tube	36	19-7	4-4	78	16.6	6	500	220	1
Ultralight Flying Machines, Inc. Box 2967 Turlock, CA 95051 (209) 634–6134	Easy Riser	Biplane hang glider	Alum./fabric	30	5	5	170	8.8	9	250	50	1
Schweizer Aircraft Box 147 Elmira, NY 14902 (607) 739–3821	2–33AK	High wing	Alum./tube	51	25-9	9-3½	219	1185	8	1,040	640	2
Volmer Aircraft Box 5222 Glendale, CA 91201 (213) 247–8718	VJ–11 Hang glider	Biplane	Wood/fabric	28	15-5	5-1	225	NA	NA	280	100	1
	VJ–23 Swingwing	High wing hang glider	Wood/tubing/fabric	32-7	17-5	6	179	NA	3	300	100	1
	VJ–24 Sun Fun	High wing hang glider	Metal	36-6	18-2	5-8	163	NA	3	310	110	1
Cirila Strojnik 2337 E. Manhattan Tempe, AZ 85282 (602) 838–1832	S-2 powered sailplane	Mid-wing	Alum./fiberglass/carbon fibers	49-2	22-5	3-6	127	19	+8/ −6	980	617	1

Top Speed (mph)	Cruising Speed (mph)	Auto Tow Speed (mph)	Airplane Tow Speed (mph)	Performance					Price Data				Comments
				Stall speed (mph)	Min. Sink Speed (mph)	Min. Sink Rate (fps)	Set Up Time (Min.)	L/D Max.	Information Packet	Plan Price per Set	Materials Kit	Time to Build	
55	35	17–35	17–35	17	19	3	20	12	$2	NA	NA	NA	Ready to assemble. Control by weight shift; roll controlled by tip rudders.
100	65	65	65	32	NA	2.6	30	24	$5	$95	Yes	500	Good first-time project; parts availability is key to length of time to build.
70	60	50	50	24	30	2.7	15	19	$5	$90	Yes	200	High stall and spin resistance. Three axis controls; can be powered; will be available after testing.
120	80	NA	80	38	55	2.8	3	28	$5	$200	Yes	350	Small add-on power pod converts this to P version. Extended wing tips give 12-meter span and 34/1 glide ratio.
45	24	24	NA	16	18	NA	6	10	NC	NA	Yes	100	Well-proven design; frequently powered; recommend wing-approved power only.
98	98	69	98	31	NA	2.6	20	23	NC	NA	Yes	300	Fully FAA type-certified; can be used for flight instruction; available in kit form. Completed aircraft sells at comparable factory aircraft prices.
NA	20	NA	NA	15	NA	NA	NA	NA	$10*	$50	No	NA	Very simple to build; first with three-dimensional controls. *Contains information on all Volmer designs.
NA	20	NA	NA	15	NA	NA	NA	NA	$10*	$100	No	NA	A most advanced design; three-axis controls.
NA	20	NA	NA	15	NA	NA	10	NA	$10*	$100	No	200	Not as esthetic looking as Swingwing but has the same performance.
149	100	NA	NA	38	34	NA	2.1	20	$6	$200	Yes	500 kit/ 1,000	A powered sailplane using the newest materials; building time cut in half using kit; optional engines.

Rotary-Wing Aircraft

Publisher or Distributor	Aircraft Name and Model Number	Type of Construction	Specifications						
			Engine(s)	Length (ft.-in.)	Height (ft.-in.)			Gross Weight (lbs.)	Empty Weight (lbs.)
Bensen Aircraft Corp. Box 31047 Raleigh, NC 27622 (919) 787–4224	Gyrocopter Model B–8HD	Alum.	McCul. 4318 GX 90 hp.	11-3	6-9	24-2	NA	650	290
	Gyrocopter Model B–80	Alum.	McCul. 4318–AX or GX 70–90 hp.	11-3	6-9	22-6	NA	600	247
	Gyrocopter Model B–8M	Metal	McCul. 4318–AX or GX 70–90 hp.	11-3	6-9	22-6	NA	600	247
International Helicopters, Inc. P.O. Box 107 Mayville, NY 14757 (716) 753–2113	Commuter II	Steel tube/ alum.	Lyc. 150 hp.	29	8-2	25	NA	1,300	700
Ken Brock Mfg. 11852 Western Ave. Stanton, CA 90680 (714) 898–4366	KB–2 Gyroplane	Alum.	VW 1835 cc or McCul.	11-3	6-8	22	NA	650	250
Rotorway Aircraft, Inc. 14805 S. I–10 Tempe, AZ 85284 (602) 961–1001	Rotorway Executive	Fiber-glass/ steel	RW–145 (145 hp.)	21-6	7-10	25-4	4-2	NA	830
	Scorpion 133	Fiber/ steel	RW–145 (145 hp.)	21	7-3	25	3-9	1,200	800
Winther-Hollman Aircraft, Inc. 11082 Bel Aire Ct. Cupertino, CA 15014 (408) 255–2194	Sky Dancer	Steel	Revm. 2,100 cc 64 hp.	10-10	7-8	23	NA	540	280
	HA–2M Sportster	Alum.	Lyc. 0–320 150 hp.	12	7-8	28	NA	1,100	620

Fuel Capacity (gal.)	Number of Seats	Top Speed (mph)	Cruising Speed (mph)	Initial Climb (sl)(fpm)		Ceiling (ft.)		Information Packet	Plan Price per Set	Materials Kit	Time to Build (hrs.)	Comments
		Performance						**Price Data**				
12	1	90	65	1,400	NA	NA	200	$10	NA	Yes	300	This gyrocopter has in-flight powered rotor; first of its kind in the world; top of the line. Plans included with kit.
6	1	85	60	1,000	NA	NA	100	$10	NA	Yes	200	All-metal version of the popular model B–8M Gyrocopter, with plans and materials supplied in the kit.
6	1	85	60	1,000	NA	NA	100	$10	$100	Yes	600	Most popular design; more than 1,000 copies built.
22	2 sbs	100	90	NA	NA	NA	225	$10	$75	Yes	NA	A well-proven design. Many finished components and materials kits available.
8.5	1	90	65	1,000	NA	NA	140	$7	$75	Yes	100	Can be transported to and from the airport; approx. 15 minutes assembly time.
15	2 sbs	105	75	1,200	6,500/4,000	10,000	228	$15	$150	Yes	600	Only piston-powered helicopter to employ an asymmetrical airfoil rotor system; range is obtained with auxiliary tanks.
10	2 sbs	85	75	800	4,500/5,500	10,000	120	$15	NA	Yes	600	Over 100,000 flight hours on this model; amateur-built helicopter plans provided with kits.
6	1	90	55	1,000	NA	NA	120	$5	$58	Yes	1,000	A well tested and proven gyroplane.
17	2 sbs	90	65	1,000	NA	NA	120	$5	$150	Yes	1,000	Rotor pre-rotator and rotor brake are standard.

Ultralight Powered Aircraft

Publisher or Distributor	Aircraft Name and Model Number	Configuration	Type of Construction	Engine(s)	Wingspan (ft.-in.)	Length (ft.-in.)	Height (ft.-in.)	Wing Area (sq. ft.)	Number of Seats	Gross Weight (lbs.)	Useful Load (lbs.)
Advanced Aviation Rt. 7, Box 569–D Orlando, FL 32305	Hi Nuski Huski	High wing	Tube/ Dacron	Cuyuna 30 hp. 430–D	33-6	16-9	9-9	169	1	440	250
Aircraft Specialities Co. Box 1074 Canyon Court Canyon Country, CA (805) 252-4054	Hovey Delta Bird	Biplane	Alum. tube/fabric	Cuyuna 30 hp. 430–D	24	15	6	160	1	425	189
	Hovey Wing Ding WD II	Biplane pusher	Wood/ alum./ fabric	Mac 101 12 hp.	18	12	5	106	1	310	185
Airmass Hillside Airport 16845 Kenneth Road Stillwell, KS 66085 (913) 897-9797	Airmass Sunburst	High wing pusher	Alum. tube/ Dacron	Cuyuna 430 30 hp.	36	16	9-5	156	1	465	245
CGS Aviation 4252 Pearl Road Cleveland, OH 44109 (216) 348-5272	Hawk	High wing pusher	Alum. tube/ Dacron	Cuyuna 430–D 30 hp.	29.3	19.5	5-5	145	1	460	240
American Aerolight Inc. 700 Commanche Road Albuquerque, NM 87107 (505) 822-1417	Eagle Ultra-lite	High wing pusher	Alum./ Dacron	Cuyuna 30 hp. 215R, 20 hp.	36	14	10	188	1	380	215
	Double Eagle	High wing pusher	Alum./ Dacron	Cuyuna 430R, 35 hp.	36	14	10	188	1	515	315
Barnstormer Mfg. RR #2 Hiway 37S Mitchell, IN 47446 (812) 849-3242	Barnstormer	High wing pusher	Alum. tube/ Dacron/ sailcloth	Lloyd 400 cc 22 hp.	31-6	13	5-6	176	1	528	352
Gordon Bedson & Associates Oliver St. Bundarra, NSW Australia 2359	Resurgam	High wing	Metal/ foam/wood	Konig 430 cc 30 hp.	28	18-6	8-6	112	1	400	210
Cascade Ultralites 1750–12th N.W. Issaquah, WA 98027 (206) 392-0388	Kasperwing 1–80	Parasol	Tube/fabric	Zenoah G250B 20 hp.	35	12-8	7-6	180	1	380	220

Empty Weight (lbs.)	Fuel Capacity/Consumption (gal.)	Load Factor +/-	Top/Cruise/Stall Speed (mph)	Initial Climb (fpm)	Take-off/Landing Roll	Performance				Price Data				
						L/D, Sink Rate	Set-up Time	Control System	FAA License Req.	Information Packet	Plan Price per Set	Materials Kit	Time to Build (hrs)	Comments
190	3.5/2+	NA	50/40/20	800	100/NA	6/NA	NA	Comb.	No	NC	NA	Yes	NA	Popular; sold only as a kit.
215	3.5/2+	4.5	55/45/27	300	250/250	NA	40	3–AX	NA	$4	$40	No	300	A new Hovey design.
122	1/1.5	4.59	50/45/26	250	150/150	6/300	20	3–AX	No	$3	$25	No	400	Unlike most ultralights, this is for ground effects flying.
220	5/1.2	NA	60/50/23	800	100/100	10/5	60	3–AX	No	NC	NA	Yes	40	V tail; rudder pedal and steerable nosewheel; reduction drive.
220	4/1.8	4.5/2.5	75/55/25	600	100/150	6.5/NA	30	3–AX	Yes	$4	125	Yes	40–100	Excellent control and stability; new design.
165	2.5/.9	8/2.5	50/32/18	550	100/75	8/300	45	Comb.	No	$2	NA	No	*	*Factory built; every unit test flown. Personalized flight training required with purchase.
200	2.5/1.5	7/2.5	55/36/22	800	150/100	8/400	45	Comb.	No	$2	NA	No	*	*Factory built; for pilots weighing more than 200 lbs.
180	5–1½	NA	55/35/18	NA	40–100	NA	15	3–ax.	No	$5	NA	Yes	*	*90% factory custom built; assembled at factory and shipped disassembled.
190	3/2	3.8	72/55/33	460	260/210	13/NA	10	3–ax.	Yes	$10	$95	No	800	Meets FAA requirements for home-built aircraft, and all Australian DOT requirements.
160	2.5/1	7/4	60/37/19	700	50/50	10/3.3	30	Comb.	No	$5	NA	Yes	40	Only ultralight that maintains control independent of forward speed.

Publisher or Distributor	Aircraft Name and Model Number	Configuration	Type of Construction	Engine(s)	Wingspan (ft.-in.)	Length (ft.-in.)	Height (ft.-in.)	Wing Area (sq. ft.)	Number of Seats	Gross Weight (lbs.)	Useful Load (lbs.)
				Specifications							
Delta Sailplane Corporation 13161 Sherman Way	DS–26A Nomad Type A	High wing	Alum. tube/fabric	210 solo 18 hp.	36-1	18-5	5-8	147	1	408	246
North Hollywood, CA 96105 (213) 765–0144	DS–26B Nomad Type B	High wing	Alum. tube/fabric	Lloyd 386 cc 26 hp.	36-1	18-9¼	9-3	147	1	408	213
	DS–27 Honcho Type A	High wing	Fabric/ Alum. tube	Lloyd 26 hp. DS1	32-2	17-5	9-3	131	1	407	218
	DS–27A Honcho Type B	High wing	Fabric/ alum. tube	Lloyd 26 hp. DS1	32-2	17-5	9-3	131	1	420	215
Eastern Ultralights Box 424 Chatsworth, NJ 08019	Snoop	Parasol	Alum. tube/ Dacron	Cuyuna 30 hp. 430R	33	18	8	165	1	523	285
J.M. Fay Mfg. Co. 1821 South Shore Road Ocean View, NJ 08230	Ronair G25B–1	High wing	Alum. tube/ Dacron	Zenoah 20 hp.	34	NA	NA	170	1	440	260
Eipper Formance Inc. 1070 Linda Vista Drive	Sea Quick	High wing	Alum. tube/ Dacron	Cuyuna 30 hp.	34	18-1	9-8	160	1	480	220
San Marco, CA 92069 (714) 744–1514	Double Quick	High wing	Alum. tube/ Dacron	Cuyuna 30 hp.	34	18-1	9-8	160	1	465	260
	Quicksilver	High wing	Alum. tube/ Dacron	Cuyuna 20 hp.	34	18-1	9-8	160	1	425	240
	Quicksilver MX	High wing	Alum. tube/ Dacron	Cuyuna 30 hp.	34	18-1	9-8	160	1	480	260
Flight Designs, Inc. 1328 Burton Saunas, CA 93901 (408) 758–3844	Jetwing ATV	High wing	Alum. tube/ Dacron	Kawasaki TA 440 40 hp.	33-6	6-5	7-7	176	1	438	235

Empty Weight (lbs.)	Fuel Capacity/Consumption (gal.)	Load Factor +/-	Performance							Price Data				Comments
			Top/Cruise/Stall Speed (mph)	Initial Climb (fpm)	Take-off/Landing Roll	L/D, Sink Rate	Set-up Time	Control System	FAA License Req.	Information Packet	Plan Price per Set	Materials Kit	Time to Build (hrs)	
162	2.5/.8	7/2.6	55/45/25	340	165/150	14.5/2.8	20	3–ax.	No	NC	NA	Yes	160	Kits supply everything in ready-to-use form for assembly.
195	2.5/.8	7/2.6	55/54/25	600	80/150	14.3/2.8	20	3–ax.	No	NC	NA	Yes	160	Engines and gear optional; simple assembly uses modular units.
189	2.5/1.2	7/2.6	60/60/27	620	85/150	13.6/3.3	20	3–ax.	No	NC	NA	Yes	160	Sophisticated motor gliders; can be hauled and stored on modified boat trailer; complete kits.
205	2.5/1.2	7/2.6	70/62/28	630	80/150	13.6/3.4	20	3–ax.	No	NC	NA	Yes	160	Same as for DS-27 Honcho Type A
238	3/1¼	3.2	50/45/18	600	75–100/50	7	NA	3–ax.	No	NC	NA	Yes	25	Aircraft comes with many finished parts; spoilers and rudder pedals for control.
180	3/2.5	NA	45/35/18	400	20–110/50	7/NA	NA	3–ax.	No	NC	NA	Yes	NA	Aircraft is delivered in ready-to-fly condition; easy maintenance.
260	3.4/2.2	4.5/2.5	45/40/25	600	60/30	5/6	45	3–ax.	No	$3	NA	Yes	25	Aircraft is almost completely built; equipped with non-tipping floats.
205	3.4/1.9		50/40/21	900	50/50	6.6/4.8	35	Comb.	No	$3	NA	Yes	16	Purchasers must go through dealer training; variable C.G. control; custom parts, floats, optional gears, cowling, skis available.
185	3.4/2.5	5/3	45/35/20	450	75/50	6.5/4.3	30	Comb.	No	$3	NA	Yes	16	
220			50/43/22	800	50/50	6/5	40	3–ax.	No	$3	NA	Yes	25	
203	5/1.2	6/3.7	50/35/22	600–700	50/50	8/5	20	Wt. shift	No	NC	NA	No	None	Optional parachute recovery systems; STOL ability; ready to set up and fly.

Publisher or Distributor	Aircraft Name and Model Number	Configuration	Type of Construction	Engine(s)	Wingspan (ft.-in.)	Length (ft.-in.)	Height (ft.-in.)	Wing Area (sq. ft.)	Number of Seats	Gross Weight (lbs.)	Useful Load (lbs.)
				Specifications							
Goldwing, Ltd Box 1123 Jackson, CA 95642 (209) 223–0384	Gold Duster	Canard mid-wing	Composite	Cuyuna 430 30 hp.	30	12	5	128	1	640	380
	Goldwing	Canard mid-wing	Composite	Cuyuna 430 30 hp.	30	12	5	128	1	490	250
Gemini International 75 Bank Street #13 Sparks, NV 89431 (702) 331–3638	Humming-bird	High wing	Alum. tube/ Dacron	2 Partner Gemini K1200 8 hp.	34	NA	NA	157	1	413	250
Kolb Co., Inc. RD. #2 Box 38 Phoenixville, PA 19460 (215) 948–3264	Kolb Flyer	High wing	Alum/ Dacron/ steel tube	2 Solo 15 hp.	29	20	5	160	1	450	250
La Mouette La rue de la petite Fin Fontaine les Dijon, France 21121	Dragster	High wing	Alum. tube/ Dacron	Fuji Robin 250 cc	33	11	8-6	180	1	376	200
Manta Products 1647 E. 14th Street Oakland, CA 94606 (415) 536–1500	Foxbat FL 2 and 3	High wing	Alum. tube/ Dacron	Zenoah reduction drive	32-6	8-6	9	157	1	450	270
Mattison Aircraft 204 Front St. Perry, KS 66073 (913) 597–5972	MAC 200	High wing	Alum. tube/ Dacron	Kohler 15– 40 hp.	34	20	9-10	170	1	475	300
	MAC 300	High wing	Alum. tube/ Dacron	Kohler 30 hp. Cuyuna 40 hp.	34-5	20	9-10	170	1 and 2	610	400
	MAC 400	High wing	Alum. tube/ Dacron	Kohler 30 and 40 hp.	34	20	9-10	170	1	465	300
Maxair Sports, Inc Box 95 (Winter Ave) Glen Rock, PA 17327 (717) 235–2107	Hummer	High wing	Alum./ Dacron	Zenoah 20 hp.	34	19	8	128	1	395	215

Empty Weight (lbs.)	Fuel Capacity/Consumption (gal.)	Load Factor +/−	Performance							Price Data				Comments
			Top/Cruise/Stall Speed (mph)	Initial Climb (fpm)	Take-off/Landing Roll	L/D, Sink Rate	Set-up Time	Control System	FAA License Req.	Information Packet	Plan Price per Set	Materials Kit	Time to Build (hrs)	
260	2.5/1.5	6/4	70/50/25	500	150/200	15/4.6	15	3–ax.	No	$6	NA	Yes	100	Ultralight crop duster. Alternate engines.
240	6/1.5	6/4	70/60/24	600	150/200	16/4.1	10	3–ax.	No	$6	NA	Yes	100	Full 3-axis controls. Floats, wheel parts, and canopy are available.
163	1.75/1	3.5	50/35/18	600	100–150 both	11/6	35–40	3–ax.	No	$5	NA	Yes	NA	Twin engine; easily disassembled and carried on car top.
185	1.75/1.25	4/2.5	53/40/20	450	150/100	NA	15	3–ax.	No	$2	$65	Yes	350	Gentle stalls; two surface airfoils; docile handling.
176	2.5/NA	4	50/35/15	600	70/30	10/1.1	10	Wt. shift	No	NC	NA	Yes	5	Tricycle landing gear; uses Azur glider wing.
180	5/1	6/5	55/35/25	NA	65/40	8/3.6	25	Comb.	No	$2	NA	No	None	Aircraft comes ready to set up and fly; Cuyuna engine optional.
175	3/1	NA	45/35/15	650	20–40 both	6/NA	15–30	Comb.	No	NC	$100	Yes	5–20	Shock-absorbing gear; custom parts; steerable nose gear.
210	3/1.5	NA	55/40/18	750	20–40 both	6/NA	15–30	3–ax.	No	NC	$125	Yes	15–30	Stick controls; five-way harness.
165	3/1	NA	45/30/15	650	20–40	6/NA	15–30	Comb.	No	NC	$100	Yes	5–20	Many custom features.
170	5/1.5	NA	55/40/22	400–600	200–300 both	8/3	10–15	3–ax.	Yes	$6	$75	Yes	80–100	FAA student license required. Cowl, parts, engine-reduction drive available.

Publisher or Distributor	Aircraft Name and Model Number	Configuration	Type of Construction	Engine(s)	Wingspan (ft.-in.)	Length (ft.-in.)	Height (ft.-in.)	Wing Area (sq. ft.)	Number of Seats	Gross Weight (lbs.)	Useful Load (lbs.)
Mitchell Aircraft Corporation 1900 South Newcomb Portville, CA 93257 (209) 781-8100	P–38 Lightning	Mid-wing	Alum./steel/wood/fabric	Cuyuna 30 hp.	29	16	5	116	1	620	320
	Mitchell Wing B–10	Flying wing	Wood/fabric	Zenoah 23 hp.	34	7	5	136	1	475	300
	U–2 Super Wing	Flying wing	Wood/fabric	Zenoah 23 hp.	35	9	3	138	1	610	350
Pterodactyl Ltd. P.O. Box 191 Watsonville, CA 95076 (408) 724-2233	Pterodactyl Fledge	High wing	Alum. tube/Dacron	Cuyuna 430D	33	13-8	9-10	162	1	475	240
	Ptiger	High wing	Alum/fabric/foam	Cuyuna 430R	29	14	9	150	1	550	310
	Ascender	High wing	Alum/Dacron	Cuyuna 430R	33	16-8	9-10	173	1	465	250
	Ptraveler	High wing	Alum/Dacron	Cuyuna 430R	33	16-9	9-10	173	1	465	265
Striplin Aircraft Corp. P.O. Box 2001 Lancaster, CA 93539 (805) 945-2522	Long Ranger	High wing	Composite	Zenoah 20 hp.	34	15-8	5	154	1	450	225
	Sky Ranger	High wing	Fiberglass/composite	Cuyuna 40 hp.	37	17	6-4	166.5	2	800	410
Swallow Aeroplane Co. Pistol Shop Road Rockfall, CT 06481 (203) 397-9543	Swallow	High wing	Alum./steel/Dacron	Cuyuna 30 hp. or 2 Yamaha 15 hp.	34-1	18-1	8-9	138	1	515	295
Ultraflight Sales Box 370 Port Colborne, Ont. Canada L3K 1B7 (416) 735-8352	Lazair	High wing	Alum. frame/Mylar	2 Rotax 9.5 hp.	36-4	14	6-4	142	1	433	250
Ultralight Flying Machines of Kentucky, Inc. E.P. Tom Sawyer State Park Louisville, KY 40218 (502) 458-6912	Aeroplane	Biplane	Alum. tube/Dacron	Cuyuna 20 hp.	30	NA	NA	170	1	NA	220
SR–1 Enterprises 2323 Endicott St. Paul, MN (612) 646-3884	Hornet SR–1	Biplane	Alum. tube/Dacron	20–40 hp.	34-4	18	6-8	223	1	423	Var.

Empty Weight (lbs.)	Fuel Capacity/ Consumption (gal.)	Load Factor +/−	Top/Cruise/Stall Speed (mph)	Initial Climb (fpm)	Take-off/Landing Roll	Performance L/D, Sink Rate	Set-up Time	Control System	FAA License Req.	Price Data Information Packet	Plan Price per Set	Materials Kit	Time to Build (hrs)	Comments
300	6/2.5	6	60/50/32	500	200/120	7/8.3	NA	3–ax.	Yes	$7	$125	Yes	60	Sporty design; easily completed.
175	3/1.5	3	70/50/22	800	150/120	15/4.5	15	3–ax.	No	$7	$125	Yes	350	Unique flying-wing design.
260	6/1.5	3	95/65/32	500	250/200	25/4.5	15	3–ax.	Yes	$7	$125	Yes	450	Motor glider, ultralight or airplane; high performance.
185	5/1.5	NA	55/35/23	400+	125/50	9/6.6	40	Comb.	No	$5	NA	Yes	50	Hang glider can be converted to ultralight.
240	5/1.5	NA	NA/55/30	800	150/120	12/NA	30	3–ax.	Yes	$5	NA	Yes	100	Regular aircraft controls.
215	5/1.5	NA	55/35/23	1,000+	80/50	9/7	45	3–ax.	No	$5	NA	Yes	75	Very quiet; can tow hang gliders and banners aloft.
200	5/1.5	NA	55/35/23	400	125/50	9/7	45	3–ax.	No	$5	NA	Yes	75	Moderate price; excellent trainer.
218	4.5/1.5	4.5/3	80/65/26	550	200/250	16/NA	20	3–ax.	Yes	$7	NA	Yes	200	Both have completely enclosed cockpits with heater; regular aircraft controls.
330	10/3	Auto.	95/85/38	550	350/400	14/4.5	30	3–ax.	No	$7	NA	Yes	250	
220	4/1.5	3.7/NA	55/50/26	800	100/50	6/8.3	30	3–ax.	No	$3	NA	Yes	40–60	Low wing loading of 3.7 lb./ft. is based on a 285 lb. pilot.
183	2/1	4	55/40/17	400	50/75	13/3.8	25	3–ax.	No	$5	NA	Yes	150	Has overhead stick; soaring capability; disassembles easily for transporting.
110 less eng.	5/.9	NA	50/35/NA	NA	NA	NA	60	3–ax.	No	$3	No	Yes	150	Extremely strong and stable; uses easy power wing cell.
133 less eng.	3/1	5.5/2.7	60/55/18	400–800	80/80	10/NA	20	3–ax.	No	NC	NA	Yes	40	Almost completely built at factory; dealers offer training.

Publisher or Distributor	Aircraft Name and Model Number	Configuration	Type of Construction	Engine(s)	Specifications						
					Wingspan (ft.-in.)	Length (ft.-in.)	Height (ft.-in.)	Wing Area (sq. ft.)	Number of Seats	Gross Weight (lbs.)	Useful Load (lbs.)
Teman Aircraft 10092 Northampton Ave. Westminister, CA 92683 (714) 531–2655	Mono-Fly	High wing	Alum. tube/ composite/ Dacron	Onan 18 hp.	30-9	17	6-7	124	1	550	270
Ultralight Flight Inc. 480 Hayden Station Road Windsor, CT 06095 (203) 683–2760	Mirage Mk II C	High wing	Alum. tube/ Dacron	Cuyuna 430RL 37 hp.	33	18	8-11	149	1	500	280
Vector Aircraft Corp. Industrial Park Box 304 Turners Falls, ME 01376	Vector 610	High wing	Alum/ Dacron	Zenoah G25B–1 22 hp.	35-2	18	NA	154	1	445	250
Volmer Aircraft Box 5222 Glendale, CA 91201	VJ–23 Swing Wing	High wing	Alum./ wood/ fabric	Mc101 10 hp.	32-7	17-5	6	179	1	330	200
	VJ–24E Sun Fun	High wing	All metal and fabric	Mc101 10 hp.	36-6	18	5-8	163	1	330	200
	VJ–24W Sun Fun	High wing	All metal and fabric	Mc101 10 hp.	36-6	18	6	163	1	345	180
Waspair 1881 Enterprise Boulevard West Sacramento, CA 95691 (916) 372–5791	Tom Cat	Parasol canard	Metal/ fabric	Cuyuna 30 hp. 43 cc	30	15-4	7	175	1	395	220
Weedhopper of Utah, Inc. Box 2253 1148 Century Drive Ogden, UT 84404	Popular Mechanics Woodhopper	High wing	Wood/ foam/fabric	Chotia 460D	32	17-6	NA	157	1	350	200
	Weedhopper Model C JC 24C	High wing	Alum/ Dacron	Chotia 460D	28	19	6-6	168	1	400	220

Empty Weight (lbs.)	Fuel Capacity/Consumption (gal.)	Load Factor +/-	Top/Cruise/Stall Speed (mph)	Initial Climb (fpm)	Take-off/Landing Roll	L/D, Sink Rate	Set-up Time	Control System	FAA License Req.	Information Packet	Plan Price per Set	Materials Kit	Time to Build (hrs)	Comments
						Performance					**Price Data**			
280	3 or 6/1.5	9/6	50/38/20	400	165/100	8–5	14	3–ax.	Yes	$5	$40	Yes	300 for plans; 150 for kit	Uses a 4-stroke engine; large tires, pilot pod, wheel units, etc. available.
220	3.5/1.5	5.6/2.8	65/50/25	1,000	60–100 both	8/7.5	20	3–ax.	No	$1	NA	Yes	30–40	Double surface wing; conventional controls; can be used as crop duster.
195	5/12	NA	50/40/27	600	100/NA	8/NA	NA	3–ax.	No	$2	No	Yes	30	Upright V-tail; double surface wings; full three-axis controls.
130	1/1.5	2	30/25/17	NA	2 steps in 12 mph. wind	9/NA	20	3–ax.	No	$10	$100	No	200	Popular motorized hang glider; simple to build, maintain, and repair; metal structure; improved engine instructions; separate plans; wheeled landing gear, tractor engine.
130	1/1.5	2	30/28/17	NA	same	9/NA	20	3–ax.	No	$10	$100	No	200	
165	1/1.5	2	30/28/17	NA	same	9/NA	20	3–ax.	No	$10	$100	No	300	
175	5/1.5	6/4	56/45/24	600	90/NA	9–5	20	3–ax.	No	$4	No	Yes	NA	All-canard wing provides inherent longitudinal stability, and controls pitch and roll/yaw.
145	1/1	3.5	45/35/21	250–450	80/60	9/4.1	20	2–ax.	No	NC	$50	No	300	Extremely low cost; designed for *Popular Mechanics* readers.
160	3.5/1	5/2	50/40/22	600	100/75	8/5	30	2–ax.	No	NC	NA	Yes	8	Sold as prefabricated kit only; nose wheel brake; double surface wings.

Ultralight Powered Aircraft continued

Publisher or Distributor	Aircraft Name and Model Number	Configuration	Type of Construction	Engine(s)	Wingspan (ft.-in.)	Length (ft.-in.)	Height (ft.-in.)	Wing Area (sq. ft.)	Number of Seats	Gross Weight (lbs.)	Useful Load (lbs.)
Starflight Manufacturing, Inc. Route 3, Box 197 Liberty Landing Airport Liberty, MO 64068	Tri Star Mark II	Parasol	Alum./ Dacron	Cuyuna 20 hp.	32-6	14	9-6	165	1	450	250
	Star	Parasol	Alum./ Dacron	Cuyuna 20 hp.	32-6	14	9-6	165	1	450	250

In the Wings

Publisher or Distributor	Aircraft Name and Model Number	Configuration	Type of Construction	Engine(s)	Wingspan (ft.-in.)	Length (ft.-in.)	Height (ft.-in.)	Wing area (sq. ft.)	Number of Seats	Load factor +/−	Gross Weight (lbs.)	Useful Load (lbs.)
American Aerolights, Inc. 700 Comanche Road Albuquerque, NM 87107 (505) 822-1417	Falcon AA-1A	High wing canard ultralight	Fiberglass/ alum./ Dacron	Cuyuna 215R 20 hp.	34–7	10-5	7	161	1	7.5/ 3	460	240
Harland Experimental Aircraft 2118 Kansas St. Carson City, NV 89701	Buzzard T-8	Biplane	Wood/ Dacron	Chaparral 42 hp.	31–2	20	5-8	202	1	NA	550	249
Helicraft P.O. Box 16988 Baltimore, MD 21217	Helicraft Jet	Helicopter	Steel/alum.	EMG. G8-2-20	25 rotor	5-2	NA	NA	1	NA	500	249
Horizon Aviation 200 W. Hampton St. Pemberton, NJ 08068 (609) 894-8980	Condor	High wing ultralight	Alum. tube/ Dacron	Cuyuna or KFM 30 hp.	34	17-6	5-6	151	1	4.9/ 2.4	460	235
Rick and Sue McWilliams 908 Rich Ave #9 Mountain View, CA 94040	Triperon	High wing canard pusher	Foam/fiberglass/ steel	Lyc. 0-235 118 hp.	30	18-7	6-6	88	2 sbs	NA	1,300	NA

234

Empty Weight (lbs.)	Fuel Capacity/ Consumption (gal.)	Load Factor +/−	Performance							Price Data				Comments
			Top/Cruise/Stall Speed (mph)	Initial Climb (fpm)	Take-off/Landing Roll	L/D, Sink Rate	Set-up Time	Control System	FAA License Req.	Information Packet	Plan Price per Set	Materials Kit	Time to Build (hrs)	
200	2.5	5.5/ 3.5	55/35/ 20	500	150/ 50	7/5.3	45	3–ax.	No	$5	NA	Yes	NA	Sail cut span-wise; includes sunken buttons; stainless steel bushings used in all high-stress areas.
200	2.5	5.5/ 3.5	40/27/ 18	600	150/ 50	8/4.5	30	Wt. shift	No	$5	NA	Yes	NA	

Empty Weight (lbs.)	Fuel capacity (gal.)	Baggage (lbs.)	Performance								Price Data				Comments
			Top Speed (mph)	Cruising Speed (mph)	Initial Climb (S.L.) (fpm)	Stall Speed (mph)	Take-off Run (ft.)	Landing Run (ft.)	Service Ceiling (ft.)	Range (miles)	Information Packet	Plan Price per Set	Materials Kit	Time to Build (hrs)	
220	5	0	75	65	400	30	250	200	NA	325	NA	NA	NA	150	In pre-production flight testing; design intended to be stall and spin resistant.
301	2	0	44	34	NA	23	50–75	20–30	NA	NA	NA	NA	NA	450	Uses wing warp instead of ailerons; ready for flight testing.
180	10	NA	80	55	NA	NA	NA	NA	7,000	100	NC	$9	No	Var.	For the true experimenter; plans offer construction options and alternatives.
198	5	NA	NA	55	800	19 with flaps	NA	NA	NA	NA	NA	NA	NA	NA	Aircraft in testing stages; first shown at Sun 'n Fun 1982.
780	30	NA	210	170	1,340	65	NA	NA	23,000	NA	NA	NA	NA	2,000	New aircraft design of unusual configuration; first flight planned July 1983.

Publisher or Distributor	Aircraft Name and Model Number	Configuration	Type of Construction	Specifications								
				Engine(s)	Wingspan (ft.-in.)	Length (ft.-in.)	Height (ft.-in.)	Wing area (sq. ft.)	Number of Seats	Load factor +/-	Gross Weight (lbs.)	Useful Load (lbs.)
Monnett Experimental Aircraft, Inc. P.O. Box 2984 Oshkosh, WI 54903	Monex	Low wing V-tail	Alum. and bonding	Monnett Aero Vee 2,180 cc	16–8	15-2	4-8	48	1	6	650	270
Barney Oldfield Aircraft, Inc. P.O. Box 83 Gates Mills, OH	Buddy Baby Lakes	Biplane	Tube/ wood/ fabric	Cont. 85–100 hp. Lyc. 108–118 hp.	18	14-8	6-3	94	2 tand.	8/6	1,000	450
Renegade Aircraft Prods. 2129 S. 107 St. West Allis, WI 53227	Polter-geist-1	Low wing	Tube/ wood/ fabric	VW 1600 cc and up	17	15	Var.	75	1	8.7	655	255
Sequoia Aircraft Co. 900 West Franklin Street Richmond, VA 23220	Kodiak Model 302	Low wing	Steel tube/ alum./ comp.	235–300 hp. turbo	30	25	9-6	130	2 sbs or tand.		3,200	1,350
Nick Smith RR #3 Thorndale, Ont. Canada NOM 2P0	Super Citabria Homebuilt	High wing	Steel tube/ alum.	Cont. 100 hp.	32–40	20-6	7	160/ 200	2 tand.	NA	1,700	700–800
Molt Taylor P.O. Box 1171 Longview, WA 98632	Smith Super Acro	Mid-wing	Steel tube/ wood/ fabric	Lyc. 205 hp.	24–1	20	4-1	124	2 tand.	12	1,270	550
	Bullet-2100	High wing pusher	Paper/fi-berglass	Revm. 65 hp.	31	18-9	4-4	120	2 sbs	NA	1,100	550
Thompson Aircraft 336 Fitzwater St. Philadelphia, PA	Thompson Boxmoth	Tandem wing bi-plane	Alum. tube/ Dacron	Hirth 65 hp.	24	28	11	480	1	NA	550	220
Thurston Aero-marine Corp. 16 Jericho Drive Old Lyme, CT 06371	Model TA16 Trojan	High wing amphibian	Metal/fi-berglass	160–250 hp	37	27-2	NA	183	2–4	NA	3,000	1,200
Winther-Hollman Aircraft Co. 11082 Belaire Ct. Cupertino, CA 95014	Condor	Mid-wing pusher	Fiberglass/ graphite/ metal	Revm. 2100 cc	18	6	NA	32	2 tand	NA	1,250	500

Empty Weight (lbs.)	Fuel capacity (gal.)	Baggage (lbs.)	Top Speed (mph)	Cruising Speed (mph)	Initial Climb (S.L.) (fpm)	Stall Speed (mph)	Take-off Run (ft.)	Landing Run (ft.)	Service Ceiling (ft.)	Range (miles)	Information Packet	Plan Price per Set	Materials Kit	Time to Build (hrs)	Comments
															Performance / **Price Data**
380	10	NA	230	210	2,000	52	600	1,000	NA	500	NA	NA	NA	NA	New high-performance aircraft; prototype displayed at Oshkosh but not flown.
550	15	NA	135	118	1,500–1,800	55	400	400	17,000	250	$5	$150	NA	NA	Plans and kits will be revised after flight tests; unique tandem seating arrangement.
400	13.5	Var.	170	130	1,000	50	NA	NA	NA	390	$5	$125	Yes	NA	Aircraft similar to Cassutt racer but set up for VW engines.
1,850	96	100	NA	255	2,270	72	NA	NA	18,000	1,280	$5	$400	Yes	NA	Specifications for sbs seating; can be built as tandem; plans are sold only to experienced builders.
850–1,050	41	20	160	120	NA	50	200–400	400	NA	500–1,000	NC	$180	Yes	NA	Similar to Citabria; float fittings will be shown.
720	30	10	250	180	3,000	60	600	600	NA	720	NC	$150	Yes	NA	Aircraft patterned after another Acro, but as a two-seater.
550	18	50	150+	NA	750	50	NA	NA	NA	NA	NC	NA	NA	NA	Folding wings, retracting gear; transportable.
NA	5	NA	40	30	1,000	20	200	100	5,000	50	$10	$125	Yes	150	A patented design; has patented adjustable propeller.
1,800	40	80	NA	145	1,100	57	NA	NA	NA	NA	NC	$550	Yes	NA	Aircraft is being certified for production.
730	NA	NA	120	95	800	46	NA	NA	NA	600	NA	NA	NA	NA	Aircraft almost completed; will be available as a kit after flight testing.

Index

Note: **Boldface** numbers indicate photographs.